LETTERS TO POWER

Edited by Cheryl Glenn and J. Michael Hogan
The Pennsylvania State University

Editorial Board:

Robert Asen (University of Wisconsin–Madison)
Debra Hawhee (The Pennsylvania State University)
Peter Levine (Tufts University)
Steven J. Mailloux (University of California, Irvine)
Krista Ratcliffe (Marquette University)
Karen Tracy (University of Colorado, Boulder)
Kirt Wilson (The Pennsylvania State University)
David Zarefsky (Northwestern University)

Rhetoric and Democratic Deliberation is a series of groundbreaking monographs and edited volumes focusing on the character and quality of public discourse in politics and culture. It is sponsored by the Center for Democratic Deliberation, an interdisciplinary center for research, teaching, and outreach on issues of rhetoric, civic engagement, and public deliberation.

Other books in the series:

Karen Tracy, *Challenges of Ordinary Democracy: A Case Study in Deliberation and Dissent*

LETTERS TO POWER

PUBLIC ADVOCACY WITHOUT PUBLIC INTELLECTUALS

SAMUEL McCORMICK

The Pennsylvania State University Press | University Park, Pennsylvania

Library of Congress Cataloging-in-Publication Data

McCormick, Samuel, 1978–
    Letters to power: public advocacy without public intellectuals / Samuel McCormick.
        p.   cm. — (Rhetoric and democratic deliberation; 2)
    Includes bibliographical references and index.
    Summary: "Discusses the role of the intellectual in public life. Argues that the scarcity of public intellectuals among today's academics is a challenge to us to explore alternative, more subtle forms of political intelligence. Looks to ancient, medieval, and modern traditions of learned advocacy"—Provided by publisher.
    ISBN 978-0-271-05074-4 (pbk. : alk. paper)
    1. Rhetoric—Political aspects.
    2. Intellectuals—Political activity.
    I. Title.

PN239.P64M33 2012
808—dc23
2011020734

Copyright © 2011 The Pennsylvania State University
All rights reserved
Printed in the United States of America
Published by The Pennsylvania State University Press,
University Park, PA 16802-1003

The Pennsylvania State University Press is a member of the Association of American University Presses.

It is the policy of The Pennsylvania State University Press to use acid-free paper. Publications on uncoated stock satisfy the minimum requirements of American National Standard for Information Sciences—Permanence of Paper for Printed Library Material, ANSI Z39.48–1992.

CONTENTS

Acknowledgments | vii

1 MINOR POLITICAL RHETORIC, MAJOR WESTERN THINKERS | 1

2 REMAINING CONCEALED:
   LEARNED PROTEST BETWEEN STOICISM AND THE STATE | 19

3 MIRRORS FOR THE QUEEN:
   EXEMPLARY FIGURES ON THE EVE OF CIVIL WAR | 52

4 PERFORMATIVE PUBLICITY:
   THE CRITIQUE OF PRIVATE REASON | 81

5 HIDDEN BEHIND THE DASH:
   TECHNIQUES OF UNRECOGNIZABILITY | 109

6 OPPOSITIONAL POLITICS IN THE AGE OF ACADEMIA | 142

   Notes | 171

   Index | 191

ACKNOWLEDGMENTS

This project has benefited from many readers. David J. Depew, James P. McDaniel, and John Durham Peters provided crucial encouragement at its outset and invaluable feedback during its early stages of development. Barbara A. Biesecker, Kristine L. Muñoz, Bruce E. Gronbeck, and Daniel M. Gross waded through substantial portions of the work in progress. Dieter J. Boxmann, Robin Patric Clair, Gerard A. Hauser, John Louis Lucaites, Felicia D. Roberts, and Michael Vicaro commented on drafts of chapters along the way. And audiences at the University of Iowa, Northwestern University, and Purdue University helped me work through several difficult sections of the manuscript.

Portions of this study appeared in early form as articles: part of chapter 2 as "In Defense of New Stoicism: Public Advocacy and Political Thought in the Age of Nero" in *Advances in the History of Rhetoric* 14 (2011): 49–64; much of chapter 3 as "Mirrors for the Queen: A Letter from Christine de Pizan on the Eve of Civil War" in the *Quarterly Journal of Speech* 94, no. 3 (August 2008): 273–96; some of chapter 4 as "The Artistry of Obedience: From Kant to Kingship" in *Philosophy and Rhetoric* 38, no. 4 (2005): 302–27; and sections of chapter 6 as "The Political Identity of the Philosopher: Resistance, Relative Power, and the Endurance of Potential" in *Philosophy and Rhetoric* 42, no. 1 (2009): 71–91. I am grateful to the editors of these journals for permission to use this material.

I also wish to thank to everyone at the Pennsylvania State University Press, especially Kendra Boileau, Cheryl Glenn, J. Michael Hogan, Stephanie Lang, Patricia A. Mitchell, Laura Reed-Morrisson, Nicholas Taylor, and Sanford G. Thatcher; as well as my assistants at Purdue University—Adam Lerner, Michael Maione, and Corey Palmer—for their diligent work on the index. And I am particularly grateful to Robert Hariman, whose invaluable feedback on the entire manuscript saved me from a variety of pitfalls.

As always, though, my greatest debt is to my wife, Heather June Gibbons, without whose patience (and impatience) this project never would have found completion.

I

MINOR POLITICAL RHETORIC, MAJOR WESTERN THINKERS

It seems to me that we are now at a point where the function of the specific intellectual needs to be reconsidered. Reconsidered but not abandoned, despite the nostalgia of some for the great "universal" intellectuals.

—MICHEL FOUCAULT

The Usable Past

When did "intellectual" become a noun? Isolated instances of the term date from 1652, but it did not enter into popular usage until the 1890s. The catalyst seems to have been the Dreyfus Affair—a decadelong political scandal surrounding the wrongful conviction of a Jewish artillery captain, Alfred Dreyfus. Among its defining moments was the 13 January 1898 publication of Émile Zola's open letter to the president of France, in which the renowned novelist accused military officials of anti-Semitism and obstruction of justice. Support for Zola's letter arrived a day later in a "Manifesto of the Intellectuals" signed by 1,200 artists, writers, and academics, all of whom, in an act of solidarity, now identified themselves as "intellectuals." It was the radical political rhetoric of these educated elites—more than their artistic, literary, and scholarly achievements—that crystallized the social category of "the intellectual."

Much has been written about the subsequent history of intellectuals in conflict with public authorities. But the history of these conflicts before the Dreyfus Affair has not been sufficiently traced. This book attempts to provide such a tracing. It is at once a genealogy of learned advocates prior to Zola and the Dreyfusards; an inventory of the persuasive techniques, resistant practices, and ethical sensibilities on which they relied; and, to this extent, a recovery of their status as rhetorically skilled and morally inclined political actors. My aim is neither to exhaust nor even to delimit the political tradition in which these educated elites participate. Instead, I attempt to bring several of this tradition's key moments into alignment with one another, and in so doing to arrive at a constellation of situations and strategies in which to reenvision the political potential of today's learned men and women. At issue in the following chapters, then, is not a comprehensive historical survey, but a version of the past that is useful to learned advocates in the present.

The utility of this past is nowhere more apparent than in today's colleges and universities. From Russell Jacoby's classic lament for *The Last Intellectuals* to Richard Posner's more recent eulogy for *Public Intellectuals*, scholars have accused late-modern academics of relinquishing much of their former authority, especially in the realm of public affairs.[1] So much authority, in fact, that many now doubt the ability of American academic culture to sustain anything like "the intellectual"—a political identity that continues to derive its meaning from open and often radical opposition to the state. Although certainly a cause for concern, the scarcity of intellectuals among today's academics is also a challenge to explore alternate, more elusive forms of political intelligence. And many of these forms, as we shall see, await discovery in ancient, medieval, and modern traditions of learned advocacy. Only by venturing beyond the historical and conceptual limits of "the intellectual," I argue, can we begin to address the political predicament of late-modern academics.

In service to this argument, the following chapters focus on the political and theoretical writings of four renowned scholars: the Roman Stoic Seneca the Younger, the late-medieval feminist Christine de Pizan, the key Enlightenment thinker Immanuel Kant, and the Christian anti-philosopher Søren Kierkegaard. What separates these educated elites from other figures in the history of ideas is also what connects them to late-modern academics: their use of epistolary rhetoric as a semipublic form of address in which to contest, without directly challenging, established figures of authority. Anticipating much of today's online advocacy, in which educated elites have only begun to participate, their letters help us understand the economy of personal and public address at work in existing relations of power, suggesting that the art of lettered protest—like letter-writing itself—involves appealing to diverse, and often strictly virtual, audiences. As the public sphere continues to dissolve into the blogosphere, few modes of political contention could be more relevant to American academics.

Seneca perfected this subtle form of dissent in a rhetoric of withdrawal. Written at the height of Nero's tyranny, his *Letters to Lucilius* (64–65 CE) are lessons in the art of abandoning abusive authorities without arousing their suspicion. Christine framed her protest in a rhetoric of exemplarity. Arriving on the eve of civil war, her letter to the queen of France (1405) is a masterpiece in the art of prodding without offending unpopular public officials. Kant's correspondence with the Friedrich Wilhelm II (1794)—the occasion for which was a dramatic increase in state censorship—figures his opposition in a rhetoric of obedience. His letter suggests that rather than abandoning or provoking the authorities, the art of resistance consists in balking their commands without failing to obey them. And Kierkegaard's missive to literate Denmark (1848)—which appeared amid a dramatic transfer of public authority from the monarch to the masses—is coded in a rhetoric of identification, the artistry of which involves aligning oneself with certain relations of power while simultaneously alienating others.

If indeed these persuasive techniques are relevant to learned advocates in the academic era, it is not because they comport with the political intelligence and ethical sensibilities of today's educated elites. In fact, the rhetorical maneuvers and resistant practices of Seneca, Christine, Kant, and Kierkegaard look nothing like those characteristic of our era's politicized professors. And this is precisely why they are worthy of recuperation. Each is an antidote to one of four basic dilemmas of learned advocacy in late modernity. As we shall see, Seneca's rhetoric of withdrawal counteracts the politics of desertion implicit in the specialized, disciplinary language of contemporary academics; Christine's rhetoric of exemplarity challenges their tendency to rely on linear, abstract, and hyperrational forms of argument; Kant's rhetoric of obedience offsets their Dreyfusard inheritance of overt dissent and radical opposition; and Kierkegaard's rhetoric of identification short-circuits the Marxist standards of vanguard leadership to which many of them aspire.

In addition to disrupting several norms of learned political culture, the epistolary rhetorics of Seneca, Christine, Kant, and Kierkegaard supplement their major theoretical writings, at once augmenting and intervening in many of their canonical works. Seneca's letters amend his earlier discussions of political withdrawal in *On the Shortness of Life* (49–55 CE), *On Retirement* (61 CE), and *On Tranquility of Mind* (62 CE). Christine's missive to the queen of France strategically excises certain passages from her well-known *Book of the City of Ladies* (1405). Kant's correspondence with the king of Prussia poses a counterargument to his *Lectures on Ethics* (1775–80), his famous "Answer to the Question: 'What Is Enlightenment?'" (1784), and the *Critique* of *Practical Reason* (1788). And Kierkegaard's missive to the Danish reading public crosshatches the religious and political theories outlined in *Two Ages* (1846), *Works of Love* (1847), and *Practice in Christianity* (1850). To this extent, analyzing these figures' letters to power not only allows us to recuperate forms of political intelligence other than those of "the intellectual" but it also gives us new access to a range of canonical arguments and characteristic attitudes in the history of Stoic, feminist, rationalist, and Christian moral philosophy. That many of these arguments and attitudes continue to inform the ethical sensibilities of today's educated elites makes their reassessment all the more important.

In addition to these political and theoretical objectives, this book has a methodological agenda. By reconsidering the moral and political thought of Seneca, Christine, Kant, and Kierkegaard in light of their letters to power (and vice versa), I hope to avoid traditional approaches to intellectual history, as well as two of their most formidable critiques: Marxism and deconstruction. In place of twentieth-century quarrels over the rhetorical and political unconscious of Western thought, I attempt to provide a line of inquiry into the overt political rhetoric of its key figures. In so doing, I hope to advance the cultural history of ideas and the broader, multidisciplinary tradition known as "the new cultural history." Building on the work of microhistorians, new historicists, and rhetorical scholars—especially work that walks the line between intellectual and cultural history—the following chapters aim to return us to the great men and women of learned culture without the traditional, Rankean emphasis on their great ideas.

The Prolonged Letter: Addressing Power, Anticipating Publics

From lead tablets to Listservs, letters have often troubled the boundaries between intimate and impersonal forms of address. It is here, in these troubled boundaries, that Seneca, Christine, Kant, and Kierkegaard honed their skills as learned political agents. In publishing his apparently intimate *Letters to Lucilius*, Seneca was able to expand his audience from a single addressee—Lucilius Junior—to all of literate Rome. As chapter 2 demonstrates, he was especially keen to address two readers, both of whom he also aimed to resist: the Roman senator Thrasea Paetus, who had recently stormed out of the curia in protest against imperial corruption, insisting that his Stoic ethics obliged him to do so; and the emperor Nero, who, now jeopardized by Thrasea's abstention, was compelled to deny other Stoics' requests to retire from public life, including those of Seneca. Thanks to Thrasea, Stoicism had become the face of resistance, and in 62 CE—the same year in which Seneca attempted to retire from Nero's court—adherence to the school's doctrines became a criminal offense. Not even Seneca's theoretical writings in support of public service and peaceful withdrawal could vindicate his request to retire. It was in response to these political circumstances that Seneca penned *Letters to Lucilius*. In addition to redeeming Stoicism as a compliant moral philosophy and discouraging other Romans from joining Thrasea, Seneca used his letters to begin a slow, piecemeal retreat from court life, at once revising his philosophy of public service and contesting Nero's authority as emperor.

Christine's 1405 letter to Queen Isabeau also insinuates public discourse in personal correspondence. Although addressed to "the Excellent, Revered and Powerful Princess, My Lady Isabella, Queen of France," her letter was probably delivered by John the Fearless, Duke of Burgundy, a task that, in keeping with medieval epistolary conventions, would have required him to transmit its content orally. And John was not the only witness to Christine's appeal. Another was his sworn enemy, the duke of Orléans, with whom the queen had recently fled Paris and, at the time of John's arrival, was still abroad. The likely addition of these rival dukes to Christine's audience is especially significant given the purpose of her letter: to legitimate and effect the queen's intervention in their political quarrel. How Christine does this without offending the queen is the topic of chapter 3. Among her rhetorical devices was the exemplary figure. In reciting tales of admirable and infamous women—all of whom either successfully managed or failed to control unruly male figures—Christine suggests that, depending on how Isabeau exercises her authority as queen, the virtues or vices of these predecessors will recur, thereby writing her into the annals of history as an example of judicious or immoderate leadership. In this sense, the public audience of her personal letter was not only the dukes of Orléans and Burgundy, but also exemplary women throughout history, all of whom Christine positioned as judging witnesses to the queen's conduct.

Kant also widened his audience for political effect. What began as a correspondence with the king of Prussia, the readership of which was limited to court officials, ended up in the preface to his *Conflict of the Faculties*, along with several explanatory footnotes in which he strategically reinterprets this exchange of letters for the general reading public. Four years earlier, Kant explains, he had received a royal dispatch ordering him to remain silent on religious topics, to which he responded with a promise to obey, this being his duty as "Your Majesty's loyal subject." Because his letter was addressed to the king himself, however, and because this regal addressee had recently died, he was now free to resume his discussion of religious topics. Thus, Kant used his preface to the *Conflict* as a public forum in which to reinscribe his correspondence with the king as an intimate exchange of letters, thereby justifying and concluding a lengthy period of silence in his philosophical theology. Chapter 4 explores the intellectual and cultural conditions, as well as the political consequences, of this maneuver. Of particular use to Kant, I argue, was the modern expectation that letters be personal, informal, and private. When coupled with late eighteenth-century challenges to "the king's two bodies," these epistolary conventions allowed him to sidestep Enlightenment norms of civic duty—many of which, interestingly enough, he had helped to establish with his philosophical writings.[2]

Unlike Seneca, Christine, and Kant, all of whom expanded their readerships by infusing personal correspondence with public discourse, Kierkegaard contracted the audience of his 1848 missive to literate Denmark by encrypting it with moments of private address. In addition to readers of the newspaper in which it appeared, his "Crisis and a Crisis in the Life of an Actress" had two specific addressees: the celebrated stage actress Johanne Luise Heiberg, with whom he hoped to align himself; and her widely reviled elitist husband, Johan Ludvig Heiberg, against whom he hoped to oppose himself. In praising Fru Heiberg and critiquing her husband, Kierkegaard aimed to renew public interest in his own work, especially among middle- and lower-middle-class readers, many of whom esteemed the Royal Danish Theater almost as much as they enjoyed newspaper screeds against intellectual and cultural elitism. Despite its clarity of purpose, the execution of this promotional stunt was remarkably complex. Kierkegaard mentions neither of the Heibergs by name; nor does he identify himself as the article's author, attributing it instead to the pseudonym "Inter et Inter," meaning "between and between." Only later, in a series of private letters to the Heibergs, did he reveal "The Crisis" for what it was: a missive to Fru Heiberg and, by extension, her husband. As we shall see in chapter 5, however, they were not its primary addressees. More than an open, albeit ciphered, letter to the Heibergs, the article was a calculated appeal to the emerging sovereign of democratic Denmark: public opinion. As a letter to power, its addressee was neither a crowned prince nor the cultured elite, but instead a mass society.

By troubling the boundaries between personal and public address, Seneca, Christine, Kant, and Kierkegaard all multiplied their audiences. In addition to individual recipients, their letters were written for wider publics. And among these wider publics were three distinct groups: auditors, witnesses, and eavesdroppers. Unlike *addressees*, who are known, ratified, and engaged directly (e.g., Lucilius, Isabeau, Friedrich Wilhelm, literate Denmark), *auditors* are known and ratified, but not engaged directly (e.g., Nero and Thrasea, the dukes of Orléans and Burgundy, Prussian court officials, Johanne Luise Heiberg). *Witnesses* are those audience members who are known but neither ratified nor addressed (e.g., literate Romans, other members of the queen's entourage, the Prussian reading public, Johan Ludvig Heiberg). At the furthest reach of this wider public are *eavesdroppers*, who are neither known nor ratified nor addressed, their identities being strictly potential (e.g., readers of this book, all of whom, from the vantage points of Seneca, Christine, Kant, and Kierkegaard, were still to come).[3] Here, as the intentionality of the writer gives way to an indefinite range of readers, the structural vocation of letter-writing becomes apparent: *letters are always addressed and essentially nomadic*. In keeping with the theme of this book, they represent a decisive interface between occasioned discourse (political rhetoric) and transhistorical exchange (learned culture).

Taken together, these four audiences—addressees, auditors, witnesses, and eavesdroppers—make up the participation framework of the letters discussed in this book. Interestingly, Seneca, Christine, Kant, and Kierkegaard all prefigured these audiences in their letters to power, actively anticipating the likely interpretations of each group. More than other major Western thinkers, many of whom also found themselves in correspondence with power, these letter-writers capitalized on the public dimensions of epistolary discourse, allowing the absent presence of wider audiences to inform and strengthen their arguments. The relevance of this persuasive technique to late-modern academics cannot be overstated, especially given their emerging role in online advocacy, where auditors, witnesses, and eavesdroppers often determine the significance of their discourse. "The idea of an imagined community has suddenly acquired a very literal, if virtual, dimension," writes Edward Said of today's new media environment. "All of us should therefore operate today with some notion of very probably reaching much larger audiences than we could have conceived of even a decade ago."[4] Seneca, Christine, Kant, and Kierkegaard were among the first learned political agents to master this rhetorical skill, and letter-writing was the medium of communication in which they did so.

This is not to suggest, of course, that the "absent presence" of their wider publics was merely spatial, as though the *epistulae* discussed in this book, like early Christian *apostoloi*, were simply "sent forth" or "sent out" into the world as substitutes for the proximal presence of their authors. Of more concern to Seneca, Christine, Kant, and Kierkegaard were the *temporal* aspects of letter-writing, notably the irreducible meantime between their letters' composition, delivery, interpretation, and response. Although the spatial dimensions of epistolography may vary (a note on the kitchen counter being as likely to find its addressee as one mailed across town), these writers shrewdly realized that its relation to time never changes. Like all letters, theirs were addressed to the future. Because the public and personal affairs that were present to them as learned political actors would soon be past, they wrote in anticipation of moments still to come. For each, letter-writing involved imagining a not-yet-present from the standpoint of a will-have-been. Future anteriority was the tense in which they contested, without directly challenging, established figures of authority.

If Christianity highlights the spatial attributes of epistolary culture, admonishing its followers to be "in but not of the world," Stoicism accents its future anteriority, the oracle's advice to Zeno being to "take on the complexion of the dead."[5] Seneca inherited this advice from Zeno and bequeathed it to posterity in his *Letters to Lucilius*, encouraging his readers to live each day as though it were their last, ever glancing back on their lives in advance of their deaths. Christine counseled the queen of France similarly, encouraging her to consider her emerging legacy before deciding whether to intervene in the Orléans-Burgundy conflict. Kant accepted this advice for himself, insisting that he prefigured the death of Friedrich Wilhelm—and thus a return to religious debates—in his promise to the king. And Kierkegaard even went so far as to consider "From the Papers of One Dead" as the subtitle of his address to literate Denmark—a prognostic throwback to his first publication, *From the Papers of One Still Living*, which he hoped would contribute to the restoration of his earlier fame as an aesthetic writer.[6]

The ethical and political implications of this tense are profound. "By considering oneself as at the point of death," Michel Foucault observes, "one can judge the proper value of every action one is performing."[7] As both practical embodiments of this consideration and strategic pronouncements of the judgment with which it comes, the letters of Seneca, Christine, Kant, and Kierkegaard warrant our attention—maybe even our imitation as well. For each, letter-writing was a uniquely foresighted medium of dispute, well suited to the tasks of conceiving, coordinating, and capitalizing on several personal and public relationships at once. With ample time for deliberation and design, these major Western thinkers were able to disrupt even the most exacting relationships—namely, those with established figures of authority, in which expressions of dissent were ever in need of careful adjustment to expectations of deference. That they staged these adjustments for a variety of auditors, witnesses, and eavesdroppers only added to their efficacy as political actors. Indeed, as the final chapter of this book indicates, their letters brilliantly illuminate the economy of personal and public address at work in contemporary relations of power, suggesting that the art of lettered protest in the age of academia, like the art of letter-writing itself, consists in synchronizing diverse, and often strictly virtual, audiences.

Rhetoric, Politics, and Philosophy Redressed

It is easy to locate Seneca, Christine, Kant, and Kierkegaard in the history of ideas. Their letters to power, however, are more difficult to place. This is not because they lack theoretical complexity, but because traditional approaches to intellectual history rarely venture beyond their authors' canonical tracts and treatises. The history of this limitation is worth noting, for it provides a condition of possibility for the critical-historical method of this book.

Like Dante, who famously observed the "philosophic family" walking and talking its way through Limbo, intellectual historians have often seen themselves as eavesdroppers on this timeless discussion—as though the history of Western thought were, as Richard Rorty once quipped, "a family romance involving, e.g., Father Parmenides, honest old Uncle Kant, and bad brother Derrida."[8] What enabled this romance to continue, and thus to occasion scholarly comment, was the clarity, coherence, and continuity with which its participants transcribed their thoughts, bequeathing to posterity an immortal corpus of philosophical texts. In explicating these texts, so the argument went, intellectual historians could engage their authors in further discussion and debate. "We shall understand them best," Karl Jaspers explained, "by questioning them, side by side, without regard for history and their place in it."[9]

The twentieth century saw two great critiques of this attitude toward the "philosophic family." The first was Marxist and leveled against efforts to subtract philosophical texts from their sociopolitical contexts. For critical theorists such as Lukács and Adorno, the distinguishing feature of philosophy was neither its timelessness nor its universality, but its function as a highly refined political practice, the structure of which was not ideational but ideological. In addition to acknowledging the likeness between ruling ideas and the ideas of rulers, philosophical inquiry needed to refute this historical trend, at once abandoning the torpors of bourgeois thought and reinstating itself as an agent of radical social change. For too long, they argued, philosophy and its practitioners—as well as many of its historians—had been allowed to sit back and interpret the world. Their task was now to change it.

The second great assault on the history of ideas was deconstruction. Unlike their Marxist predecessors, who attended to the *historicity* of philosophical texts, notably their sociopolitical conditions, deconstructive critics focused on the *rhetoricity* of these works, paying special attention to the figurative language, oppositional hierarchies, and counter-patterns of meaning at work in the texts themselves. Recalling Nietzsche's famous critique of metaphysics, scholars such as Derrida and de Man sought to destabilize the idealist subordination of textuality to thought and, more broadly, of language to consciousness. Inscribed in the discourse of philosophy they found an economy of metaphors, the unruliness of which, they wagered, was what had inspired Plato and his heirs to consider their discipline external to its own language. More than proprietors of ideas, philosophers were to be disclosed rhetoricians in denial. And more than vehicles for conscious ideality, their writings were to be revealed as elaborate efforts to control the disfiguring influence of figuration itself.

Revelations of this sort did not come cheap. In the wake of Marxist and deconstructive critiques, members of the "philosophic family" could be treated as political actors only so long as they remained circumscribed by texts bearing the recognizable marks of "philosophy." Only insofar as they could be shown to struggle for clarity, coherence, and continuity in arguments addressed to a timeless readership was it possible to disclose the rhetorical and political agency of which these thinkers were unaware. As the history of Western thought came to resemble a mechanism of false consciousness, so also did the study of its key figures come to function as a lifeless, surgical procedure. "Cut open the patient with the critical scalpel and operate under impeccably sterile conditions," Peter Sloterdijk quipped in the early 1980s. "The opponent is cut open in front of everyone, until the mechanism of his error is laid bare. The outer skin of delusion and the nerve endings of 'actual' motives are hygienically separated and prepared."[10]

In maintaining the sterility and ensuring the success of their procedures, Marxist and deconstructive treatments of philosophy encouraged scholars to minimize, and at times to preclude, the possibility that many "philosophers" were well aware of the rhetorical and political functions of their theoretical works. According to Leo Strauss—one of the most striking, and sometimes strident, scholars to consider this issue—philosophers have "always and everywhere" written with an awareness of their political circumstances, often relying on a persuasive technique known as "philosophic politics," the purpose of which is to convince the public that "philosophers are not atheists, that they do not desecrate everything sacred to the city, that they reverence what the city reverences, that they are not subversives, in short, that they are not irresponsible adventurers but good citizens and even the best of citizens."[11]

In order to fulfill this task without abandoning their discipline, Strauss went on to argue, philosophers also have a tendency to engage in "a peculiar technique of writing, and therewith to a particular type of literature, in which the truth about all crucial things is presented exclusively between the lines."[12] Thus, more than sites of unwitting rhetoric in need of deconstruction or moments of political contradiction in need of Marxist critique, canonical works of philosophy were strategically polysemous texts in which to analyze and admire the persuasive artistry of major Western thinkers, notably the skill with which they conveyed unorthodox views to potential sympathizers while simultaneously concealing these views from established figures of authority.[13]

Despite their many disagreements, Straussians, Marxists, deconstructionists, and early intellectual historians shared a common interest in canonized works of philosophy. From the dialogues of Plato to the commentaries of Aquinas to the meditations of Descartes to the arithmetics of Frege—the pantheon of "classic texts" to be commemorated by historians of ideas, profaned by their Marxist and deconstructive critics, and memorialized anew by Straussian scholars was extensive. But it was also exclusive. As revisionist historians like J. G. A. Pocock and Quentin Skinner pointed out, it was a mistake to limit the history of thought to the discourse of theory. The proper object of study, they argued, was nothing less than *all* the linguistic practices characteristic of any given political culture. Their unlikely ally, Michel Foucault, took this argument a step further, abandoning the history of ideas in search of the rules of formation according to which it—and a variety of other statements (*énoncés*)—could be shown to operate. To the extent that anything resembling the discourse of philosophy remained, it was to be studied alongside other, more ordinary discursive practices and institutions.

Among the "non-philosophy" that Pocock, Skinner, and Foucault have enabled us to study, but which we have yet to explore, is the overt political rhetoric of philosophers themselves. Public speeches, personal correspondence, newspaper articles, radio broadcasts, political activism, and the like—for too long, intellectual historians and their critics have either ignored these noncanonical works or relegated them to biographical anecdotes, not realizing that, although addressed to situated lay audiences, many of these works were also crafted alongside, in terms of, and frequently in tension with their authors' canonical writings.

Much has been lost along the way. In disavowing the overt political rhetoric of philosophers, we have forgone numerous opportunities to document the political speech and action of those who have made thinking their profession—not only iconic members of the "philosophic family" but also contemporary members of academic culture. And by confining this discourse to biographical accounts, we have forfeited an array of resources for studying the complex, and occasionally explosive, relationship between educated elites and their political cultures. The following chapters are an attempt to recover some of these opportunities and resources. By mediating the philosophical texts and historical contexts of Seneca, Christine, Kant, and Kierkegaard through their letters to power, I hope to shed new light on the theoretical programs out of which these letters emerged, as well as the public controversies in which they intervened—all along the way illuminating modes of political intelligence and persuasive artistry available to late-modern academics.

Casuistic Stretching

Methodologically, this line of inquiry takes its start from Walter Benjamin, who premised his attitude toward history on a simple axiom: "Nothing that has ever happened should be regarded as lost for history." For Benjamin, historiography was an exercise in the recovery of an "oppressed past," the success of which depended on an ability "to blast a specific era out of the homogeneous course of history," and frequently involved the more exacting task of "blasting a specific life out of the era or a specific work out of the lifework." When properly sparked, Benjamin claimed, detonations of the later sort would result in an intertextual *Aufhebung*: "The lifework is preserved in this work and at the same time canceled."[14]

It is here, in the use of forgotten speech and action to sublate an author's famous lifeworks, that the critical-historical method of this book becomes legible. But make no mistake: In foregrounding the letters of Seneca, Christine, Kant, and Kierkegaard, my aim is neither to canonize these "minor" works nor to attenuate, and thereby to devalue, the "major" lifeworks of their authors. Rather, I attempt to destabilize the hierarchy in which "major" and "minor" texts derive their significance. Instead of allowing the traditional philosophical opposition between thought and action, principle and politics, to determine the meaning of their epistles, I read them as persuasive appeals that, while still anchored in this venerable opposition, are no longer simply subordinate to it.[15]

Taken together, these appeals constitute a "minor literature," the function of which is to deterritorialize, without in turn abandoning, the learned traditions in which their authors participate. More specifically, they constitute a "minor rhetoric."[16] What qualifies the epistolography of Seneca, Christine, Kant, and Kierkegaard as a *rhetoric* is its supply of persuasive techniques, resistant practices, and ethical sensibilities available for use by other educated elites, be they philosophers or fiction writers, scientists or spiritual leaders, contingent instructors or coffee-house intellectuals. What defines it as a *minor* rhetoric is not the marginalization of these various practitioners, all of whom, after all, are distinguished by the linguistic and cultural capital of "learnedness." Rather, it is their investment of this capital in political speech and action, a leveraging of sorts that stretches tensors through the discourses of science, religion, philosophy, aesthetics, and the like, effectively "minoritizing" the major languages from which they derive their authority to speak and act.

Consider Seneca, Christine, Kant, and Kierkegaard. In addressing letters to power, they neither exposed philosophy as a mode of politics (Marxism) nor unmasked its initiates as rhetoricians in disguise (deconstruction). Instead, they displaced themselves and their letters—and by extension their addressees, auditors, witnesses, and eavesdroppers—from the history of ideas to its rhetorical and political outer limits, where the protocols of this tradition could be set in variation, yielding subsystems or outsystems of public discourse. For each, letter-writing was not a rejection of their major language but rather its *minor political practice*—a becoming-minor-and-political of the Stoic, Feminist, Enlightenment, and Christian philosophies for which they were already well-known.[17] In recuperating this minor political practice, I hope to make it available to learned advocates in the age of academia, at once enabling and encouraging them to translate the discursive formations from which they derive linguistic and cultural authority into opportunity structures for political speech and action. If indeed, as Foucault insists, "the function of the specific intellectual needs to be reconsidered," we must begin by mapping and traversing fields of possible conduct between today's learned and political cultures.[18]

From what, then, do I propose to recover the minor political rhetoric of Seneca, Christine, Kant, and Kierkegaard? "Not only, and not in the main, from the discredit and neglect into which they have fallen," Benjamin knowingly replies, "but from the catastrophe represented very often by a certain strain in their dissemination, their 'enshrinement as heritage.'"[19] Interestingly, what protects their letters to power from oblivion is also what guards them against canonization: their undecidable allegiance to both the *bios politikos* and the *bios theōrētikos*. Seneca's letters to Lucilius, Christine's epistle to the queen of France, Kant's correspondence with Friedrich Wilhelm II, Kierkegaard's newspaper address to literate Denmark—all are productively split between the exigencies of specific historical events and the prescripts of broader moral theories, public controversies in which their authors were compelled to intervene and ethical sensibilities for which they were already famous.

The result is a kind of "casuistic stretching," whereby their letters introduce and instantiate new principles of conduct while simultaneously attempting to maintain earlier ethico-political agendas.[20] Seneca's rhetoric of withdrawal develops a new concept of retirement (*otium*) atop his earlier Stoic philosophy; Christine's rhetoric of exemplarity provides an alternate take on her own feminist critique of patriarchy; Kant's rhetoric of obedience exploits a loophole in his categorical rebuke of lying; and Kierkegaard's rhetoric of identification adds political intelligence to his theory of indirect communication. In each instance, we see a cagey, and at times fractious, articulation of moral theory and political practice, in terms of which each causes the other to stammer, insinuating in their historically separate places "*a regulated, continuous, immanent process of variation.*"[21] To recover the minor political works of these major Western thinkers is thus to recover lines of conduct in which right living and realist politicking are no longer mutually exclusive.

But we were discussing Benjamin. Between his critical-historical method and that of this book are two intermediate lines of inquiry—microhistory and new historicism—both of which inform the following chapters. Like microhistory, my reading strategy focuses on circumscribed events, individual lives, and minute political actions, especially as they intersect with and within broader social structures and latent economies of signification. And like new historicism, my reading strategy attempts to generate unusually intense, nuanced, and sustained interest in these minute political actions in hopes of redirecting scholarly attention from canonized works to a broader and less familiar range of texts. Unlike either of these methodological predecessors, however—both of which tend to feature the remarkable achievements of marginalized and often untaught political subjects—the critical-historical method of this book centers on the great men and women of learned culture and yet in such a way that avoids the traditional emphasis on their great ideas. It is their minor political activities more than their major philosophical agendas that warrant our attention.

In this sense, there is more at stake in the methodology of this book than a line of escape from the history of ideas and its Marxist and deconstructive critiques. With this escape comes an opportunity to advance the new cultural history—the broader, multidisciplinary tradition of inquiry in which microhistory and new historicism participate. More important, the methodology of this book allows critical inquiry to transgress one of the remaining frontiers between intellectual and cultural history—namely, the ill-defined relationship between major works of Western thought and the minor political engagements of their authors. By defining this relationship, I hope to strengthen and substantiate hybrid methods such as the cultural history of ideas. In particular, I hope to supplement these methods with reading strategies characteristic of rhetorical scholars. Building on the work of Ernest Wrage, a seminal critic and theorist of public address, I read the minor political rhetoric of Seneca, Christine, Kant, and Kierkegaard as a kind of "fugitive literature," the significance of which has long been obscured by our "exclusive devotion to monumental works," notably "major works in systematized thought."[22] By explicating literature of this sort, Wrage claimed, rhetorical scholars could bridge the gaps between intellectual and cultural historiography. Bolstering this claim is among the primary tasks of this book.

The Order of Things

By focusing on the political correspondence of Seneca, Christine, Kant, and Kierkegaard, I do not mean to suggest that they are the only major Western thinkers to have written letters to power worthy of analysis. Isocrates's missives to Philip of Macedon, Laura Cereta's dispatch to Bibulus Sempronius, Francis Bacon's exchange of letters with the earl of Essex, Descartes's correspondence with Princess Elizabeth of Bohemia—all could have found their way into this book. Nor do I mean to suggest that the study of minor political works by major Western thinkers ought to stop at the analysis of their letters. Theocritus's poetry, Aquinas's sermons, Fichte's speeches, Kafka's office writings, Benjamin's radio broadcasts—all lend themselves to the critical-historical method of this book. In each case, we see a network of political intelligence, persuasive artistry, and moral thought that is at once subtracted from the tradition of "the intellectual" and relevant to contemporary men and women of letters.

I also should note that, even though the following studies proceed chronologically, I do not mean to suggest a philosophical progression from

Seneca to Christine to Kant to Kierkegaard. Rather, I have organized these learned political agents according to their rhetorical maneuvers. The result is a loosely dialectical sequence of chapters. Seneca's rhetoric of withdrawal offers advice on how to extricate oneself from hazardous political disputes. Christine's rhetoric of exemplarity provides an incentive to intervene in them, as well as a linguistic device for encouraging others to do the same. Kant sublates both of these techniques in his rhetoric of obedience, preparing readers then and now for the difficult task of withdrawing from hazardous political disputes in order to return to them later. And Kierkegaard perfects this return strategy in his rhetoric of identification, effectively reinstating Kant's mediation of Seneca and Christine as the immediate basis for a new dialectic, the animating force of which is not a classical Stoic longing for philosophical leisure but a modern, democratic urge for public discussion and debate—the same urge that Zola and his intellectual heirs would later harness for purposes of moral protest.

In this sense, Kierkegaard's rhetoric of identification is at once the final moment in the dialectic of this book and the first moment in a new dialectic, the vitality of which would not become apparent until the Dreyfus Affair. It is a synthesis-turned-thesis in which the political detachment prized by Seneca and endured by many of today's academics has given way to an unwavering demand for its opposite. At issue in the following chapters, then, is not a systematic return to yesterday's engaged scholars but several preliminary strides toward new forms of learned advocacy. Between today's academics and tomorrow's intellectuals, I suggest, are four specific modes of political intelligence, each of which, although anchored in circumstances prior to the Dreyfus Affair, is replete with persuasive techniques and ethical sensibilities for use in the interim between contemporary academic life and intellectual cultures still to come—an interim in which learned advocacy continues to suffer from jargon-clotted vocabularies, hyperrational forms of argument, nostalgia for radical dissent, and ideologies of vanguard leadership.

In addition to conceptualizing the rhetorics of withdrawal, exemplarity, obedience, and identification, I hope to heighten our awareness of the situations in which to deploy them. To be sure, imperial Rome, feudal France, Enlightenment Prussia, and Golden Age Denmark look nothing like contemporary democratic public culture. But the specific rhetorical situations in which Seneca, Christine, Kant, and Kierkegaard intervened bear a striking resemblance to those in which late-modern academics now find themselves. As systems of tenure continue to devolve into economies of contingent labor, and traditions of shared governance continue to buckle under the weight of corporate managerial styles, the ivied walls of the modern university have begun to crumble, exposing contingent instructors and tenured professors alike to administrative, industrial, governmental, and populist abuses of power.[23] It is here, in this complex network of authority, that the rhetorical situations discussed in this book find their late-modern analogues. The disempowerment of the Roman Senate and the concentration of executive power during Nero's reign parallel the increasing circumvention of elected faculty governance by centralized college administrations.[24] The ducal attempt to privatize and profit from the king's public authority in late-medieval France resembles the privatization and exploitation of the university's traditionally public services (knowledge production and dissemination) by powerful corporate sponsors.[25] The acceleration of state censorship in conservative Prussia during the French Revolution accords with post-9/11 attempts by the national security state to monitor and regulate outspoken scholars at home and abroad.[26] And the outburst of populist reason and anti-intellectual sentiment in nineteenth-century Denmark mirrors the ongoing effort of right-wing advocacy groups to incite public opinion against "tenured radicals."[27]

Many of today's academics have learned to live with these abuses of power, resigning themselves to "the necessity for constant, disabling wariness and for intellectual choices shaped by estimates of personal and political vulnerability."[28] But this does not mean they are incapable of dissent. It just means that their persuasive techniques and resistant practices are likely to be more subtle and indirect than those of the public intellectual. Even as early as 1902, in an essay on "Academic Freedom," John Dewey realized the importance of subtlety and indirection to politically engaged academics. Consider, for instance, ongoing efforts to counteract the commercialization of knowledge. Instead of allowing our critiques "to rasp the feelings of everyone exercising the capitalist function," Dewey explains, we might phrase them so as "not to excite the prejudices or inflame the passions even of those who thoroughly disagreed."[29] Not since the McCarthy era has this subtle form of political contention—"the technique of protective coloration," as one of Dewey's commentators famously described it—been more crucial to the public and professional lives of American academics.[30] In an age of willful college administrators, avid corporate sponsors, paranoid government officials, and overzealous advocacy groups, Dewey's words continue to echo through the halls of academe: "*Watch what you say.*"[31]

What this means for learned political action in late modernity is the subject of my final chapter. In service to recent depictions of American academics as "legitimists in some areas of political discourse and action, and contesters in others," I suggest that one of the defining features of their resistance is its undecidability, specifically its habit of toggling indeterminately between rhetorics of deference and dissent, resulting in ambiguous and at times inconsistent articulations of personal, professional, and public interests.[32] To illustrate this curious form of political contention, I consider the "thinking man" in Bertolt Brecht's *Stories of Mr. Keuner*, notably the relationship between Mr. Keuner, his students, and his superiors. At stake in this relationship, I argue, is a mode of resistance by which today's academics can position themselves in and against existing systems of authority, tactfully yet effectively mobilizing certain power relationships in order to oppose others. In theorizing this oppositional technique, I hope to provide a summative, albeit still incomplete, answer to the question that led me to the letters of Seneca, Christine, Kant, and Kierkegaard: How can learned men and women in the age of academia, when the tradition of "the intellectual" has been reduced to ruins, pose a meaningful challenge to abusive figures of authority?

2

REMAINING CONCEALED:
LEARNED PROTEST BETWEEN STOICISM AND THE STATE

There is a very well-known saying by a man who had grown old in royal service. Asked how he had achieved that rarest of distinctions at court, old age, he answered, "By suffering wrongs and saying 'Thank-you.'"

—SENECA THE YOUNGER

Suicide and Strategy

With one swift pass of the knife, he opened the veins of four wrists. While the blood of his wife pooled freely at her feet, Seneca the Younger refused to hemorrhage. So he severed the arteries of his legs and knees. With blood still escaping slowly, he ordered a stock of hemlock to be prepared. And when even this failed to subdue him, Seneca entered a cauldron of heated water and ordered his servants to carry him into a bath, where steam and suffocation eventually claimed his life.

Seneca never intended to end his career so dramatically. Twice he requested permission to retire from court life, presenting Nero with claims of old age, poor health, and absorption in philosophy, and twice the *princeps* refused. Between his first failure to retire in 62 CE and his state-ordered suicide three years later, Seneca lost more than the persuasive leverage needed to retire unscathed into philosophical leisure. Having fallen from Nero's good graces, he also lost the political influence needed to sway imperial affairs.

All along the way, Seneca was addressing letters to his friend, Lucilius Junior. More than a collection of "carelessly written" notes, as Seneca famously described them, his *Letters to Lucilius (Ad Lucilium epistulae morales)* offer a correspondence course in the art of securing retirement and, where the path to retirement is blocked, remaining concealed in hazardous political landscapes.[1] Cataloging and conceptualizing these persuasive techniques, especially as they lend themselves to purposes of learned activism, is the primary task of this chapter.

Letter-Essays to Lucilius

Seneca's *Letters to Lucilius* rely on the epistolary techniques of Demetrius and Cicero, both of whom understood the letter as one side of a naturally occurring conversation. "You have been complaining that my letters to you are rather carelessly written," Seneca remarks to Lucilius. "Now who talks carefully unless he also desires to talk affectedly? I prefer that my letters should be just what my conversation would be if you and I were sitting in one another's company or taking walks together,—spontaneous and easy; for my letters have nothing strained or artificial about them."[2] And with artlessness comes intimacy, Seneca goes on to insist: "I never receive a letter from you without being in your company forthwith." Unlike "pictures of our absent friends," which only "lighten our longing by a solace that is unreal and unsubstantial," letters bring with them "real traces, real evidences" of their remote authors: "For that which is sweetest when we meet face to face is afforded by the impress of a friend's hand upon his letter—recognition."[3] Casual, impulsive, and personal—these are the attributes with which Seneca inscribes his letters.

Nevertheless, the authenticity of these letters is doubtful. This is partly because Seneca wrote them for posterity.[4] But it has more to do with the pace of philosophical education and epistolary exchange in imperial Rome. Given that Seneca probably wrote his letters between winter 63 and autumn 64 CE, it is unlikely that Lucilius could have made the kind of spiritual progress ascribed to him.[5] That Lucilius—a Roman knight with Epicurean tendencies—could come of age as a stoic in a matter of months would have surprised even the most accomplished pedagogue. And because Seneca's correspondence comprises 124 extant letters, and Lucilius's letters sometimes took months to arrive, the legitimacy of their exchange depends on Seneca having written to Lucilius before receiving replies to previous posts, and frequently sending many letters at once.[6] To this extent, the epistolarity of his letters may be little more than a formal attribute. Indeed, when coupled with his gestures toward posterity, these traces of fabrication suggest that, despite his claim to have written carelessly, as though engaged in an intimate conversation, Seneca's letters are highly stylized texts designed for audiences other than Lucilius.[7]

Seneca's letters are neither intimate nor official, their purpose being neither to manage interpersonal relations nor to conduct affairs of state. They more closely resemble what M. Luther Stirewalt calls "letter-essays." As a subgenre of professional and technical letter-writing, the letter-essay is anchored in epistolary form but aimed at "extended settings" in which "writers publicize non-epistolary topics for a group of people, identified or unidentified, and known or unknown."[8] The philosophical letters of Plato and Epicurus, the letters on rhetoric by Isocrates, and the letters of literary criticism by Dionysius of Halicarnassus are all species of this kind. In each case, we see a "participation framework" not unlike that discussed in chapter 1, in which authors stage dialogues with addressees before a variety of third and fourth parties.[9]

In addition to addressing extended recipients, letter-essays were often used to supplement previously published work. Like Epicurus, who addressed his first letter to students eager to master his more formal writings, Seneca positions his correspondence in the wake of three earlier treatises: *On the Shortness of Life* (*De brevitate vitae*), *On Tranquility of Mind* (*De tranquillitate animi*), and *On Retirement* (*De otio*). Each of these dialogues, as we shall see, tried and largely failed to counteract the use of Stoic doctrine to justify political abstention in imperial Rome. *Letters to Lucilius* can and should be read as an ethico-political addendum to these failed philosophical labors. In contrast to Miriam T. Griffin, who finds "no clear development" in these works, I read Seneca's correspondence as the fourth and final statement in a decadelong discussion of philosophical leisure and the limits of political participation.[10]

That Seneca characterizes his letters as "spontaneous and easy" texts, with "nothing strained or artificial about them," is in keeping with their supplemental function. As Stirewalt observes, stylists of the letter-essay often seem "conscious of using a plain style in contrast to the parent works which are of a higher style." Embracing their "minor literary merit," Seneca strives for *scriptio humilis* in his letters to Lucilius.[11] Recalling *Ad Nicoclem*, in which Isocrates plainly advises the young king of Cyprus, Seneca cultivates a casual style, counseling readers then and now in "the low-toned words of conversation [*submissiora verba*]."[12]

Interestingly, the tone of these letters is only partially reflected in the persona of their author. Throughout his correspondence, Seneca toggles between the role of a teacher, supplying posterity with proverbial insights ex cathedra (proverbs being "the only philosophy admissible" in epistolary discourse, according to Demetrius), and that of an *imperfectus* who, like Lucilius, is still in search of Stoic virtue.[13] "When I saw your abilities, I laid my hand upon you, I exhorted you, I applied the goad and did not permit you to march lazily, but roused you continually," Seneca explains. "And now I do the same; but by this time I am cheering on one who is in the race and so in turn cheers me on."[14]

At once teacher and student, coach and competitor, Seneca models the subject position of today's educated elites. In his struggle to address posterity as a Stoic sage and at the same time to identify himself with first-century imperial subjects, we glimpse some of the persuasive techniques and ethical sensibilities with which "learnedness" comes. In particular, we see a rhetoric of withdrawal that enables learned men and women to exercise linguistic authority without, in turn, forfeiting their moral integrity in corrupt political cultures. At issue here is not only a line of escape from scurrilous figures of authority, as scholarly comment on Seneca's *Letters to Lucilius* often suggests, but also a strategy for remaining concealed in their presence. In order to understand this strategy, we must first explain the historical circumstances in which Seneca perfected it.

Imperial Drama, 54–62 CE

With the passing of Claudius in 54 came the imperial ascent of his seventeen-year-old adopted son, Nero. His rule began well enough under the guidance of Seneca the Younger and Burrus, prefect of the guard. But the good times did not last long. In 55, Nero poisoned Claudius's son Britannicus. He then went on to abandon his wife, Octavia, the daughter of Claudius, for the freedwoman Acte, whom he later replaced with Poppaea Sabina, the wife of his good friend Otho. Then, in 59, Nero murdered his mother, Agrippina. Soon thereafter, Burrus suffered a mysterious death. And next came Octavia, whom Nero had recently exiled.

Matters were only slightly better for Seneca. With Burrus gone, Nero had begun receiving counsel from his successor, Tigellinus, and the empress in waiting, Poppaea. Together, they brought a variety of charges against Seneca, insisting that he was bent on surpassing Nero in wealth, admiration, and eloquence. They even went so far as to accuse him of bemoaning Nero's skill as a charioteer and his voice as a singer. When news of these charges reached Seneca, he immediately sought an audience with the emperor. Tacitus recounts his appeal to Nero:

> It is fourteen years ago, Caesar, that I was first associated with your prospects, and eight years since you have been emperor. In the interval, you have heaped on me such honors and riches that nothing is wanting to my happiness but a right to use it. . . . As I should pray for support in warfare, or when wearied by the road, so in this journey of life, an old man and unequal to the lightest of cares, I ask for succor: for I can bear my riches no further. Order my estates to be administered by your procurators, to be embodied in your fortune. Not that by my own action I shall reduce myself to poverty: rather, I shall resign the glitter of wealth which dazzles me, and recall to the service of the mind those hours which are now set apart to the care of my gardens or my villas. You have vigor to spare; you have watched for years the methods by which supreme power is wielded: we, your older friends, may demand our rest. This, too, shall redound to your glory—that you raised to the highest places men who could also accept the lowly.

Seneca's request met with a frosty reception from the *princeps*:

> On the contrary, not only is yours a vigorous age, adequate to affairs and to their rewards, but I myself am but entering the first stages of my sovereignty. Why not recall the uncertain steps of my youth, if here and there they slip, and even more zealously guide and support the manhood which owes its pride to you. Not your moderation, if you give back your riches; not your retirement [*quies*], if you abandon your prince; but *my* avarice, and the terrors of *my* cruelty, will be upon all men's lips. And, however much your abnegation may be praised, it will still be unworthy of a sage to derive credit from an act which sullies the fair fame of a friend.

Veiling his hatred in gestures of care, Nero is said to have followed his rebuttal with an embrace and kisses, to which Seneca replied with gratitude, this being the "the end of all dialogues with an autocrat."[15] Make no mistake: appearances were to be kept up.

We could do worse than interpret this exchange in terms of politeness theory. Seneca and Nero are both competing for the right to determine their relationship. In particular, each is vying for control of his relation to the public persona of his interlocutor. Face threats abound. Consider, for instance, the tension between negative- and positive-face wants, the former of which indicate a desire for personal autonomy, and the latter of which mark a desire to be valued by others.[16] In these terms, the mechanics of this exchange are readily apparent: Seneca uses negative politeness to reduce his threat to Nero's positive face, which is implicit in his request to distance himself from the principate, and Nero responds with a point-by-point denial of the negative-face wants ascribed to him in Seneca's request. Thus, by refusing to accept "the glitter and wealth" offered to him, Nero is able to withhold "the service of the mind" that Seneca hopes to receive in exchange, thereby blocking his path to retirement.

But we might also do better than politeness theory. In order to understand why Seneca's petition failed, its nature as rhetorical act, and the scar it left on his political career, we cannot limit ourselves to the study of its linguistic structure. Although interesting in its own right, his conversation with Nero is symptomatic of a broader intellectual and cultural milieu, in which the concept of retirement (*otium*) was hotly disputed and dangerously enacted. What makes Seneca's request to retire so interesting, then, is neither the subtlety of his appeal nor the harshness of Nero's reply, but the instability of the rhetorical situation in which it occurred. Mapping this situation is the task to which we now turn.

Quinquennium Neronis

In the years leading up to his appeal for retirement, Seneca accomplished many feats of public service. Among his most dubious achievements was the defense of Nero's decision to assassinate his mother. In a letter to the Senate, almost certainly written at the emperor's request, Seneca accused Agrippina of plotting against her son and gave thanks for Nero's delivery from her murderous lust—and he encouraged his addressees to do the same. As Tacitus reports, "Thanksgivings were to be held at all appropriate shrines; the festival of Minerva, on which the conspiracy had been brought to light, was to be celebrated with annual games; a golden statue of the goddess, with an effigy of the emperor by her side, was to be erected in the curia, and Agrippina's birthday included among the inauspicious dates."[17]

The hypocrisy of Seneca's letter probably outraged many senators. But only Thrasea Paetus, a would-be Stoic from the upper echelons of Roman society, was willing to act on his anger. Upon hearing Seneca's defense of

Nero, Thrasea stormed out of the curia, thus beginning an oppositional campaign against the principate. What bothered him was not only the desertion of Nero's earlier program of *clementia*, which Seneca had dutifully outlined in the mid-50s, but also the Senate's increasing subordination to the principate. Just a few years before Agrippina's murder, the tribunes had been barred from the judicial functions of higher magistrates, and the authority to fine among the tribunes and magistrates had been reduced. On top of this, the senatorial treasury had been brought under the control of special prefects chosen by the emperor. Imperial officials were gaining power at the expense of their republican counterparts, and everyone knew it.

If this shift in power startled members of the Senate like Thrasea, it was because it stood in sharp contrast to first few years of Nero's reign, a period of generous leadership and shared governance that would later come to be known as the "quinquennium Neronis."[18] After his ascension speech of 54, in which Nero promised to avoid the autocratic tendencies of his predecessor and to uphold the traditional authority of the Senate, the teenage emperor scaled back his personal jurisdiction, allowing the Senate and its appointed representatives not only to settle quarrels in and between Italian cities but also to handle more appeals in civil cases. No longer would the *princeps* conduct trials of prominent Romans behind closed doors. Nero was careful to insist that "his private establishment and the State should be kept entirely distinct."[19] Inspired by this gesture toward shared governance, the Senate immediately overturned two measures of the previous regime—one allowing forensic orators to receive gifts in exchange for their services, and another requiring the quaestors-elect to stage gladiatorial exhibitions at their own expense. As a sign of his continued support, Nero granted impoverished senators an annual allowance, thereby allowing them to hold games of their own and, more important, to maintain their wealth qualification. He even went so far as to strike his precious metal coinage with the formula "EX S C," meaning "ex senatus consulto" or "in conformity with a decree of the Senate." Although Nero never actually relinquished his control over the minting of gold and silver, it is difficult to imagine a more significant act of deference to the Senate. That he meant what he said in his accession speech would be readily apparent to everyone with a coin in his or her purse.

Just as Nero went out of his way to indicate his respect for the Senate, so, too, did the Senate go out of its way to indicate its support of Nero. Gold and silver statues of himself, the honor of having the Roman calendar begin with his birth month, the title of pater patriae ("father of the fatherland"), and even the honor of consulate for life—all were freely offered to the young *princeps*.

And all were prudently refused. Accepting these honors (like allowing Seneca to retire from court life) would have jeopardized the *persona civilis* of the new principate—namely, its public appearance as a communal form of governance "held together by the bond of law, existing for the mutual benefit of its members, and incompatible with the injustice and pride of tyranny."[20] Although Cicero's *societas civilis* was nowhere to be seen, imperial senators wanted Nero to play the part of a democratic leader. He was to act "as if under a republic" (*hōs en dēmotikos*), as Cassius Dio aptly noted.[21] It was the performance of republican sentiment, not a restoration of its political institutions, that the Senate expected from Nero. And much to its members' delight, nothing came easier to the young emperor than political stagecraft.

That the quinquennium Neronis involved a good bit of performance almost goes without saying. Like Gaius and Claudius before him, both of whom also promised to share executive power with the Senate, Nero worked hard to maintain the illusion of a Roman dyarchy. Not only did the imperial Senate retain the constitutional powers assigned to it during the republic, but it actually improved on these powers. Since the reign of Augustus, the legislative, judicial, and electoral powers of the imperial Senate had all increased.[22] And yet, its political and administrative authority never escaped the grasp of the principate. Although decrees of the Senate could assume the force of law, all were subordinate to imperial pronouncements. Although the Senate acquired decisive power over elections, the *princeps* exercised great influence over the candidacy. And even though the Senate became an important criminal court, Nero still reserved the right to hear appeals. "Whereas once the Senate had exercised a *de facto* control greater than its formal powers and its *auctoritas* was often contrasted with the people's *potestas*," argues Miriam Griffin, "its increased legal powers were now subject to the *auctoritas* of the Princeps."[23] Add to this the overwhelming military, financial, and provincial power of the emperor, and the republican ideal of shared governance can be seen for what it was during the Julio-Claudian principate: an ideological state apparatus.

Coincident with the increase in senatorial power was a discernible loss of its political influence. Like many of today's academic senates, the Neronian Senate was little more than an advisory board. "The Emperor might take its advice on matters of home and foreign policy, but he was not bound to follow it, and always reserved the right of final decision."[24] This is not to suggest, of course, that the imperial Senate had no part to play in affairs of state. As the young *princeps* well knew, it was a repository of political intelligence and administrative experience, both of which were crucial to the management of his new principate. Only by maintaining a *persona civilis* could he conceal the absolutism inherent in his office and, in so doing, convince members of the senatorial order to assist him in the difficult and precarious task of administering his vast empire, which now reached as far north as Britain. "The Principate as a system of government could only remain efficient and secure if it had the consent and co-operation of the senatorial order," Griffin explains. "Without its co-operation in assuming commands and governorships, there would be a shortage of administrative manpower which could only be met by retaining the willing in their posts for long terms, thereby increasing the chances of successful rebellion."[25] Thus, although the Roman Senate had been reduced to an advisory council, its individual members had become invaluable human resources, not unlike committee members and faculty senators in the late-modern university system.

When Thrasea stormed out of the curia, he posed a direct political challenge to the imperial order of things. And in a very real sense it was the only senatorial mode of resistance available to him. Because "the *princeps* controlled the discussion and the action of the senate," Frank Frost Abbott notes, "a senator could indicate his disapproval of a measure only by staying away from the meeting when the bill in question was to be presented."[26] Seneca's defense of matricide before the Senate hardly constituted a new bill, but it was certainly an opportunity for Thrasea to express his disapproval of the young *princeps*. And given the communal sentiments with which membership in the Senate often came, his disapproval had the potential to inspire other acts of defiance, and perhaps even a wave of absenteeism.[27] Nothing would have been worse for the new principate, the administration of which was still heavily reliant on the public service of the Roman ruling class. This is precisely why Thrasea's abstention and political inertia amounted to revolutionary propaganda. And it was Nero's harsh response to this revolutionary propaganda that brought the quinquennium Neronis to a close.

Serving States: Inwardness, Publicity, and the Order of the Cosmos

That Thrasea claimed to be a devoted Stoic implicated all who walked the porch. "In order to subvert the empire," one government official said of the Stoics, "they make a parade of liberty: the empire overthrown, they will lay hands on liberty itself."[28] Thanks to Thrasea, Stoic *constantia* had become the face of resistance. And in 62 CE, the same year Seneca requested permission to retire from court life, adherence to Stoicism became a criminal offense.

Much to the embarrassment of other Roman Stoics, Thrasea's opposition did not seem to derive from his philosophical commitments. And even if it had, the complexity of first-century Stoicism precluded any clear endorsement of political sedition.[29] But neither did it provide a definitive argument to the contrary. If Socrates redirected philosophy from the physical universe to human affairs, early-imperial Stoics diverted it from the sphere of moral thought to the practice of everyday life. First-century malcontents took it even further, pressing philosophy into the service of their own political agendas.[30] With Stoicism up for grabs, activists like Thrasea were able to exploit it for the tropes and topoi they needed to frame and justify acts of moral disapproval. Whether this disapproval derived from serious philosophical commitments or desperate political circumstances was beside the point.

Although Seneca and Thrasea found a common enemy in Nero's new administration (and otherwise seemed to respect each other), they could not have disagreed more on the use of Stoicism to legitimate acts of political resistance.[31] For Seneca, nothing could be more disastrous than a political culture in which philosophy had become a sign of dissent, and public service the outer limit of practical wisdom.

In defense of this position, he penned three treatises, each of which, in light of our previous discussion of the autocratic inheritance and administrative demands of the Neronian principate, warrants careful consideration: *On the Shortness of Life*, *On Tranquility of Mind*, and *On Retirement*. In an effort to dissociate political withdrawal from moral protest, Seneca's treatise *On the Shortness of Life* purges philosophical leisure of all political activities, literary achievements, and pursuits of luxury, leaving in their stead only a rigorous devotion to wisdom. Written sometime between 48 and 55 CE, this treatise provides its addressee, Paulinus, with a conditional set of warrants for gradually withdrawing from imperial politics: advanced age and a desire to return to liberal studies. A spirited and popular work, *On the Shortness of Life* is addressed not only to Paulinus, however (whose virtuous career as *praefectus annonae* had long been "displayed in laborious and unceasing proofs"), but also to a wider Roman readership, before whom Seneca sought to defend his father-in-law, who had recently been forced to surrender his political position.[32]

Recalling Plato and Aristotle, both of whom stressed the relative autonomy of the *bios theōrētikos*, Seneca offers "the philosopher" as an exemplary figure of political withdrawal: "He is not confined by the same bounds that shut others in. He alone is freed from the limitations of the human race." For this reason, Seneca writes, "all ages serve him as if a god."[33] And nowhere are conditions of this servitude nastier than in the realm of public affairs, which is overrun by "those who labor at engrossments that are not even their own, who regulate their sleep by that of another, their walk by the pace of another, who are under orders in case of the freest things in the world—loving and hating."³⁴ If public life seems short, Seneca concludes, it is because such a small portion of it is ours to live.

By the beginning of 62, Seneca had written his treatise *On Tranquility of Mind*, an exercise in applied Stoicism encouraging his friend, Annaeus Serenus, to consider how best to live in "a time when it is not at all easy to serve the state."³⁵ Rebutting Athenodorus, the moral adviser to Augustus, who recommended avoiding the forum when circumstances are less than ideal, Seneca argues that he "seems to have surrendered too quickly to the times, to have retreated too quickly. I myself would not deny that sometimes one must retire, but it should be a gradual retreat." On this point, the treatise is explicit: "If Fortune shall get the upper hand and shall cut off the opportunity for action, let a man not straightaway turn his back and flee, throwing away his arms and seeking some hiding-place, as if there were anywhere a place where Fortune could not reach him, but let him devote himself to his duties more sparingly, and, after making [this] choice, let him find something in which he may be useful to the state."³⁶ That civic life is far from perfect does not erase our moral duty to engage in it: "He will truly be a man who, when perils are threatening from every side, when arms and chains are rattling around him, will neither endanger, nor conceal, his virtue [*non alliserit virtutem nec absconderit*]."³⁷ How are we to understand this line of conduct? What does it mean to avert without avoiding the hazards of public life? Seneca wastes no words in his reply: "Combine leisure with business" (*miscere otium rebus*, where *miscere* means to mingle, and *rebus* is a term for public affairs).

Over and against his earlier distinction between the lordship of philosophers and the bondage of politicians, Seneca goes on to redefine public service as the medium of wisdom: "All life is servitude. And so a man must become reconciled to his lot, must complain of it as little as possible, and must lay hold of whatever good it may have; no state is so bitter that a calm mind [*aequus animus*, where *aequus* indicates a state of impartiality, patience, and contentment] cannot find in it some consolation."³⁸ Here, the wretched partiality of public life discussed in *On the Shortness of Life* becomes the basis for a run-of-the-mill Stoic withdrawal to the inner world of self-consciousness: "Most of all, the mind must be withdrawn from external interests into itself [*Utique animus ab omnibus externis in se revocandus*]. Let it have confidence in itself, rejoice in itself, let it admire its own things, let it retire [*recedat*] as far as possible from the things of others and devote itself to itself, let it not feel losses, let it interpret kindly even adversities."³⁹

Cultivating this inner state involves organizing the contents of personal experience (e.g., desires, feelings, judgments) into a coherent, harmonious network of rational precepts and attitudes *in the place of* an independent world of appearances. "The trick discovered by Stoic philosophy is to use the mind in such a way that reality cannot touch its owner even when he has not withdrawn from it," Hannah Arendt explains, echoing Hegel and Zeller before her. "Instead of withdrawing mentally from everything that is present and close at hand, he has drawn every appearance inside himself, and his 'consciousness' becomes a full substitute for the outside world presented as impression or image."[40] More than a line of escape from public life, then, *tranquillitas animi* is an intellectual resource for enduring its various hardships.[41]

Unlike *Tranquility of Mind*, which presumes the potential for right living even in the most depraved political landscapes, the extant portion of Seneca's treatise *On Retirement* outlines several conditions in which political disengagement is acceptable:

> If the state is too corrupt to be helped, if it is wholly dominated by evils, the wise man will not struggle to no purpose, nor spend himself when nothing is to be gained. If he is lacking in influence or power and the state is unwilling to accept his services, if he is hampered by ill health, he will not enter upon a course for which he knows he is unfitted, just as he would not launch upon the sea a battered ship, just as he would not enlist for service in the army if he were disabled.[42]

Without negating the advice contained in *Tranquility of Mind*, Seneca suggests that when political turmoil begins to interfere with the maintenance of Stoic consciousness, it is appropriate to remove oneself from the realm of human affairs.

But political abstention does not mark the end of public service, as *On the Shortness of Life* suggests. On the contrary, Stoic doctrine posits two res publicae in which to exercise political agency: a "lesser" realm of social interaction among members of a particular speech community, and a "greater" realm of worldly affairs in which membership crosses terrestrial and heavenly lines of difference:

> Let us grasp the idea that there are two commonwealths [*res publicas*]— the one, a vast and truly common state, which embraces alike gods and men, in which we look neither to this corner of earth nor to that,

but measure the bounds of our citizenship by the path of the sun; the other, the one to which we have been assigned by the accident of birth. This will be the commonwealth of the Athenians or of the Carthaginians, or of any other city that belongs, not to all, but to some particular race of men. Some yield service to both commonwealths at the same time—to the greater and to the lesser—some only to the lesser, some only to the greater.[43]

Underpinning this theory of dual citizenship is a classical tension between the Cynic ancestry and the imperial ascent of Stoic moral theory. Informing Seneca's notion of the "greater" commonwealth is a radical Cynic rejection of conventional ethics, according to which the guiding ideas of personal and political life should be those established by philosophy, regardless of prevailing social conventions. And shoring up his theory of the "lesser" commonwealth is a middle-Stoic insistence that "life according to nature"—and with it the natural process of ethical development (*oikeiōsis*)—takes place within existing configurations of the family and the state. Historically speaking, this tension between intransigent Cynicism and malleable Stoicism marks the transition from late Hellenistic to early Roman political thought, especially as it found expression in the works of the Greek philosopher Panaetius and his student Posidonius. With these two at the helm, "Zeno's radical quasi-Cynicism was replaced, increasingly (though not uniformly) with a tendency to accommodate core Stoic ideals with at least qualified validation of conventional social structures."[44]

This is not to suggest that Zeno and his successor, Chrysippus, understood the "greater" commonwealth as a site of ideal morality lying at the historical and anthropological roots of civilization (as Panaetius, Posidonius, and their followers suggested). Nor is it to suggest that they understood it as an emerging world-state in which the unity of humankind would eventually become apparent, as though their theories of cosmopolitanism were analogous to Alexander's struggle to obliterate cultural differences between the Greeks and their neighbors (this being Plutarch's interpretation). Rather, for these early Stoics, the "greater" commonwealth was a morally admirable community of gods and sages united across space and time by their daily practice of the same internalized law of right reason. In this republic of Stoic virtue, participating in local forums of collective life was paramount, but locality was unconstrained by physical proximity and mutual acquaintance. Philosophers and laypeople, citizens and noncitizens, men and women—all had the potential to become *kosmopolitai*.[45]

In positing two commonwealths—one for philosophy and another for politics—and allowing Stoics to participate in both, Seneca aimed to reconcile these two ethical sensibilities, at once recuperating the Cynic insights of Zeno and Chrysippus and reinforcing the philosophic politics of Panaetius and Posidonius. Over and against the modern tendency to "dislocate" cosmic order in favor of etiological theory or, as is more often the case, transnational flows of capital and culture, *On Retirement* suggests that virtue cultivated in withdrawal and contemplation (particularly through the study of moral and natural philosophy) can contribute to the development of a Stoic cosmopolis by enabling the philosopher (*sapiens*) to advise the layperson (*proficiens*) in the terms and interests of a cosmic *logos*. "Who will deny that Virtue ought to test her progress by open deed," Seneca asks—prefiguring the arguments of Jacoby, Posner, and other apologists for the public intellectual—and "at times apply her hand and bring into reality what she has conceived?"[46]

Also prefigured in his treatise *On Retirement* are the communicative ethics of Kantian rhetorical theory. As Seneca is careful to point out, the advice of the sage should not cater to the ethos of any given audience, as recommended by Aristotelian theories of persuasion, but instead ought to address itself to the reasoning capacity of all humans.[47] Nor should Stoic philosophers limit their addressees to other human beings, for it is often themselves who stand to benefit from their personal service to the "greater" commonwealth. "It is of course required of a man that he should benefit his fellow-men—many if he can, if not, a few; if not a few, those who are nearest; if not these, himself," Seneca notes. For in bettering ourselves, we anticipate the betterment of others: "Just as the man that chooses to become worse injures not only himself but all those whom, if he had become better, he might have benefitted, so whoever wins the approval of himself benefits others by the very fact that he prepares what will prove beneficial to them."[48]

It is here, where dialogue with the self has become a condition of possibility for the moral uplift of others, that the political upshot of dual citizenship becomes apparent: "Even the contemplative life is not devoid of action."[49] Thus, if *The Shortness of Life* subordinates public service to philosophical leisure, and *Tranquility of Mind* advocates their intermingling, *On Retirement* refines both arguments, insisting that political activity is a crucial aspect of philosophical leisure. Recalling Chrysippus before him (who argued that although we should choose the active life, we should not contrast it with the contemplative life, because wisdom acts itself out in our social nature), Seneca invites his readers to understand philosophy as a *commune bonum*, practitioners of which, because they are "always in action," ever engaged in "the business of wisdom" (*sapientiae negotium*), are able and obliged to guide ordinary citizens through even the most trying political circumstances.[50]

But this is not their only task, as his treatise *On Retirement* plainly states. In addition to Stoics who serve both commonwealths at once, there are those who offer their assistance "only to the lesser" and those who yield it "only to the greater." What are we to make of this apparent loophole in the theory of dual citizenship? Although he insists that political activity is a crucial aspect of philosophical leisure, Seneca remains committed to the possibility of their noncoincidence. Advising others in the terms and interests of a cosmic logos is not a necessary condition but a contingent function of Stoic philosophy. And yet, it is not a simple continuation of philosophical thought. On the contrary, this advice marks a break or departure from contemplation, a momentary *respectus*, in which *otium* diverts its attention from "the things of heaven" to "human affairs," and in so doing "brings what it has learned into the open [*quod didicit, ostendens*]."[51] If indeed Stoic philosophers have a part to play in civic life, as Seneca suggests, it is because they spend most of their lives in worlds apart from it.

The Part That Has No Part

By publishing *The Shortness of Life*, *Tranquility of Mind*, and *On Retirement*, Seneca hoped to forestall the conflict between Stoic doctrine and imperial governance, if only long enough for him to retire unscathed into philosophical leisure. By purging *otium* of all political activities, literary achievements, and pursuits of luxury, leaving in their stead only a rigorous devotion to philosophy, his treatise on the brevity of life aimed to dissociate political withdrawal from moral protest. In arguing against hasty, emotional flights from civic life, advocating instead a slow, piecemeal retreat, his dialogue on mental tranquility recommended public service in even the stormiest political cultures. And by highlighting the relevance of philosophical leisure to affairs of state, his tract on retirement disavowed any direct opposition between the Stoic sage and imperial order.

Taken together, these arguments form a coherent political program whose adherents look nothing like Thrasea and his *rigidi et tristes satellites*. Where the retirement we have earned cannot be claimed, serving our communities in a state of tranquil inwardness is a prudent alternative; and where our Stoic psyche cannot endure the conditions of public service, mediating our political and philosophical commitments through civil acts of right reason is a fitting option. Even in retirement, where the call of the cosmos is loudest, Stoics can be good citizens—perhaps even the best citizens.

Although certainly relevant to contemporary academic culture, in which college administrators, private advocacy groups, and the national security state are ever on alert for "bad citizens," it is difficult to understand Seneca's political agenda apart from the first-century conflict between Stoicism and the principate in which it was designed to intervene. Nor is it easy to understand his conversation with Nero apart from the intervening efforts of his philosophical writings. Indeed, to overlook the intellectual and cultural surroundings of his request to retire is to overlook the mode of rhetorical agency for which it stands. Over and against the opportunistic and newly criminalized use of Stoicism to justify political abstention, Seneca's exchange with Nero was an opportunity to transform the philosophical commitments outlined in his treatises *The Shortness of Life, Tranquility of Mind,* and *On Retirement,* into a set of categories capable of legitimating his request to retire.

Nero did more than deny this request. He also reminded Seneca of his role as a "friend of the Emperor" (*amicus principis*)—an advisory position that, once secured, afforded no escape.[52] With Stoicism outlawed and his path to retirement blocked, Seneca found himself shackled to the principate. And with Burrus gone and Tigellinus at Nero's ear, he found himself devoid of political power. By 63 CE, Seneca was neither "an old man and unequal to the lightest of cares," as he claimed to be in his request to retire, nor of "a vigorous age, adequate to affairs and their rewards," as Nero coldly rejoined. Seneca spent his final years in hopeless suspension between these two personae, lacking not only the political influence needed to sway imperial affairs but also the persuasive leverage needed to retire unscathed into philosophical leisure.

As a courtier and a philosopher, he came to embody the tension between imperial governance and Stoic doctrine. Neither the arguments of his theoretical treatises nor his personal appeals to Nero could relieve him of this abject position. It was in response to this political abjection that Seneca penned his famous *Letters to Lucilius,* presenting readers then and now with an array of strategies for right living and clever politicking in the interstices between imperial politics and philosophical leisure. Punctuating the events of 63–64, when Seneca was struggling to "combine leisure with business" (much as he had advised Serenus to do in *Tranquility of Mind*), his correspondence toggles productively between the demands of "greater" and "lesser" commonwealths, arguing by example for the interpenetration of learned and political cultures.

Although several of his epistles recall the basic arguments of *On Retirement*, notably the claim that Stoics can serve two res publicae by forfeiting their places in one, much of Seneca's letter-writing erodes the distinction between "greater" and "lesser" commonwealths. Consider, for instance, this puzzling excerpt from his sixty-eighth epistle:

> When we have assigned to our wise man that field of public life which is worthy of him,—in other words, the universe,—he is then not apart from public life, even if he withdraws [*non est extra rem publicam, etiam si recesserit*]; nay, perhaps he has abandoned only one little corner thereof and has passed over into greater and wider regions; and when he has been set in the heavens, he understands how lowly was the place in which he sat when he mounted the curule chair or the judgment-seat. Lay this to heart,—that the wise man is never more active in affairs than when things divine as well as things human have come within his ken.[53]

If *On Retirement* theorizes public life as an aspect of philosophical leisure, letter 68 upends this relationship, reclassifying philosophical leisure as an aspect of public life. Moreover, if *On Retirement* allows for the existence of *otium* apart from *res civiles*, letter 68 insists on their convergence, even going so far as to define *otium* as an irremovable part of *res civiles*. How are we to understand this mandatory inclusion? What does it mean for Seneca's theory of dual citizenship? And how does it relate to the self- and state-imposed exclusion of Stoic thought from imperial politics?

Two things are obvious at this point. First, despite their animosity, Thrasea and Nero share a common belief: Stoic philosophers have no part to play in imperial governance. They are the part of Roman society that has no part in Roman politics. And second, in Seneca's treatise *On Retirement*, this exclusion from the "lesser" commonwealth becomes a negative condition of possibility for their positive identification with the "greater" commonwealth. The result is a curious form of political agency, in which this part of Roman society that has no part in Roman politics, by laying claim to the cosmic whole in which all forms of civic life take part, is able to recover a modicum of public authority.[54] If Thrasea's conflict with the principate forced the Stoic philosopher into a game of all or nothing, in which communion with the "greater" commonwealth presupposed estrangement from its "lesser" variant, *On Retirement* changed the rules of this game, redoubling the cast-out philosopher as a *nothing that is all*—a void in Roman politics through which all things political eventually pass. More than an outspoken deserter of the "lesser" commonwealth, the Stoic philosopher is a metonymic stand-in for the "greater" commonwealth, a singular civilian embodiment of the universal order of the cosmos.

Letter 68 takes this argument a step further by asserting that the "greater" commonwealth from which the *sapiens* contemplates the "lowly" state of human affairs (and occasionally intervenes in them) is actually an extension of Roman civic life. Without subtracting from its status as the cosmic whole of which Roman politics is merely a part, Seneca reduces the "greater" commonwealth to one among many parts of Roman political culture. It is included in civic life as one of its exclusions, counted as uncounted by the imperial order of things. That the wise man "non est extra rem publicam, etiam si recesserit" is a testament to this paradoxical inclusion. As the container of Roman politics and one of its political contents, the "greater" commonwealth becomes a zone of indiscernibility in which Stoic philosophers, while beating their retreat from public life, ultimately discover another way to reenter it.

And the paradox does not stop here. By identifying Stoicism with the "vast and truly common state" to which all political subjects have a rightful claim, Seneca establishes a lateral connection between the Stoic philosopher and the Roman citizen. Channeling the *persona civilis* with which Nero began his reign, he argues that philosophers and citizens have an equal stake in the "greater" commonwealth. For, like all "great and true goods," those of the cosmos "are not divided in such a manner that each has but a slight interest." In contrast to meat and grain, which are unevenly distributed among individuals, the "goods" of which the philosopher partakes are "indivisible" and "belong in their entirety to all men just as much as they belong to each individual." No longer is the wise man a part of Roman society that has no part to play in Roman politics, an infra-citizen to be banished from public life and degraded, even criminalized, for his adherence to Stoic doctrine. As a stakeholder in the "common property" to which all citizens have access, he is nothing less than their equal.

But the wise man does more than partake of this common property. As Seneca is careful to point out, he attributes this property to himself, claiming as his proper lot what in fact belongs to all. Unlike the Roman citizenry, which "believes that it has ownership in nothing in which the general public has a share," the Stoic philosopher "considers nothing more truly his own than that which he shares in partnership with all mankind."[55] In this sense, he is not an infra-citizen, shamefully excluded from affairs of state. Nor is he simply one among many Roman citizens. As the only political subject with privileged access to the "greater" commonwealth, the Stoic sage is an ultra-citizen—a citizen above and beyond the rest, equal only to the universal concept of citizenship itself. More than a stakeholder in the "vast and truly common state," he is its true proprietor.

In service to this expropriation, Seneca troubles the boundaries between public and private property, notably the citizen's habit of separating possession (*possessiō*) from ownership (*proprietās*). Unlike possessions, which are defined by their ability to change hands—specifically their ability to receive various occupants (e.g., subway seats, hotel rooms)—things owned are normally thought to be the exclusive property or, more literally, the *peculiar quality* of an individual or a group. Contrary to ordinary citizens, who always crave more than they have, ever longing to own more than they possess, Stoic philosophers are content with whatever comes their way, accepting as their own only that which eludes the logic of ownership. To illustrate this distinction between the citizen's greed and the Stoic's contentment, Seneca quotes and refines a simile he attributes to Attalus:

> "Did you ever see a dog snapping with wide-open jaws at bits of bread or meat which his master tosses to him? Whatever he catches, he straightaway swallows whole, and always opens his jaws in hope of something more. So it is with ourselves; we stand expectant, and whatever Fortune has thrown to us we forthwith bolt, without any real pleasure, and then stand alert and frantic for something else to snatch." But it is not so with the wise man; he is satisfied. Even if something falls to him, he merely accepts it carelessly and lays it aside.[56]

Unlike gluttonous members of civic life, Stoics know how to receive the gifts of Fortune. Take peace, for instance. For "many of our toga-clad citizens," Seneca laments—probably referring to members of the Roman ruling class, for whom the toga was a sign of social status and civic engagement—"peace brings more trouble than war," hurtling them downward into "the Chaos of Epicurus," where, sunken in empty and boundless circumstances, they resort to "drunkenness," "lust," and "other vices."[57] Only the Stoic philosopher, who has learned "to scorn as trivial everything that the crowd covets as supremely important," knows what to do with peace.[58] It is not a common good to be squandered by members of the "lesser" commonwealth, but a unique opportunity to inquire into the "greater" commonwealth. Virtue, nature, art, matter, God, the heavens, eternity—all occupy the *sapiens* during times of peace.[59]

With these extraordinary pursuits come extraordinary profits, and with these extraordinary profits come extraordinary debts. Consider, for instance, the obligations incurred by various sailors of the same peaceful sea:

> Just as, out of a number of persons who have profited by the same stretch of calm weather, a man deems that his debt to Neptune is greater if his cargo during that voyage has been more extensive and valuable, and just as the vow is paid with more of a will by the merchant than by the passenger, and just as, from among the merchants themselves, heartier thanks are uttered by the dealer in spices, purple fabrics, and objects worth their weight in gold, than by him who has gathered cheap merchandise that will be nothing but ballast for his ship; similarly, the benefits of this peace, which extends to all, are more deeply appreciated by those who make good use of it.

To whom is this deep appreciation addressed? If sailors are beholden to the gods who control the sea, philosophers are beholden to the rulers who control the state. It is their willingness to accept this obligation that ultimately sets them apart from other citizens. What distinguishes the wise man as an ultra-citizen, then, is not only his ability to "make good use" of the peace enjoyed by all. Moreover, it is his appreciation for "those who have made it possible for him to do this in security," specifically "the ruler who makes it possible, by his management and foresight, for him to enjoy rich leisure [*otium*], control of his own time, and a tranquility uninterrupted by public employments."[60]

As peace becomes the condition of possibility for *otium*, and the unusually moderate appetites and remarkably useful abilities of the wise man give way to an extraordinary appreciation for the ruler, the simile of dog begins to make sense. More than a passing comment on the insatiable greed of the citizenry, it is a powerful testament to the unremitting gratitude of the philosopher. In support of this interpretation, Seneca even goes so far as to refigure the simile in terms of civic life, openly bemoaning "those restless [*inquieti*] persons who are always in the public eye, who owe much to the ruler, but also expect much from him, and are never so generously loaded with favors that their cravings, which grow by being supplied, are thoroughly satisfied." And lest his audience miss this parallel between the thankless citizen and the insatiable dog, Seneca ends his complaint with a pointed axiom: "He whose thoughts are of benefits to come has forgotten the benefits received; and there is no greater evil in covetousness than its ingratitude."[61]

It is difficult to read this passage apart from the personal and political turmoil it sought to abate. In sharp contrast to citizens like Thrasea, who all too often serve themselves at the state's expense, philosophers like Seneca never forget the debts they owe to public authority. Nor do they ever fail to repay them. "This is what philosophy teaches most of all," Seneca concludes, returning to the fiscal rhetoric of his request to retire from Nero's court: "Honorably to avow the debts of benefits received, and honorably to pay them."[62] Miss the connection between his earlier exchange with Nero and this overweening praise of the ruler, and we miss the personal agenda implicit in Seneca's degradation of thankless citizens to insatiable dogs. At stake in this analogy is not only a defense of Stoicism from Thrasea, and any other citizens who might be inclined to follow his example, but also a defense of Seneca from any further abuse that he might suffer at the hands of Nero. Unlike those "inquieti" members of the Roman citizenry, who derive their identity from the Latin verb *inquietare* (meaning "to harass," "to disturb," "to trouble," and even "to press legal claim against"), Seneca remains willing and eager to relinquish his wealth in exchange for the peace and quiet—the *quies*—that Nero had previously denied him.

Vita abscondita: Publicity as Protection

The function of *Letters to Lucilius morales* as political rhetoric is obvious. By relocating the "greater" commonwealth in its "lesser" variant, Seneca places in common the wrongful exclusion of Stoic philosophers from imperial governance, forcing two distinct worlds—one that partakes of Roman civic life and one that does not—into a single, though hardly selfsame, order of the political. Stoic philosophers are not just good citizens. Moreover, as Seneca is at pains to demonstrate, they are among the *best* citizens. More modest in their demands, more remarkable in their skills, more exuberant in their gratitude—they are not the part of Roman society with no part to play in Roman politics, as Thrasea and Nero suggest, but the only part of Roman politics with privileged access to the whole of which all forms of civic life partake.

In this sense, it is tempting to read Seneca's correspondence as the logical next step in his philosophical defense of Stoicism. Doing so, however, would require us to ignore one of the key differences between his letters to Lucilius and the writings that preceded them. Unlike *The Shortness of Life*, *Tranquility of Mind*, and *On Retirement*, all of which were highly wrought theoretical arguments, Seneca's letters were "carelessly written" political texts.[63] At times, Seneca recalls his treatise *On the Shortness of Life*, urging Lucilius to retire on grounds that philosophical leisure is more valuable than public service. At other times, he channels *Tranquility of Mind*, suggesting that because Lucilius is an old man, he should secure *otium* while he still can.[64] As a letter-writer, however, Seneca is not interested in vindicating retirement, much less in theorizing its conditions of possibility. On this point, many of his commentators agree. "The *Letters* are not a theoretical treatise," Paul Veyne comments.[65] The "truth" of retirement, Vasily Rudich explains in his study of the *Letters*, "seems now to transpire as a matter of intimate experience rather than theoretical speculation."[66] Indeed, as Miriam T. Griffin observes, "the Letters are furthest from the theoretical dialogue *De Otio*."[67]

How, then, are we to read this correspondence? For citizen-subjects like Seneca, who are in close proximity to political power but ultimately excluded from its exercise, *Letters to Lucilius* offers lessons in the art of personal and professional advancement during periods of conflict between learned and political cultures. From letter to letter, Seneca prepares his addressees for the daunting task of securing advantage in the borderlands between *otium* and *res civiles*, a region strewn with opportunities and resources for learned political action. Even a cursory glance at his correspondence yields practical advice: let your movements be gradual and inconspicuous (22.3–9, 26.4); surround yourself with claims of mental and bodily insufficiency (68.3); do not upset the customs of the people with novel ways of living (5.2–3, 14.14, 19.2, 103.5); avoid saying, doing, or possessing anything that would incur resentment (19.11–12, 103.5, 105.3), court applause (52.9–15), flattery (66.14–15), or the offense of authority (14.7–8).

As we have seen, *Tranquility of the Mind* advocates public service in a state of Stoic inwardness when the retirement described in *On the Shortness of Life* cannot be realized. And *On Retirement* recommends mediating political commitments through philosophical leisure when our tranquil interiors cannot endure the moral condition of public service. Seneca's letters stretch this argument to its outermost limits, providing readers then and now with equipment for living through political circumstances in which classical notions of *otium* are no longer applicable. Where philosophical leisure is no longer an option, Seneca recommends a rhetoric of withdrawal.

In order to understand this rhetoric, we must first attempt to grasp the mode of political intelligence out of which it emerges. Nowhere is this intelligence more apparent than in Seneca's use of the verb *abscondere*, meaning "to conceal," "to obscure," or "to shelter" (from *abs*, meaning "off" or "away," and *condere*, meaning "to stow" or, more literally, "to put together"). On first glance, the letters seem ambivalent in their use of the term. Consider, for instance, letter 43, in which variations on *abscondere* help Seneca advocate for publicity and self-display:

> Do not, however, deem yourself truly happy until you find that you can live before men's eyes, until your walls protect but do not hide you [*non abscondent*]; although we are apt to believe that these walls surround us, not to enable us to live more safely, but that we may sin more secretly. I shall mention a fact by which you may weigh the worth of a man's character: you will scarcely find anyone who can live with his doors wide open. It is our conscience, not our pride, that has put doorkeepers at our doors; we live in such a fashion that being suddenly disclosed to view is equivalent to being caught in the act. What profits it, however, to hide ourselves away [*recondere*], and to avoid the eyes and ears of men? A good conscience welcomes the crowd, but a bad conscience, even in solitude, is disturbed and troubled. If your deeds are honorable, let everybody know them; if base, what matters it that no one knows them, as long as you yourself know them? How wretched you are if you despise such a witness![68]

Now consider letter 94, in which *abscondere* lends itself to a counterargument, offsetting letter 43 with an imperative to retreat from the world of appearances:

> A quiet life does not of itself give lessons in upright conduct; the countryside does not of itself teach plain living; no, but when witnesses and onlookers are removed, faults which ripen in publicity and display sink into the background. Who puts on the purple robe for the sake of flaunting it in no man's eyes? Who uses gold plate when he dines alone? Who, as he flings himself down beneath the shadow of some rustic tree, displays in solitude the splendor of his luxury? No one makes himself elegant only for his own beholding, or even for the admiration of a few friends or relatives. Rather does he spread out his well-appointed vices in proportion to the size of the admiring crowd. It is so: claquers and witnesses are irritants of all our mad foibles. You can make us cease to crave, if you only make us cease to display. Ambition, luxury, and waywardness need a stage to act upon; you will cure all those ills if you seek retirement [*absconderis*].[69]

How are we to read these competing epistles? In letter 43, public appearance is a sign of candor and good conscience, and concealment from others an indicator of sin and psychic turbulence. In letter 94, public appearance is unhealthy and deceitful, while concealment is an occasion for honesty and right living. A closer look at these letters suggests that it possible to reconcile these diverging treatments of the *vita abscondita*: despite their glaring differences, both characterize the self as an inescapable witness to its own conduct, and identify solitude as the "site" at which witnessing of this sort occurs.

But solitude does not come easy for political actors, as Seneca reiterates throughout his correspondence. Nowhere is this more apparent than in letter 19, where he sublates the advice of letters 43 and 94 in a broader phenomenology of withdrawal, effectively scrambling the theories of *otium* presented in his earlier theoretical works:

> Not that I would advise you to try to win fame by your retirement [*otio*]; one's retirement should neither be paraded nor concealed [*nec iactare debes nec abscondere*]. Not concealed, I say, for I shall not go so far in urging you as to expect you to condemn all men as mad and then seek out for yourself a hiding-place and oblivion; rather make this your business, that your retirement [*otium*] be not conspicuous, though it should be obvious [*non emineat, sed appareat*].[70]

It is difficult to read this advice apart from that of *Tranquility of Mind*: "He will truly be a man who, when perils are threatening from every side, when arms and chains are rattling around him, will neither endanger, nor conceal, his virtue [*non alliserit virtutem nec absconderit*]."[71] What was true of *virtus* in years past was now also true of *otium*. As Seneca well knew, neither political oblivion nor a glorious retirement was available to him after Thrasea's conflict with Nero. But there is more than autobiography at work in letter 19. Seneca is also laying the groundwork for a new conception of retirement, a mode of withdrawal that, like walls that "protect but do not hide," at once endures and eludes the broad daylight of public appearance, enabling political subjects to occupy a zone of indiscernibility between fanfare and concealment—*iactare* and *abscondere*.

Rather than theorize this mode of withdrawal, letter 19 goes on to describe its opportunity structure. For "those whose choice is unhampered," the question remains "whether they wish to pass their lives in obscurity." For citizen-subjects like Lucilius, however, who have made a name for themselves in public discussion and debate, "there is not a free choice." Obscurity—and with it, the Roman concept of *otium*, which in turn indexes the Greek *bios theōrētikos*—is not an option: "Your ability and energy have thrust you in the work of the world; so have the charm of your writings and the friendships you have made with famous and notable men. Renown has already taken you by storm. You may sink yourself into the depths of obscurity and utterly hide yourself [*recondaris*]; yet your earlier acts will reveal you. You cannot keep lurking in the dark; much of the old gleam will follow you [*sequetur*] wherever you fly."[72]

From the verb *sequor*, Seneca's use of *sequetur* in this excerpt further illuminates the common ground between letters 43 and 94. If indeed we are inescapable witnesses to our own conduct, it is because our "earlier acts" follow us everywhere, even into states of solitude—or, as Seneca puts it, "the depths of obscurity." But *sequor* means more than "to follow from one place to another." It also means "to come after in time," often indicating a causal relationship between an action and its (logical) consequence. In this sense, "lurking in the dark" is not only the condition in which our "earlier acts" find us, but also an impetus for their return in the first place. More precisely, it is a catalyst for the "old gleam" in whose light these "earlier acts" reveal us "lurking in the dark." The deeper we plunge into obscurity, the brighter our previous deeds shine; and the brighter they shine, the more brazenly they open us to an outward appearance. The witness from whom we cannot escape is not our selves as we have come to know them, as letters 43 and 94 suggest, but our selves as they have come to be known by others. It is the publicity of our past, not our politicking in the present, that ultimately precludes our obscurity.

The rhetoric of withdrawal is founded on this insight. Where oblivion is unavailable, our next best option, it seems, is to strike a balance between *otium* and *res civiles*, neither fully disclosing nor entirely obscuring our withdrawal from affairs of state. How is this possible? The trick, Seneca argues, is to conceal ourselves in public appearance, a maneuver that, rather than simply offsetting obscurity with openness, involves redoubling the act of concealment itself. Again, *abscondere* is the operative term, as Seneca indicates in the opening lines of his sixty-eighth epistle—just before his argument that the wise man, even when he withdraws to the cosmos, is not apart from public life: "Retire and conceal yourself in repose. But at the same time conceal your retirement [*Absconde te in otio. Sed et ipsum otium absconde*]." To clarify this mode of withdrawal, Seneca goes on to offer a series of illustrations:

> There is no need to fasten a placard upon yourself with the words: "Philosopher and Quietist." Give your purpose some other name; call it ill-health and bodily weakness, or mere laziness. To boast of our retirement is but idle self-seeking. Certain animals hide themselves

from discovery by confusing the marks of their footprints in the neighborhood of their lairs. You should do the same. Otherwise, there will always be someone dogging your footsteps. Many men pass by that which is visible, and peer after things hidden and concealed; a locked room invites the thief. Things which lie in the open appear cheap; the house-breaker passes by that which is exposed to view. This is the way of the world, and the way of all ignorant men: they crave to burst in upon hidden things. It is therefore best not to vaunt one's retirement. It is, however, a sort of vaunting to make too much of one's concealment and of one's withdrawal from the sight of men.[73]

At issue here is the appearance of our absence, or, more precisely, the status of our withdrawal as a privation (*sterēsis*) of public life.[74] Hiddenness of this sort finds its definitive expression in Edgar Allan Poe's "The Purloined Letter," where openness doubles as an occasion for concealment.[75] It also recalls book 8 of the *Odyssey*, where Odysseus, with a covered head, and thus unbeknownst to those around him, weeps during the public performance of a song detailing his clash with Akhilleus and his victory at Troy.[76] In each case, we see the negation of a negation of public appearance—or, as Seneca would have it, the withdrawal of a withdrawal from human affairs. The effect of this withdrawal of a withdrawal is neither a politics of desertion like that of Thrasea nor a simple regression into the world of appearances like that of the citizen, but instead *a tactical enfoldment of ourselves in publicity*. As the Minister D—, Odysseus, and Seneca well knew—and as learned advocates in the age of academia have yet to learn—remaining concealed in surveilled circumstances has less to do with "lurking in the dark" than it does with hiding in the light. Publicity can also be a source of protection.

The forensic tilt of letter 68 calls us even further. Remaining concealed in the world of appearances involves scrambling the evidence of our withdrawal from public life. Like animals that "hide themselves from discovery by confusing the marks of their footprints in the neighborhood of their lairs," we can conceal ourselves as well as our concealment by dissembling the public traces of our previous conduct. To be sure, "earlier acts" admit no escape. But with a bit of cunning, their "old gleam" can be turned to our advantage. Without rescinding letter 19, in which Seneca mandates the return of our past, letter 68 accents our ability to determine how it will appear upon arrival, suggesting that the rhetoric of withdrawal consists in shaping the appearance of our previous deeds before they can return to us as specters of history.

Artistry of this sort transforms political actors into activist historians. Their task becomes one of assessing and intervening in what might otherwise have remained a simple sequence of actions and their effects. To illustrate this curious line of conduct, in which historical judgments and political activities coincide, let us consider "the account"—a speech act in which interlocutors restructure initial responses to their "earlier acts" in order to reduce their culpability as actors. In accounting for previously or potentially offensive conduct, we *performatively interpret* the intentionality of which this conduct was supposedly a poor reflection. The post-utterance phrase "I mean," as in, "What I meant to say was . . .," " is a case in point, as the following excerpt from a contemporary city council meeting well indicates:

> I'd just like to say that regarding there was one paragraph in our letter that we sent to you and city staff that had a statement in it that was probably the way we intended it was not the way it was sounded when it read back. And that was regarding the language of our letter which referred to an unspoken agreement, we really meant kind of the way things have operated not necessarily an unspoken agreement. When I got the reply from city staff it hit me right in the head, I thought wow how did we put that in there? But so we certainly didn't intend to imply that's there anything under the table that were, we have any unspoken agreements we just meant to say that the way things have generally operated in the past as far as development and we present our developments to you or the developers do and you know there's kind of things that we know that we're responsible for that kind of thing.[77]

Here, variations on "I mean" serve a preventative purpose, mending a potentially confusing letter before city council members have a chance to bring it up. The speaker uses his authorship of this text as a warrant for its authoritative interpretation, effectively converting his meaning-to-say into a meta-interpretive norm, in accordance with which readers can and should understand his epistolography. In so doing, he encourages city council members to offset their initial assessments of his letter with a new set of judgments, the object of which is not only the letter in question but also these initial assessments, all of which are now under the rule of a meta-interpretive norm. In this way, his account is able to insinuate and multiply interpretations in the communicative gap between an earlier act of epistolography and its various moments of reception.

Seneca champions this persuasive technique. Like an account, the art of remaining concealed involves manipulating the public appearance of our previous conduct—the "old gleam" of our "earlier acts"—before it can come back to haunt us. And with this artistry comes a specific mode of political intelligence. Implicit in the account is a willingness to see our speech and action as potentially offensive, as well as a readiness to suspend this horizon, if only to avoid the woe with which offense so often comes. Is this not the gist of Seneca's advice? Let your movements be gradual and inconspicuous; surround yourself with claims of mental and bodily insufficiency; do not upset the customs of the people with novel ways of living; avoid saying, doing, or possessing anything that would incur resentment, court applause, flattery, or the offense of authority—all these strategies are designed to attenuate and, in the best-case scenario, to preclude effronteries to which we might otherwise need to respond with an account.

To be sure, remaining concealed has everything to do with avoiding offense. As Seneca indicates in letter 14, "The wise man will never provoke the anger of those in power." Instead, "He shuns [*vitat*] a strong man who may be injurious to him, making a point of not seeming to avoid him [*ne vitare videatur*], because an important part of one's safety lies in not seeking safety openly; for what one avoids, one condemns." As an enfoldment of publicity, the *vita abscondita* is well suited to this task. Unlike ordinary political actors, who court the it-seems-to-me of an audience (the *dokei moi* on which their *doxa* depends), Seneca's luminously self-concealed sage is at once anchored in the world of appearances and shielded from the watchful eyes of others—an ideal position from which to avert the powers that be without seeming to do so. Thus, if the advice of letters 43, 94, 19, and 68 culminates in a rhetoric of withdrawal, this rhetoric culminates in an ethic of wisdom: "A man may be wise without parade and without arousing enmity."[78]

Philosophy and Power Aslant

However elucidating, the political kinship between remaining concealed and avoiding offense—the rhetoric of withdrawal and the ethics of wisdom—belies another perplexity: why would Seneca publish this insight? Given the hazards of mid-first-century political culture in which lines of escape were always fraught with danger, and the obvious fragility of his own circumstances in which any sign of withdrawal could be taken as a statement against the principate, why would Seneca risk offending Nero by advocating an exit strategy designed to manipulate the powers that be? "This is the mystery—lying in plain sight—of the *Letters to Lucilius*," Veyne rightly notes: "Their character as oppositional writing in such circumstances."

In order to solve this mystery, we must look beyond the persuasive techniques discussed in Seneca's letters to the political rhetoric of the correspondence itself. For these letters are more than a *lexicon rhetoricae* for avoiding offense; they are also an exercise in avoidance of this sort: "Not hiding his light under a bushel, while at the same time not provoking the tyrant, is what Seneca *does* in his published correspondence with Lucilius. More than that, he *states* that this is what he is doing, taking care to reveal his game so that no one could misunderstand."[79]

To whom did Seneca address this statement? At the very least, he was hailing Nero, Thrasea, and public officials with imperial or Stoic leanings. To clarify this participation framework, let us return to Seneca's advice on avoiding offense to the powerful. The surest way to proceed, he argues, is to "take refuge in philosophy." For unlike "speechmaking at the bar, or any other pursuit that claims to people's attention," and in so doing "wins enemies for a man," philosophy is always "peaceful and minds her own business." He even goes so far as to characterize the life of the mind as a "protecting emblem"— an *infularum loco*, from the Latin *infula*, meaning "bandage" and, more precisely, a veil worn by priests and sacrificial victims, normally displayed as a sign of submission. And no one is more deserving of such submission than the ruler, Seneca claims, all but indicting Thrasea for his use of Stoicism to resist imperial governance:

> It seems to me erroneous to believe that those who have loyally dedicated themselves to philosophy are stubborn and rebellious, scorners of magistrates or kings or of those who control the administration of public affairs. For, on the contrary, no class of man is so popular with the philosopher as the ruler is; and rightly so, because rulers bestow upon no men a greater privilege than upon those who are allowed to enjoy peace and leisure [*tranquillo otio licet*]. Hence, those who are greatly profited, as regards their purpose of right living, by the security of the State, must needs cherish as a father the author of this good.[80]

Griffin reads this reconciliation of philosophy and power as "a warning to philosophers" and "an assurance to the government," the goal of which was to remind both parties of the attitudes toward public service outlined in Seneca's earlier treatises *Tranquility of Mind* and *On Retirement*. "A man who bases his retirement into philosophical leisure on disapproval of the government would rightly be viewed as a political dissenter," she surmises.[81] But there is another way to read this letter. As Rudich observes, "the lavish praise Seneca bestows on the ruler may appear not only ironic, but even derisive," especially when viewed "against the background of his personal relations with Nero."[82] Veyne carries this argument a step further, insisting that the seventy-third epistle is "in reality an open letter intended for Nero," the central issue of which was the so-called "Stoic opposition"—the movement against the principate in which Thrasea was currently embroiled and to which Nero had recently responded by outlawing Stoicism.[83] Also on Nero's side was Tigellinus, who saw the persecution of Stoics as an opportunity to increase his authority at court. Indeed, the notoriety of the "Stoic opposition" owed as much to his propaganda at court as it did to the political activity of dissidents like Thrasea.[84]

None of this was lost on Seneca. To be sure, he floundered in the wake of Thrasea's abstention. But he also was scandalized by the disinformation of Nero's new adviser. Whatever else it entailed, the "Stoicism" in which Thrasea couched his dissent was not an opposition movement, much less a warrant for the persecution of other Stoics. In claiming that philosophers "cherish" their rulers, then, Seneca did more than undermine the use of Stoicism to frame and justify acts of resistance. He also subverted the authority of the principate to criminalize Stoicism. "Was Seneca trying to distinguish himself from the arrogant Stoic opposition?" Veyne cleverly asks. "No. Instead, he denies its existence, belying the thesis of the police and recognizing philosophy's right to exist."[85] Yet the rhetoric of letter 73 is more nuanced than Veyne lets on. Subverting the ideology of the principate is not something Seneca does *instead* of distinguishing himself from the "philosophical opposition." On the contrary, marking this distinction is the condition of possibility for his subversion of state authority. Only by assuring Nero that Stoics like himself "cherish" the powers that be could he get away with dismissing the criminalization of Stoicism as "erroneous." Meekness may be the disposition of philosophers, as Seneca suggests, but only insofar as mistakenness belongs to the principate.

Is this not an exercise in the rhetoric of withdrawal? By counteracting statist attitudes toward philosophy, Seneca distances himself from Nero and the principate. And by subordinating philosophers to the state, he dissociates himself from Thrasea and the "Stoic opposition." Taken together, these maneuvers allow Seneca to insinuate himself in a hazardous political conflict, and yet in such a way that separates him from the ideologies in dispute. Neither apart from nor a part of this public affair, he remains safely concealed and politically engaged in the world of appearances.

Only by enfolding himself in publicity, cloaking his dissent in claims of deference, could Seneca distance himself from Nero without appearing to do so. In this sense, letter 73 is an embodiment of his earlier advice on avoiding offense to the powerful. And because this earlier advice was potentially offensive to public authority, letter 73 also functions as an account. In addition to offsetting his current dispute with the principate over the definition of Stoicism, it compensates for his previous endorsement of an exit strategy designed to beguile the powerful. If indeed the letters to Lucilius form "an oppositional work," as Veyne suggests, it is because Seneca at once proffers and performs maneuvers of this sort, routinely contesting without directly challenging the powers that be—and always in the broad daylight of public appearance.

Judgment and Imagination unto Death

Hiding ourselves from discovery by confusing our footprints in the neighborhood of our lairs presupposes a future in which passersby will either acknowledge or ignore these footprints. Following Seneca's advice means acting in anticipation of these passersby. As we have seen, there are two ways to proceed. The first is reactive and involves revising the "old gleam" of "earlier acts," typically by way of an account. The second is proactive and involves taking steps to avoid effrontery in the first place, thereby paving the way for a history of "earlier acts" whose "old gleam," because it will have given no offense, will warrant no future revision. Both techniques are integral to the rhetoric of withdrawal. And both illuminate the attitude toward history implicit in this rhetoric: to imagine our current steps as footprints visible to future passersby is not only to realize today's conduct as the origin of "earlier acts," but also to embrace tomorrow's judgments of these "earlier acts" as the basis for today's conduct.

In this sense, the present is not the negative limit of past and future events, but a composite moment in which what is "no longer" and what is "not yet" become resources for public advocacy. What this means for the rhetoric of withdrawal is that its practitioners have a unique ability to integrate the backward glance of judgment and the forward thrust of imagination. That life must be understood backward is for Seneca coexistent with the requirement that it be lived forward. Indeed, where Kierkegaard sees an existential bind, in which philosophy remains exterior to politics, Seneca sees an occasion for persuasive artistry.[86] The skill consists in finding our way between the retrospective insights of the historian, who sits in judgment over "earlier acts," and the representative thoughts of the spectator, who anticipates a variety of passersby before deciding how to account for his or her "old gleam." Recalling Aristotle's judge, who decides things past and future, Seneca's letters to Lucilius bespeak a Janus-faced political subject—someone capable of envisioning both tenses at once. For the present is only blind to what the future will value when it loses sight of the past.

A backward glance focused forward—this is the way of seeing at work in the rhetoric of withdrawal. Indeed, Seneca courts and cultivates the stance from which Benjamin's angel of history cannot escape: "When he sees the dangers, uncertainties, and hazards in which he was formerly tossed about, he will withdraw,—not turning his back to the foe, but falling back little by little to a safe position."[87] Although riddled with techniques for ensuring our safety from established figures of authority, *Letters to Lucilius* tells us little about the attitude toward history on which these techniques depend. How, exactly, are we to remain focused on the past without ever losing sight of the future?

Seneca's only answer is to live as though dead. In order to encompass the retrospections of the *histor* and the anticipations of the *theoros*, we must consider ourselves at the point of death, ever glancing back, in advance, so to speak, on our lives. As Foucault explains, "we should place our selves in a condition such that we live as if it is already over," which is to say, "we should have the attitude, behavior, detachment, and accomplishment of someone who has already completed his life."[88] To illustrate this ethical sensibility, let us consider one more excerpt from *Letters to Lucilius*, specifically the dialogue on death in which Seneca claims to be embroiled with himself: "As if the test were at hand and the day will have come which is to pronounce its judgment on all the years of my life, I regard and address myself thus: 'The showing which we have made up to the present time, in word or deed, counts for nothing. All this is but a varnished and deceitful relict of our character [*pignora animi*] enveloped in much allure.'" In contrast to "the opinion of the world," which is "always wavering" in its assessments of previous words and deeds, Seneca solicits "the final judgment" of death. "What you will have done in the past will become visible only when you draw your last breath," he reminds himself.[89]

That death awaits us in the future is a lesson on living in the present. From the vantage point of this "final judgment," all our acts are "earlier acts." Conduct in which we are currently engaged, and even conduct still to come—all glisten with "old gleam" when viewed through the optics of death. Politicizing this secret affinity between past, present, and future conduct is precisely what is at stake in treating our previous deeds as latent spectacles (letter 19), our ongoing activities as historic artifacts (letter 68), and the unforeseeable interests of the future as our own (letter 14). Dated footprints, occurring footsteps, and imminent passersby—all may be monitored from the standpoint of death.

"This is what I say to myself," Seneca concludes, "but I would have you think that I have said it to you also." And yet he never does. To be sure, his letters to Lucilius offer several statements on the importance of rehearsing death.[90] But none are as detailed as Seneca's dialogue with himself. Moreover, none are didactic enough to coach readers from their current position as idle spectators of this dialogue to their potential status as political actors capable of dialoguing with themselves. The result is a community of bystanders that, although regaled with persuasive techniques and moral imperatives, is largely unable to mobilize these lessons for purposes of right living. Correcting for this incapacity is the challenge now before us.

3

MIRRORS FOR THE QUEEN:
EXEMPLARY FIGURES ON THE EVE OF CIVIL WAR

Through charity, this great lady will be the advocate of peace between the prince, her husband (or her son, if she is a widow), and her people, those to whom she has a duty to offer her assistance. If the prince, because of poor advice or for any other reason, should be tempted to harm his subjects, they will know their lady to be full of kindness, pity, and charity. They will come to her, humbly petitioning her to intercede for them before the prince.

—CHRISTINE DE PIZAN

Resources of Ambiguity

Seneca probably knew what he was doing. Rehearsing death, like remaining concealed and avoiding offense, does not lend itself to abstract philosophical instruction. In keeping with the pedagogical landscape of early-imperial Rome, in which Stoic combinations of *axioma* and *exempla* thrived, Seneca relied on vivid imagery and pointed illustrations to guide his readers. His rationale was simple: "The way is long if one follows precepts, but short and helpful, if one follows examples."[1] Hence his soliloquy on death. More than a monologue to contemplate, it was an example to imitate. The same could be said for *Letters to Lucilius*. As Martha C. Nussbaum notes, the correspondence is itself "one long rich *exemplum*."[2]

It is tempting but difficult to agree with Nussbaum's characterization, if only because scholarly and popular notions of exemplarity often center on Aristotle's use of the term *paradeigma*, from the Greek verb *paradeiknumi*, meaning "to exhibit side by side," "to compare," "to indicate," "to point out."[3] The Latin *exemplum* on which Seneca relied—from the verb *eximere*, meaning "to cut out," "to subtract," "to free," "to make an exception of"—has received scant attention.[4] The contrast between these ancestral terms is too striking to ignore. Unlike the Greek *paradeigma*, which associates the example with processes of illumination, display, sight, and indication, the Latin *exemplum* identifies it with processes of selection, excision, combination, and discontinuity. To this extent, the etymological characteristic of Seneca's *exemplum* makes explicit dimensions of exemplarity not indicated in Aristotle's *paradeigma*.

Any thorough conception of the example must account for its Greek and Latin origins. This chapter attempts to do so by theorizing the example as a rhetorical figure constitutively split between the activities of illumination and detachment, signification and subtraction—the respective structural vocations of the Greek *paradeigma* and the Latin *exemplum*. As a *paradeigma*, the example shows its belonging to a class of similar objects, figures, or events. In exhibiting the intelligibility of this set, however, the example also steps out from it, marking itself as a singular exclusion, an *exemplum*. It is at once a part of and apart from the group of entities it designates.[5] In this sense, the rhetoric of exemplarity is a site at which moments of ambiguity necessarily arise. Rather than disposing of this ambiguity, I would like to study and clarify the example as a *strategic resource of ambiguity*. As we shall see, the example is a linguistic device for introducing ambiguity into any given rhetorical situation, and in so doing opening up opportunities for political judgment and social transformation.[6]

In support of this argument, I analyze the rhetoric of exemplarity in the work of Christine de Pizan, a late-medieval feminist and France's first woman of letters. Specifically, I focus on her use of exemplary figures in a 1405 letter to Isabeau of Bavaria, then the queen of France. In this letter, Christine recites tales of admirable and infamous women in hopes of persuading the queen to intervene in a political quarrel between the dukes of Orléans and Burgundy, which was then threatening the welfare of France. By pitting the virtues of Princess Veturia, Queen Esther, Bathsheba, and Blanche of Castile against the vices of Jezebel and Olympias, she encourages Isabeau to consider her relation to the history of womankind. Depending on how she exercises her authority as queen, Christine suggests, the virtues or vices of these predecessors will recur, thereby writing Isabeau into the annals of history as an example of judicious or immoderate leadership. At issue in this constellation of an exemplary past, imperative present, and emerging future is not only an occasion for the queen to exercise political judgment, but also an extension of Seneca's attitude toward history. For Christine, as we shall see, the rhetoric of exemplarity is a way of tying the present to the future through the past.

In using the term "exemplary figure" to describe Veturia, Esther, Bathsheba, Blanche, Jezebel, and Olympias, this chapter calls attention to a strand of exemplarity dating from the first century BCE and achieving vast popularity in the Middle Ages. For Christine and her contemporaries, the exemplary figure was a persuasive resource for connecting abstract virtues and vices to mythological, fictional, and historical characters. Thus, Cato could be cited as an embodiment of moral integrity, Ruth as one of devotion and loyalty, Nero as one of extravagant tyranny, and so on.[7] As a detachable fragment of time and text invested with transhistorical significance, the exemplary figure embodies the constitutive split of the example between the Latin *exemplum* and the Greek *paradeigma*. At once singular and representative, the substance of the exemplary figure is entirely ambiguous, providing learned political actors such as Christine with a powerful resource for awakening the judging faculties of lay audiences, and scholarly commentators with a unique opportunity to explore the complicated relationship between history, exemplarity, and judgment.

If the exemplary figure is among the more ambiguous forms of exemplarity, Christine's letter to the queen is among the most masterful displays of its rhetorical potential. How she transforms the inherent ambiguity of the exemplary figure into a sophisticated, proto-feminist line of argument is the central question of this chapter. When situated in the historical context of the Orléans-Burgundy conflict, and interpreted alongside Christine's canonical work of political thought, *The Book of the City of Ladies* (1405), her letter can be shown to critique the political inaction of the queen, as well as the patriarchal ideology in which she is enmeshed, without in turn exposing Christine to any regal backlash. Taken together, these rhetorical achievements allow us to read and recuperate her letter as an acute historico-political basis for the ongoing feminist commitment to identifying, valorizing, and extending the contributions of learned women to public life.

The Eve of Civil War, 1401–1405

The reign of Charles VI (1380–1422) should have begun with a balance of power. In the summer of 1374, Charles V arranged for his eldest brother, Louis of Anjou, to serve as regent during the initial years of his son's reign. He also awarded guardianship (*tutelle*) of the dauphin to a corporation of caretakers made up of his consort, Joan of Bourbon, and his two younger brothers, John of Berry and Philip the Bold of Burgundy. But this balance of power was not to be. When the king died, Louis of Anjou seized upon the royal treasury, confiscating the crown jewels and taking 32,000 golden francs for himself. In protest, the duke of Burgundy engineered to have the eleven-year-old Charles VI crowned king and declared a major, thereby annulling the regency of Louis of Anjou. By 1382, Philip the Bold had overpowered his uncles. The young king and, by extension, the French government were now under his control.

Soon thereafter, Philip began using the public authority of the king to advance the private interests of the nobles. In the spring of 1388, and almost certainly at his uncle's behest, the teenage king issued a royal ordinance exempting all persons of noble lineage from a newly apportioned land and income tax (*taille*). Its only stipulation was that the exempted nobles pursue the military profession. But even this obligation could be relaxed with gifts, pensions, and increased payments.[8] Then, in 1393, another royal ordinance appeared, this one relieving certain nobles of their responsibility to pay sales and circulation tax (*aides*) on the produce of their patrimonial estates.[9] To be sure, many ruling elites disapproved of Philip's rise to power, but few could afford to ignore the concessions he was willing to offer in exchange for their support.

Members of the royal family also took a share of the royal revenue. In 1384, Philip persuaded the young king to make him a gift of 100,000 francs, and two years later, he secured another 120,000. Then, in December 1401, Philip helped himself to a New Year's gift of 10,000 francs. By this time, he was receiving well over 200,000 francs per year from the royal treasury.[10] And he was not alone. In 1389, the king's brother, Louis of Orléans, began receiving half of the sales and salt taxes levied in his territories. In 1392, the house of Anjou secured the same privilege. And over the next few years, the dukes of Berry, Bourbon, and Burgundy followed suit. Matters grew worse in 1394, when the duke of Orléans began appropriating all sales and salt taxes levied on his lands, and worse still in the years thereafter, when the other royal princes began to do the same. By the turn of the century, it was obvious that "they could gain more by using the state than by opposing it," Joseph R. Strayer writes. What Philip the Bold had secured for himself, his relatives, and his fellow nobles was "a central government that was strong enough to fleece the weak and weak enough to placate the strong."[11]

Another site of corruption in the royal fiscal system was its local financial bureaucracy, notably its receiverships, which handled royal revenues.

That many receivers were not only wealthy French businessmen but also political clients of the royal princes made their work especially prone to conflicts of interest. "Each of these officials handling royal funds had an autonomous *caisse* and often combined the receiving and spending of royal money with a private business of his own," Edmund Fryde explains. "The royal funds controlled by them constituted their main security and the good credit that they thus enjoyed in normal times might allow them to make profitable private investments and embark on lucrative speculations."[12] Like their princely superiors, these wealthy businessmen were privatizing and profiting from the public fiscal authority of the king.

In addition to collecting and dispersing royal revenues, receivers were expected to lend money of their own to the French government, an expectation that made it easy for the crown to ignore their frequent malfeasance. In exchange for this leniency, receivers not only lent their money freely, but also released the crown from regular interest payments—and often even allowed it to forgo repayment altogether, albeit in anticipation of other governmental benefits. But not all lenders were so generous, and not all of them were wealthy royal officials. As the public authority of Charles VI became increasingly subordinate to the private interests of his entourage, the royal fiscal system became increasingly dependent on loans from Italian businessmen in Paris and Bruges, many of whom collected interest from the crown at a rate of 50 or 60 percent. By 1413, a quarter of the royal revenue generated by the *aides* was lost in this manner.[13]

From family members to local businessmen to foreign financiers, the agents of privatization at work on the king's public authority were as diverse as they were self-interested. "Everyone belonged to a special interest group (and usually to more than one)—town oligarchies, princely households, corporations of government officials—and everyone wanted to channel the income of the state toward his group (or groups), and within his group toward himself," Strayer notes, eerily anticipating the influx of private commercial interests into many of today's public institutions, including the modern research university. "The state was a useful device for redistributing the wealth, and no one wanted to destroy it, but relatively few people wanted to use its power for the general welfare."[14]

How did Charles VI allow this to happen? To limit the pitfalls of his reign to the avarice of his caretakers is to miss one of its most distinctive features: By the time he was old enough to exercise his authority as king, Charles VI was hopelessly insane. His first and certainly most violent lapse of reason came in August 1392, when he was leading an army through the province of Maine. One of his pages, who had become drowsy in the late-summer heat, allowed his lance to crash against the helmet of another page. Startled by the loud noise, Charles VI drew his sword and attacked, slaying four members of his entourage.[15] In later fits of lunacy, the king would run up and down the palace corridors howling like a wolf, refuse to bathe for months, and insist that he was made of glass, accusing all he encountered of trying to shatter him.

If the juvenility of Charles VI allowed Philip the Bold to seize control of the throne, his madness as an adult allowed another member of the dynastic family to rise to power: Louis of Orléans. As the king's younger brother, Louis was better positioned in the royal hierarchy than any of the uncles, even the preeminent Philip, and thus more entitled to stand in for the king during his many extended "absences." But Charles VI was not looking for another stand-in, so he integrated his brother into a new corporation of guardians, along with the queen, Isabeau of Bavaria, and the remaining royal uncles. Although the elder dukes protested Louis's newfound authority, they were unable to prevent his ascendance. By 1393, Louis had convinced the king to name him regent, on the off chance of his early death, which would result in another minority kingship. Almost immediately, the duke of Orléans began leveraging this honor, cleverly using it to frame and justify his right to rule when Charles was indisposed. By the end of the century, his influence at court rivaled that of Philip the Bold.

In 1401, the dukes of Orléans and Burgundy began to prepare for armed conflict. When he learned that Philip was planning to march into Paris with a small army, Louis hastened to gather his vassals for support. With open warfare on the horizon, and the sanity of the king nowhere in sight, the princes of the realm begged Queen Isabeau and John of Berry to intervene as arbiters in the affair. In early January, these regal arbiters issued their decision in the matter:

> If one Duke heard of an action that was undertaken by the other and that threatened him, he was to report it immediately to the arbiters. If they could not resolve the difficulty and the injured party wished to resort to the use of arms, first he would have to notify the other party of his intentions and then wait for a period of two months. During this time either the king would resolve the conflict by issuing an ordinance or the arbiters would work again towards a reconciliation. The Dukes, if they insisted on making war, would not be allowed to bring troops into the royal domain. If one party broke the conventions now agreed upon the arbiters would support the other one.[16]

The ordinance was delivered at a public meeting attended by the royal councilors at the residence of the duke of Berry. With the queen presiding, Louis of Orléans and Philip of Burgundy both swore to obey the terms of the ordinance.

The queen's political dexterity was in this way brought to public notice. And by the summer of 1402, it was needed again. In April, during another fit of lunacy, Charles named his brother the supreme governor of all *aides* in Languedoïl (*souverain gouverneur des aides en Languedoïl*), to which Louis responded by persuading the king to levy an enormous kingdom-wide tax. Not surprisingly, Philip voiced his frustration to the king, at which point Charles sought to appease his uncle by assigning him to the same post. In anticipation of the financial disputes that were sure to follow, he authorized Isabeau to mediate all future quarrels between the dukes of Orléans and Burgundy. Moreover, he empowered her to conduct government business of any kind in his absence. With so many eager to enrich themselves at the expense of his public authority, Isabeau seemed the only person responsible enough to manage the royal finances.[17]

But her authority did not last long. In the months that followed, Charles began to suspect Isabeau of advancing the interests of her Bavarian relatives. When her brother, Louis of Bavaria, arrived in Paris in the fall of 1402, Isabeau did everything she could to provide him with money and power. Within weeks, she had arranged for him to marry one of the king's second cousins, Anne of Bourbon, who also was a sister to the count of Vendôme and the widow of one of the duke of Berry's sons. In addition to the *seigneurie* of La Basse-March, which included seven *castellanies*, Anne brought with her two large sums of money: a dowry of 120,000 francs to be taken from the royal treasury and a widow's dower of 35,000 livres to be paid by John of Berry. On top of this, the crown awarded Louis of Bavaria an annual pension of 12,000 francs. Isabeau even went so far as to advance his candidacy for the office of French constable, a political initiative that, although agreeable to most of the dukes, did not gain the support of the duke of Orléans and soon thereafter failed.

In April 1403, roughly a month after Louis of Bavaria left Paris, Charles decided to rebalance executive power between the queen, the dukes, courtiers of royal blood, the constable, the chancellor, and "however many councilors the situation required" (*telz et en tel nombre comme il sera expedient*). Final decisions in matters of state now belonged to the majority and "sounder part" of the royal council (*la plus grant et saine partie des voix*).[18] Only affairs of the greatest import, which required written and sealed judgments from the king, were outside their jurisdiction. In tandem with this rebalance of power, Charles VI issued another ordinance requiring Isabeau, the dukes, the princes of the blood, all his royal councilors, and *gens d'estat* from prelates to squires to vow their allegiance to the king. He also required everyone to promise that, upon his death, they would recognize as king whoever was his eldest son at the time—and that they would do so immediately, "without anyone else, no matter how closely related, taking over the care, regency, or government of our kingdom."[19]

Two days later, Charles agreed to marry off his eldest son, the duke of Guyenne, to the granddaughter of Philip the Bold, Margaret of Burgundy. Louis of Orléans was irate. If the king's previous ordinance meant that he could no longer capitalize on his earlier nomination as regent in the event of a minority kingship, this marriage arrangement made it impossible for him to do the next best thing: namely, to wed one of his daughters to the throne. Within days, Louis had convinced the king to override the April ordinances and to cancel his marriage contract with the house of Burgundy. In a letter patent dated 7 May 1403, and almost certainly crafted by the duke of Orléans, Charles acknowledged that although his recent decisions might seem to compromise his brother's rights, nothing could be further from the truth. All his rights, regardless of any former or future decrees, would "remain whole without being wounded (*bleciez*) or worsened (*empirez*) in any way," the king concluded.[20] Thus, the future regency of Louis of Orléans remained intact, and the successor of Charles VI remained unengaged.

Later that week, the king changed his mind, insisting that his letter of 7 May not only compromised the honor of his immediate royal family but also posed a direct threat to the public welfare of France. In support of this realization, and despite his recent ordinances, Charles went on to issue another decree, this one reaffirming Isabeau's authority to administer the royal finances during his absences. Henceforth, all gifts given by the king during periods of mental impairment would require the queen's prior approval. Only Isabeau was capable of "guarding the property, belonging to us and to our kingdom, and to our children," Charles VI declared, reaffirming his confidence in her ability to administer the royal finances.[21]

With no hope of regaining his authority as future regent, and even less of wedding a daughter to the throne, the duke of Orléans turned his attention to the royal treasury. By June 1404, he had secured all royal rights over the county of Soissons and several other lands, the title of lord of Pisa, and the cities, *castellanies*, and lands of Châtillon-sur-Marne, Montargis, Courtenay, and Crécy-en-Brie. And he did not stop there. Between October 1404 and September 1405, Louis nearly emptied the royal coffers, securing more than

400,000 francs in royal grants for himself and his family—nearly twice the annual household income of Philip the Bold. Charles had no choice but to pawn some of his royal jewels. And Parliament could do nothing to help. Well, almost nothing. At the recommendation of Louis of Orléans, and much to discomfort of the already-impoverished lower classes, Parliament levied a new tax throughout France.

This would not have happened if Philip had lived through the spring of 1404. As his successor, John the Fearless, was getting his political bearings, Louis began diverting royal funds from the house of Burgundy to the house of Orléans. Indeed, much to his frustration, John received no pension and hardly any gifts from the king after his father's death. "The most he could hope for was occasional compensation for real or invented expenses incurred in France or on behalf of the French government, and an annual allowance of 12,000 francs for the upkeep and garrisoning of Sluis castle," Richard Vaughan notes. "Even these sums were more often promised than actually paid."[22] Outraged by his cousin's misconduct, John openly protested the recent tax, for which many held Louis responsible. Public opinion followed his lead, applauding the antitax stance of the new duke and spurning the unofficial regency of his cousin. By the spring of 1405, John the Fearless had emerged a viable populist alternative to Louis of Orléans.

Public opinion also turned against the queen, who was then spending noticeable amounts of time with the duke of Orléans. So much time, in fact, that when she was caught sending six horses laden with coin to her brother in the summer of 1405, most of France jumped to the conclusion that it was the proceeds from Louis's tax, which she and the duke were intent on concealing in Bavaria (even though the money was probably the 57,000 francs that Isabeau owed her brother for the revenues of several Bavarian provinces). "The people blamed the bad administration of the queen and the duke of Orléans," the *religieux* of Saint-Denis reports. "They were condemned publicly in the towns for their insatiable greed; it was said that, negligent of the kingdom's defense and not content with normal taxation, they had imposed a general levy the previous year."[23] Like the princes, nobles, and wealthy businessmen with whom she administered the state, Isabeau seemed more than willing to privatize and profit from the royal fiscal system, regardless of what it might cost her husband in public authority and her kingdom in general welfare.

Meanwhile, John the Fearless was defending the Flemish port of Sluis from a fleet of English ships. With victory at hand, he wrote to Paris in search of reinforcements for a counteroffensive. Louis of Orléans, acting in the king's stead, persuaded the royal council to deny his request, leaving the new duke to fend for himself. At this point, John seems to have realized that, if he were ever to regain the wealth and power of his father, he would have to depose the duke of Orléans or, at the very least, to loosen his grip on the royal council.

An opportunity arrived in July 1405, when the king summoned all the dukes to attend a council meeting. John left for Paris at the head of 1,700 men-at-arms, and with plans to rendezvous with his brother Anthony, who brought with him an additional 1,000 men. Louis and Isabeau flew into a panic. They left Paris immediately, en route to the queen's fortified château at Melun. Fearing John might persuade the king to empower his eight-year-old son, the duke of Guyenne, as his surrogate, they also arranged for the young prince and his wife, Margaret of Burgundy, to follow them. When news of this arrangement reached John the Fearless, he raced ahead of his soldiers, intercepted the royal children, and promptly returned them to Paris.

Later that day, John sent an open letter to several French cities, informing them of his intentions. In addition to paying homage to the king, he had come to Paris to discuss the current state of the French government. Louis responded with a letter of his own, in which he openly accused the new duke of attempting a coup d'état. John countered with a widely publicized request for government reform, specifically a reconfiguration of the royal council to include more trustworthy advisers. Louis replied to this subtle personal indictment by blaming the mismanagement of France on the royal uncles.

As this pamphlet war raged through the kingdom, armed forces continued to gather in and around Paris. With no fallback on the horizon, and no sign of Isabeau's willingness to intervene, a civil war seemed imminent. Parisians were ordered to illuminate the streets with lanterns, to keep water by their doors at all times, and to purchase armor for "the defense of the good town of Paris."[24] It was at this point in the Orléans-Burgundy conflict, when the welfare of France was most in jeopardy, that Christine de Pizan addressed her 5 October 1405 letter to Queen Isabeau.

Medieval Letter-Writing: The Birth of Modern Diplomacy

In the late Middle Ages, letter-writers negotiated all sorts of conflicts. That much of the propaganda surrounding the standoff between John the Fearless and Louis of Orléans appeared as an exchange of public letters is not surprising. Nor is Christine's use of a prose epistle to encourage Isabeau to intervene in their dispute. Indeed, the art of letter-writing—known among medievals as *dictamen* or *ars dictaminis*—was designed with the express purpose of equipping literate political subjects for the trials and tribulations of medieval diplomacy, be they legal, civic, or ecclesiastical.[25]

Despite the often-formulaic quality of medieval epistolography, and the multiple ranks and orders of feudal life, political leadership in the late Middle Ages was not yet in the grips of bureaucratic culture. Rulers often abandoned established protocols in search of alternate advice on how best to handle affairs of state. Visionary ascetics, popular preachers, and learned advocates like Christine frequently found their way into court life, often by way of written correspondence.[26] And like much medieval epistolography, their letters to power were characteristically public:

> Whereas intimacy, spontaneity, and privacy are now considered the essence of the epistolary genre, in the Middle Ages letters were for the most part self-conscious, quasi-public literary documents, often written with an eye to future collection and publication. In view of the way in which letters were written and sent, and also the standards of literacy in the Middle Ages, it is doubtful whether there were any private letters in the modern sense of the term. As in Antiquity, when the earliest letters were concerned with factual rather than private affairs, medieval letters were often intended to be read by more than one person even at the time they were written.[27]

Among the first readers of medieval letters were their carriers. In Christine's era, messengers not only delivered letters physically but also transmitted their content orally. Epistolography was inseparable from oratory: "The arts of letter writing include as part of their standard doctrine instructions for the *cursus*, rhythmically patterned clause endings that depend on being heard to have their effect, and the divisions of a letter are based on the parts of a Ciceronian oration."[28] By the thirteenth century, the term *nuntius*, meaning "messenger" or "message," had become functionally equivalent to *epistola*. "A *nuncius* is he who takes the place of the letter," the medieval jurist Azo explains. "He is just like a magpie and the voice of the principal sending him, and he recites the words of the principal."[29] In this sense, the medieval messenger was not only a living embodiment of the letter he carried, the voice of a remote speaker mediated through the written word. Moreover, as a simulacrum of the letter's author, he was an envoy or an ambassador—or, to put it a bit archly, an apostle.

John the Fearless probably delivered Christine's letter to the queen.[30] In addition to transporting it to her new location in Vincennes, he would have read the letter aloud to Isabeau and other members of her entourage, one of whom, as we know, was his sworn enemy, Louis of Orléans.[31] The likely addition of these rival dukes to Christine's audience is especially significant given the purpose of her letter: to legitimate and effect the queen's intervention in their quarrel. By presencing Isabeau, John, and Louis, she could begin the diplomatic effort that her letter advocated. Moreover, she could do so without violating established codes of deference. By positioning the dukes as auditors to a letter addressed to the queen, Christine was able to critique their power politics without engaging these royal cousins directly. That each duke was a potential patron meant that Christine had to handle them both with kid gloves. But they were more than sources of funding for Christine and her work. The dukes of Orléans and Burgundy were also attenuators of her advice to the queen, dyslogistic figures through which Christine could mediate and rarefy her obvious disapproval of Isabeau's recent inaction. Thus, just as her address to the queen sublimates her criticism of the dukes, so also does her criticism of the dukes sublimate her address to the queen.[32]

But this rhetoric of addressivity is not the only means by which Christine advises the queen without contesting her authority. Nor is it the primary means. More crucial to her persuasive artistry is the rhetoric of exemplary figures with which she authorizes and articulates her advice. In order to understand and explain this maneuver, we must first account for the canonical work of political thought out of which it emerges: *The Book of the City of Ladies*.

From the City of Ladies to a Few of Its Inhabitants

Christine's epistle is a direct political extension of her *Book of the City of Ladies*. In this cardinal work of early-feminist thought, which was finished just months before her letter to the queen, Christine sifts through scripture, natural philosophy, classical legends, and political history in search of emblematic women to include in a universal history of womankind. Unlike Boccaccio's *On Famous Women* (*De mulieribus claris*), which offers a chronological, nondidactic history of famous women from Eve to Johanna of Naples (1343–82), *The Book of the City of Ladies* treats the historical achievements of women as kindred moments that, despite their temporal dispersion, can be brought into fellowship with one another.

Moreover, *The Book of the City of Ladies* is overtly didactic. In cataloging the achievements of women, Christine seeks to provide her readers with equipment for living as women of virtue—*ladies*—in the male-dominated Middle Ages.

Unfettered by modern, Hegelian longings for totality and sequence, she follows Cicero in understanding history as "an aggregate of instances designed to serve as guides for behavior and action."[33] *Historia magistra vitae*—this is the attitude toward history entailed in *The Book of the City of Ladies*.

Citing the historically dispersed achievements of women not only enables Christine to instruct literate medieval women in the art of practical morality. It also enables her to argue by example for a radical new understanding of nobility: "She transposes the dignity afforded to noble women in the late-medieval French class structure to women who have proven their worthiness through their achievements, whether military, political, cultural, or religious."[34] Merit, not bloodline, becomes the basis for nobility, and in turn the basis for inclusion, in *The Book of the City of Ladies*.

These attitudes toward history and nobility find a powerful political outlet in Christine's letter to the queen. She begins by suggesting that only Isabeau can provide "the medicine and sovereign remedy for this kingdom now so pitifully wounded and injured," and that only a "humble servant" (*povre serve*) like herself can present the queen with "the common problems, in words as well as in facts, which prevail upon your subjects." In hopes of providing the queen with "an example of good behavior," Christine goes on to recite "tales of your predecessors who reigned nobly," all but two of whom also appear in *The Book of the City of Ladies*.[35] The first woman she cites is Princess Veturia:

> Just as it happened in Rome to a very powerful princess whose son had been banished and exiled very unfairly and without cause by the barons of the city; and after that, since he had, in order to avenge this injury, assembled an army so large that it was enough to destroy all, did the valiant lady, in spite of the villainy done, not face her son, and did [so] much that she pacified his anger, and made him make peace with the Romans?[36]

The second is Queen Esther:

> And still on the subject that it behooves a high princess and lady to be the mediator of a peace treaty, it is shown in the worthy ladies praised in the Holy Scriptures: thus, the worthy and wise Queen Esther, who appeased the anger of King Ahasuerus by her common sense and goodness, so much so that she had the sentence against the people condemned to death revoked.[37]

The third is Bathsheba, who, although absent from *The Book of the City of Ladies*, Christine uses to indicate queenly virtues similar to those of Veturia and Esther:

> Did Bathsheba not appease David's anger many times as well? Also a worthy queen who advised her husband that since he could not vanquish his enemies by force, he should do what the good physicians do: that is when they see that bitter medicines do not help their patients, they give them sweet ones. And in this way, the wise queen caused him to become reconciled with his adversaries.[38]

The fourth exemplary figure is Blanche of Castile:

> Of the good queens, for our purpose and in order not to search further, [there is] the very wise and good Queen of France, Blanche, mother of Saint Louis. When the barons quarreled over the regency of the kingdom, did she not take her child, still very young, in her arms, and holding him among the barons, say: "Do you not see your king? Do not do anything that, when God has guided him to the age of reason, he will blame on any one of you." And so she appeased them with her good advice.[39]

In addition to these admirable women, Christine provides Isabeau with two models of iniquity. The first she cites is Jezebel: "Similarly, could infinite examples of wise and praiseworthy queens be given, but I will leave them for the sake of brevity; the same could be done with opposite examples of perverse and cruel queens, enemies of humankind: thus, the false queen Jezebel and others of the same kind, who because of their evil actions are still and will be forever infamous, accursed, and damned."[40] The second of these two figures is Olympias. Although absent from *The Book of the City of Ladies*, she embodies vices similar to those of Jezebel: "God! Did Queen Olympias, mother of the great Alexander, think, when she had everyone under her feet, subjected and obedient to her, of the many blows that Fortune would have the power to inflict on her and to the point where she piteously and shamefully ended her days? And we could tell similar stories of many other people."[41]

Taken together, these exemplary figures form an epistolary composite of historical particulars and timeless qualities. Veturia is a character invented during the reign of Augustus; Esther, Bathsheba, and Jezebel are women from scripture; Olympias is a key figure in ancient Greek political culture; and Blanche of Castile is a contemporary French political actor. As *exempla*, all these figures monadically carry within themselves the entirety of their historical deployments. This includes the residual significance of the times and texts from which they were first "cut out" or "removed" as exemplary figures, as well as the residual significance of subsequent moments in which these women have been, and will have been, cited. Thus, in keeping with late-medieval attitudes toward intertextuality, most of the exemplary figures discussed in Christine's letter derive from her *Book of the City of Ladies*, and much of this book in turn derives from other literary and historical experiences.[42] Christine even went so far as to borrow from Boccaccio's *On Famous Women*, to which *The Book of the City of Ladies* was written in opposition. In fact, she borrowed from this work so heavily that *The Book of the City of Ladies* has sometimes been considered a translation of Boccaccio.[43] That *On Famous Women* also borrows freely from a variety of sources further demonstrates the textual and temporal mobility of the exemplary figures cited in Christine's letter. Their "proper place" in literary and historical experience is nothing if not dispersed.

Interestingly, the textual and temporal circulation of Veturia, Esther, Bathsheba, Blanche, Jezebel, and Olympias is precisely what enables these women to stand for general qualities of leadership—namely, to function as *paradeigmata*.[44] By citing their political activities in *The Book of the City of Ladies*, and then re-citing them in her letter to the queen, Christine demonstrates that although these activities occurred in distinct historical times and texts, they also participate in an extensive inventory of similar conduct. In this sense, Isabeau's predecessors are at once themselves and representative of something else. As exemplary figures, they share this basic ambiguity of substance.

Moreover, the "something else" for which these women stand is entirely undecidable, and this undecidability is integral to their function as *paradeigmata*. Only insofar as Veturia, Esther, Bathsheba, Blanche, Jezebel, and Olympias represent transhistorical qualities of leadership can they allude to an extensive historical iteration of similar conduct, and only insofar as their political activities represent an extensive historical iteration of similar conduct can they allude to transhistorical qualities of leadership.[45] At issue here, as we shall see, is a relationship between dispersed exemplary figures and abstract qualities of leadership that is not external but parasitical, one in which neither class of entities is entirely outside or independent of the other.[46]

The Rhetoric of Exemplary Figures

In contrast to *On Famous Women*, in which Boccaccio claims to find no *clarae* in Christian history, *The Book of the City of Ladies* interweaves classical, Hebrew, Christian, and contemporary exemplars into a discontinuous history of the achievements of women. The result is a comprehensive and powerfully erudite counterstatement to the broader misogynist ideology to which Boccaccio added captions.[47] In her letter to the queen, Christine telescopes this historical and ideological dispute through the optics of an emerging political crisis in which tensions between the houses of Orléans and Burgundy had reached their breaking point. Thus, in reciting exemplary women from her *Book of the City of Ladies*, Christine insinuates the broader cultural issue of medieval misogyny into a highly specific feudal dispute, the resolution of which, her letter suggests, only Isabeau can effect.

Compositionally, this reshuffling of time, text, and circumstance for purposes of rhetorical prodding is indicative of early-humanist epistolography.[48] However, to understand Christine's letter in terms of humanist standards of persuasion is to miss much of its political import. Unlike most rhetorical inductions, Christine's exemplary figures resist being characterized as paradigmatic, illustrative, or persuasive in a narrowly enthymematic sense. In fact, she seems to have chosen them for their ability to interrupt the inductive process. To be sure, these illustrious and ill-famed women impressed general qualities of leadership on the queen. But they were more than *paradeigmata*. As exceptions to common medieval belief that women were unfit to govern, they also functioned as *exempla*.[49] Over and against this "general truth," Christine focuses on the specific historical conduct of Veturia, Bathsheba, Esther, Blanche, Jezebel, and Olympias. In so doing, she preserves a moment of critique in which the discrepancy between her exemplary figures and the patriarchal assumptions of the late Middle Ages forces a modification of the latter in light of the historical specificity of the former.[50] The rule of man is hardly a timeless truth, Christine reminds the queen.

In opening up opportunities to contest the misogynist ideology of the late Middle Ages, Christine's examples also gesture toward an alternate rule. As *paradeigmata*, they suggest that women are able, and even obliged, to participate in affairs of state, especially those involving familial disputes, which were not uncommon in dynastic states such as France, where the overlap between personal and official interests was often considerable.[51] Thus, despite their textual and temporal specificity, a common theme unites these exemplary figures. Each of the women mentioned in her letter either successfully manages or fails to control an unruly male figure, often on behalf of a large group of people. Veturia saves Rome from the vengeful wrath of her son, Martius. Esther dissuades King Ahasuerus of Persia from allowing Haman to kill captive Jews and execute her cousin, Mordecai. Bathsheba, after marrying King David, helps manage his anger and plays an active role in dynastic affairs. Blanche of Castile governs France while her son, Saint Louis, is a minor, and she continues to lead his council in the years that followed. Conversely, Jezebel turns her husband, King Ahab, away from the one true God and toward the worship of her god, Baal, and after his death she goes on to rule through her sons, Ahaziah and Joram. Similarly, Olympias seizes power following the death of her son, Alexander the Great, and is soon thereafter brought to trial and put to death for ordering numerous and overly cruel executions. Like those of her admirable and infamous predecessors, Christine suggests, the situation in which Isabeau finds herself is a family affair that, when viewed from the vantage point of history, can be shown to have far-reaching political consequences.

To further illustrate the function of these exemplary figures as *exempla* and *paradeigmata*—opportunities to interrupt and to counterstate the misogynist ideology of the late Middle Ages—let us consider their relation to historical and allegorical levels of meaning in medieval hermeneutics. What enables the Latin *exemplum* to preserve a moment of critique is the historical baggage with which it comes. Before they were *exempla*, the women mentioned in Christine's letter were beings in time and text, the historicity of which was undeniable for her. In referencing these women as exemplary figures, Christine allows their literal historical significance to intervene in dominant collations of exemplary women, not the least of which was Boccaccio's book *On Famous Women*, which was then enjoying considerable success in France. In order to invest these women with abstract qualities of leadership, however, Christine must also reconcile their historical and textual particularities in a broader interpretive typology or, in keeping with medieval hermeneutics, an allegorical system of meaning. At issue here is a representational structure in which Veturia, Esther, Bathsheba, Blanche, Jezebel, and Olympias operate as concrete historical portals to a timeless reality of virtue and vice. The persuasiveness of Christine's letter is dependent on Isabeau's willingness to imagine herself in living correspondence with this representational structure.[52]

As *exempla*, these figures challenge the patriarchal assumptions of the late Middle Ages with historical and textual specificity. As *paradeigmata*, they represent the political aptitude of women in an allegorical or typological structure. As both *exempla* and *paradeigmata*, however, they fundamentally exceed the Orléans-Burgundy conflict, diverting Isabeau's attention from the issue at hand to a variety of remote historical landscapes and invisible qualities of leadership. Although this diversion certainly jeopardizes the rhetorical coherence of Christine's letter, it is also crucial to her argument. For Christine, the political activities of Veturia, Esther, Bathsheba, Blanche, Jezebel, and Olympias are evidentiary proofs—external events radiating their visibility outward to the queen ("evidence" being a combination of *ex*, meaning "out," and *videre*, meaning "to see"). More specifically, all the exemplary figures she cites, regardless of their historical and typological distinctions, serve as independent witnesses to the Orléans-Burgundy conflict. They are remote historical bystanders whose moment of testimony has finally arrived in the form of Christine's letter—an epistolary "now" in which these exemplary figures become recognizable as mirrors for the queen.

In the late Middle Ages, when letters were written in anticipation of their oral delivery, "overloading" arguments with exemplary figures and external authorities was a common way to facilitate audience interpretation. Moreover, doing so enabled writers to establish the authority of their discourse. However, because citing an exemplary figure involves diverting audience members to something "outside" the "inside" constituted by the epistolary text—thereby encouraging them to "see for themselves"—the rhetoric of exemplary figures differs fundamentally from direct, authoritarian assertion. Yet neither does it require an enunciative shift from the voice of the writer to that of the exemplary figure, as in the case of quoted discourse. In contrast, the rhetoric of exemplary figures consists in reciting the words or deeds of another in discourse of one's own.[53] Thus, although citing the conduct of Isabeau's predecessors certainly diverts her attention to figures and events beyond the frame of Christine's letter, doing so does not require her to relinquish her status as its author. Rather, it enables Christine to ambiguate her implicit critique of Isabeau's diplomatic inertia without attenuating her argument for an immediate intervention in the Orléans-Burgundy conflict. Far from jeopardizing the rhetorical coherence of her letter, then, ambiguity of this sort is the basis for its function as a persuasive text.

Preserving her authorial status further enables Christine to mediate the historical and typological functions of her exemplary figures. As the learned author of their epistolary surroundings, she is able to encompass these figures in authoritative moral commentary on the significance of the Orléans-Burgundy conflict. In so doing, she articulates them in a third level of address: a didactic statement on what *should be* the preoccupations of the queen of

France in this perilous historical moment. With the addition of this moral dimension, the underlying rhetorical structure of her letter begins to appear: as *exempla*, Christine's exemplary figures present the queen with specific historical conduct; as *paradeigmata*, they provide her with a representational structure in which to interpret this conduct; and in being surrounded by the moral commentary of a renowned woman of letters, they encourage the queen to act in accordance with this representational structure. Why Isabeau would *want* to consider the political activities of her predecessors, to contemplate the qualities of leadership for which they stand, and subsequently to intervene in the Orléans-Burgundy conflict remains to be seen.

Self-Mediating Thought, Other-Oriented Action

The rhetoric of exemplarity not only diverts attention to objects, figures, and events beyond the discourse at hand; it also brings these entities into closer proximity. To cite an example is to appropriate an object, figure, or event that is fundamentally absent from the communicative act, and not necessarily connected to the person citing it.[54] In this sense, Veturia, Esther, Bathsheba, Blanche, Jezebel, and Olympias all threaten to "contaminate" Christine's argument with excessive particularity and irrelevant signification.[55] As we have seen, however, the "otherness" of these exemplary figures is precisely what enables Christine to ambiguate her implicit critique of Isabeau's diplomatic languor without weakening her argument for an immediate intervention in the Orléans-Burgundy conflict. This ambiguity enables Christine to protect herself from any regal backlash her letter might incur. But how exactly does it facilitate her argument for an immediate intervention in the present political crisis?

Rather than insist that the queen mediate this conflict, Christine provides her with an opportunity to imagine and to judge it from viewpoints other than her own, specifically those of women who have either managed or mishandled similar circumstances. But let us make no mistake. This is not a question of empathy. In imagining the viewpoints of Veturia, Esther, Bathsheba, Blanche, Jezebel, and Olympias, the queen does not replace her own perspective with those of her predecessors. Instead, the rhetoric of exemplary figures encourages Isabeau to be and to think in *her own identity* where actually she is not, to consider *her own role* in the Orléans-Burgundy conflict vis-à-vis the roles other women have played in similar circumstances. In this sense, Veturia, Esther, Bathsheba, Blanche, Jezebel, and Olympias are not remote lenses through which Isabeau can regard the Orléans-Burgundy conflict, but rather intimate mirrors in which to reflect (on) her current relation to this conflict. Thus, although the rhetoric of exemplarity certainly moves from the inside out, diverting attention to foreign objects, figures, and events, it culminates in a movement from the outside in, allowing audiences to see themselves being seen by others. In considering Christine's exemplary figures, Isabeau must regard herself and her circumstances in their collective gaze, thereby offsetting her own personal understanding of the Orléans-Burgundy conflict (as well as any private financial interests of her own) with moments of self-reflection mediated through the worlds of her admirable and infamous predecessors—worlds that are now closer than ever to her own.

Mediated subjectivity of this sort is the basis for the political judgment Christine hopes to inspire in the queen. "The rhetorical force of example is to impose on the audience or interlocutor an obligation to judge," writes Alexander Gelley. "Whether it be in argument or narrative, the rhetoric of example stages an instance of judgment, and the reader, in order to grasp the point at issue, must be capable of occupying, however provisionally, the seat of judgment."[56] Like all political judgments, however, that which Christine stages in her letter can only occur on insufficient grounds. Unlike determinant judgments, which subsume historical particulars under universal laws or rules, and in so doing rely on general concepts to assign attributes to experience, judgments occasioned by the rhetoric of exemplarity are reflective, which means they have no determinate concepts available to them, no universal laws or rules under which to subsume the experience of historical particularity.[57] The law or rule according to which Isabeau might legitimate her intervention in the Orléans-Burgundy conflict—*women are able, and even obliged, to engage in political activity*—is nowhere to be found in early fifteenth-century France.[58] Isabeau, with the help of Christine, who in turn relies on the assistance of Veturia, Esther, Bathsheba, Blanche, Jezebel, and Olympias, must discover this rule for herself. She must somehow ascend from the historical particulars at hand—not only the exemplary figures before her, but also the surrounding details of Orléans-Burgundy conflict—to the absent rule of judgment reflected in their singular historicity.

If the queen is to succeed in discovering an identity in this multiplicity of historical particulars, she must pursue it not haphazardly, but rather on the basis of some principle. But the misogynist Middle Ages has provided her with no determinate concept that might serve as such a principle. The only source of guidance available to Isabeau is the *subjective purposiveness* of the historical particulars at hand, namely, her belief in the design of these exemplary figures for her power of judgment. It is their *being-for* the queen's assessment that unites Veturia, Esther, Bathsheba, Blanche, Jezebel, and Olympias as exemplary figures. Indeed, their persuasiveness depends on her acknowledgment of their mutual orientation to her present circumstances. This willingness to be guided by her predecessors is the principle according to which Isabeau can discover the absent rule of judgment that would legitimate, and perhaps even mandate, her intervention in the Orléans-Burgundy conflict.

Because this principle is fundamentally subjective, however, its condition of possibility being none other than the faculty of judgment itself, it cannot achieve the same objective validity as a determinant concept. The cogency of the queen's judgment is entirely dependent on the readiness with which she accepts and the impartiality with which she represents the standpoints of Veturia, Esther, Bathsheba, Blanche, Jezebel, and Olympias. To this list, Christine claims that "infinite examples of wise and praiseworthy queens" could be added, along with "opposite examples of perverse and cruel queens, enemies of humankind." Yet she does not append her list of exemplary figures. Instead, she supplements it with the collective standpoint of her fellow French subjects. In addition to encouraging Isabeau to see herself from the viewpoints of her predecessors, Christine implores her to "hear the complaints and pitiful regrets of the suffering and suppliant French people [*Françoys*] now full of affliction and sadness, and who cry with tearful voices to you."

Christine channels these tearful voices throughout her letter. She even goes so far as to identify her discourse as a "teary request ... written on behalf of your poor subjects, the loyal French people [*Françoys*]." In using her own "tearful voice" to express those of the French people, she models the self-mediating thought required of the queen, and in so doing hastens her letter's circumvention of the private interests that seem to have led Isabeau out of Paris and into her fortified château at Melun. As the letter winds to a close, Christine's "teary request" reaches a feverish pitch: "Alas! That the poor people should have to pay for the sin of which they are innocent! That the poor little infants and children should cry for their miserable and suffering widowed mothers, in a state of starvation, and their mothers, deprived of all their goods, should not have anything to appease them!"[59]

Formally, this passage is an adaption of the lyrical genre known as the *complainte*—a mode of public address in which personal, social, or institutional struggles find expression in a powerful voice, the purpose of which is to reveal an injustice suffered by the speaker or someone the speaker represents.[60] Christine politicizes this lyrical genre in her letter to the queen. Hers is a *complainte politique*. As Daniel Poirion notes, this courtly form of address "generally expresses the suffering of those who do not enjoy the consolations of glory or of the material compensations that could soften the harsh reality of war."[61] Among its leading topoi are references to ancient and mythological examples and recurring images of profusely flowing tears, both of which, as we have seen, figure prominently in Christine's letter. If her exemplary figures bring with them a sense of historical responsibility, specifically Isabeau's accountability to the history of womankind,[62] the images of flowing tears accent her duty to the French people, recalling the biblical identification of God's final salvation with the wiping away of all tears.[63]

Intervening in the Orléans-Burgundy conflict would at once preserve Isabeau's place in the *City of Ladies* and halt the flowing tears of her people. In accomplishing these objectives, Christine writes, Isabeau could rest assured that "in eternal remembrance of you [*perpetuelle memoire de vous*], you would be remembered, commanded, and praised in the chronicles and noble tales of France, twice crowned with honors, with love, presents, graces and humble and deep gratitude from your loyal subjects."[64] As we have seen, Christine's exemplary figures are invested with *historical* and *typological* meaning, and her commentary on these figures further inscribes them with *moral* significance. In keeping with medieval hermeneutics, this promise of "eternal remembrance" suggests their *anagogical* import, namely, their relevance to "higher matters belonging to eternal glory."[65] In this fourth and ultimate level of significance, the historical particularities of Veturia, Esther, Bathsheba, Blanche, Jezebel, and Olympias are rewritten in terms of the collective destiny of the French people. The typological and moral dimensions of these exemplary figures become little more than symbolic detours through which Isabeau must pass in order to understand the individuals and the groups on whose behalf these women intervened in their political cultures as prefigurations of the individuals and the groups on whose behalf Isabeau must now intervene in the Orléans-Burgundy conflict.

But there is more to the achievement of "eternal remembrance" than Isabeau's willingness to be guided by her illustrious and ill-famed predecessors. In addition to learning from these exemplary figures, she must do so in a way that subordinates her personal interest in this feudal dispute to the public welfare of her royal subjects. Christine develops this crucial qualification in her letter's conclusion, where she insists that, should Isabeau act in accordance with "the tales of your predecessors who reigned nobly," the French people "will pray for you"— and, hearing their prayers, God will "grant you a good and long life, and at the end, perpetual glory [*gloire pardurable*]."[66] At issue here is not Isabeau's eternal presence in the *City of God*, but her immortal dwelling in the *City of Ladies*. It is her potential to endure in time, to achieve what Arendt calls "deathless life on this earth," that is at stake in Christine's letter.[67] "Eternal remembrance" and "perpetual glory" are the lasting, earthly rewards for her intervention in the

Orléans-Burgundy conflict. In this sense, the anagogical import of Christine's prose is limited to its socioanagogic function.[68] Fame and glory, not communion with the eternal—the rewards of political activity, not the promise of philosophic *apolitia*—these are Isabeau's incentives to abandon her pursuit of private wealth and personal security, to follow in the footsteps of her noble predecessors, and in so doing to dry the tears of her long-suffering subjects.

The Temporal Politics of the Exemplary Figure

In the years to come, Isabeau will have managed or mishandled the Orléans-Burgundy conflict. She will have either bravely exemplified or unwittingly opposed the absent law of political engagement reflected in the exemplary figures of Veturia, Esther, Bathsheba, Blanche, Jezebel, and Olympias. What unites the exemplary figures and the images of tearful suffering that make up Christine's letter is their pronouncement of these two distant futures—one in which Isabeau will have performed her public duties, and another in which she will have continued to pursue her private interests. In either case, Christine suggests, the conduct of the queen's predecessors will have recurred, and thus written Isabeau into the annals of history as an exemplary figure of either prudent or immoderate leadership. As an *exemplum*, Isabeau will remain inexorably tied to the Orléans-Burgundy conflict. As a *paradeigma*, she will forever represent abstract qualities of leadership. Only the company of queens she will keep is now within her power to decide.

Christine develops this future anterior line of argument using the modal verb "would." With this term, she encourages Isabeau to view her present circumstances from the vantage points of two distant futures, both of which are contingent on her conduct in the immediate future. Should she follow in the footsteps of Veturia, Esther, Bathsheba, and Blanche and successfully manage the Orléans-Burgundy conflict, Isabeau can expect to receive "three great goods and benefits" in the distant future, all of which Christine uses the auxiliary "would" to articulate:

> The first belongs to the soul, whose very sovereign merit you would acquire [*seroit eschevee*] by the fact that, thanks to you, a great and shameful effusion of blood in the very Christian kingdom of France established by God could be avoided by your efforts, and so would the confusion which would follow [*ensuivroit*] if such a horror were to last [*avoit duree*]. Similarly, by the second good, you would be [*seriez*] the seeker of peace and the cause for the restitution of the goods of your

noble children and their loyal subjects. The third good, which is not to be despised, is that in eternal remembrance of you, you would be remembered, commanded, and praised [*ramenteue, recommandee et louee*] in the chronicles and noble tales of France.

Should Isabeau follow in the footsteps of Jezebel and Olympias and mishandle the Orléans-Burgundy conflict, however, she can expect "two great and horrible evils" to occur in the distant future, both of which Christine again uses the auxiliary "would" to pronounce. "One is that the kingdom would be destroyed [*convendroit*] by it in a short time," she warns. "The other is that a perpetual hatred would spring up and remain [*soit nee et nourrie*] henceforth between the heirs and children of the noble blood of France." Should Isabeau fail to address the feudal conflict now threatening her kingdom, and thus refuse to allow her "predecessors who reigned so nobly" to provide her with "an example of good behavior," she will become just like Jezebel and Olympias—"forever infamous, accursed, and damned."

The permanence of this terrible likeness is Christine's final plea for an intervention in the Orléans-Burgundy conflict. "How," she asks, "would [*seroit*] such an ugly infamy, unusual in this noble kingdom, ever be rectified or forgotten?" Christine then amplifies this question by reminding Isabeau that as her catastrophic present passes into collective memory, she remains tied to the uncertainties of fortune: "Moreover, a prince or princess who would be [*aroit*] so obstinate in sin that he/she would render no account [*n'accompteroit nulle chose*] to God or to such great sufferings, should be reminded, if he/she were not completely mad, of the very variable turns of Fortune, which can change and transform itself at any time." And with ill fortune comes ill fame, Christine concludes, further accenting the permanence of this "ugly infamy" by shifting her tense from the conditional future to the simple past:

> What happens to the powerful man thus welcomed by Fortune? If he did not act wisely in the past [*saigement n'a tant fait le temps passé*], and by the means of love, pity, and charity had not first attracted God and not done well in this world [*qu'il ait acquiz Dieu premierement et bien vueillans au monde*], then his whole life and actions are told in public and put to shame. And as a dog is pursued by all who are chasing it away, this man is trampled by all, and they all shout at him that he is being deservedly treated.[69]

"Perpetual glory" or "ugly infamy"—these distant futures could not be more distinct. As vantage points for the queen, however, they share a common attribute: both enable Isabeau to view the Orléans-Burgundy conflict as a historical event. Relative to these distant futures, her catastrophic present is located in the past. More important, because her decision to address or to ignore this catastrophic present is the condition of possibility for these two distant futures, and thus logically prior to their occurrence, the vantage points they provide also enable Isabeau to view her immediate future—one of intervention or abstention—as a historical event. Relative to these distant futures, her immediate future is also located in the past. Thus, in using the auxiliary "would" to forecast two distant realities, one of "perpetual glory" and another of "ugly infamy," Christine encourages Isabeau to understand the catastrophic present in which she now finds herself as a *present in the past* and the immediate future of this catastrophic present as a *future in the past*.

In grasping her catastrophic present and her immediate future as events in the past, Isabeau makes a slight yet significant adjustment to her experience of time. The present in which she finds herself and the future just ahead of her now bear a striking resemblance to the historical and literary experiences of Veturia, Esther, Bathsheba, Blanche, Jezebel, and Olympias. Relative to her distant future of "perpetual glory" or "ugly infamy," all three of these events—Isabeau's exemplary past, catastrophic present, and immediate future—are located in the past, as figure 1 indicates.

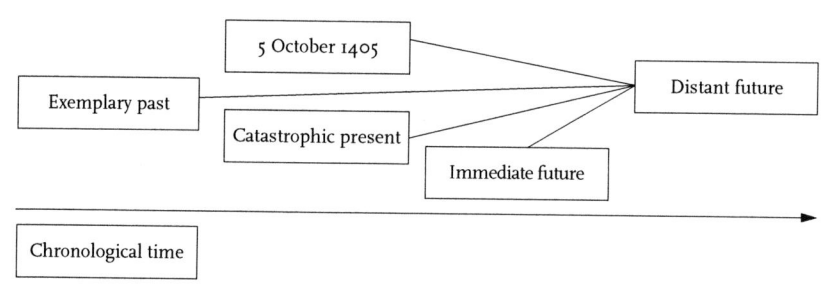

Fig. 1 The constellation of time in Christine's letter to the queen

By using the auxiliary "would" to forecast the distant future, then, Christine enables Isabeau to unite her exemplary past, catastrophic present, and immediate future in a single historical configuration, the determining feature of which is its anchorage in moments prior to her achievement of "perpetual glory" or "ugly infamy"—namely, its "future anteriority."[70] Despite this common temporal attribute, these three moments do not coincide. Instead, they form a constellation of time in which an order of relationships previously concealed within the sweep of history becomes recognizable to the queen.[71]

Although this constellation of time comes to legibility in Christine's letter, it issues from the continuum of history. And yet it is not temporal in a narrowly chronological sense. Instead, it indicates a moment of discontinuity within the continuum of history, a time within time—or in Walter Benjamin's terms, a "temporal differential" (*Zeitdifferential*).[72] The "time" in which Isabeau recognizes her exemplary past, catastrophic present, and immediate future as events of the past is not the continuum of history (*chronos*), but its contraction and abridgement, its seizure in a composite figure of time (*kairos*). It is the Pauline *ho nyn kairos*, the medieval *nunc stans*, Benjamin's *Jetztzeit*—in short, *the time of the now*.

If the exemplary figure is undecidably split between the structural vocations of the Greek *paradeigma* and the Latin *exemplum*, the constellation of time with which Christine confronts the queen also marks a zone of indiscernibility. In her letter, Isabeau's exemplary past, catastrophic present, and immediate future are all dislocated from chronological time, and thus allowed to mingle with tenses and aspects other than their own. In being clasped to her catastrophic present and her immediate future, Isabeau's exemplary past rediscovers the possibility and incompletion of the future; and in being clasped to her exemplary past and her catastrophic present, Isabeau's immediate future acquires the finality and completion of the past. In this sense, the catastrophic present in which Veturia, Esther, Bathsheba, Blanche, Jezebel, and Olympias become recognizable as mirrors for the queen is also the moment in which Isabeau's impending management or mishandling of the Orléans-Burgundy conflict is, as Heidegger would put it, in "the process of having been [*gewesende*]."[73] It is precisely here, in and as the interface between these two activities—the becoming-incomplete of her exemplary past and the becoming-complete of her immediate future—that the exigency of the "now" in which Isabeau finds herself becomes apparent. If she is to make a difference in the Orléans-Burgundy conflict, she must accept this inversion of past and future as a constituent feature of her present.

What is at stake in this acceptance? What difference does it make to the endangered citizens of Paris whether she accepts or rejects Christine's inversion of past and future? One thing is certain: in understanding her exemplary past as becoming-incomplete and her immediate future as nearing-completion, Isabeau changes the structure of their relation to each other. No longer is it temporal in a narrowly chronological sense. Rather, the structure of their relationship becomes dialectical or, in keeping with the terms of this chapter, *figural*. The catastrophic present in which Isabeau's exemplary past and immediate future trade aspects no longer functions as a simple transition between determined and indeterminate events. No longer does it serve as an idle juncture of events that are "no more" and events that are "not yet." In recognizing this inversion of past and future, and with it the dislocation of chronological time, Isabeau must realize her catastrophic present as an occasion for political judgment (*krisis*). No longer one among many moments in chronological time, the Orléans-Burgundy conflict is now a singular historical exigency, the negotiation of which is of the utmost political concern. It is the formulation of this exigency that ultimately distinguishes Christine's letter as a persuasive appeal.

By understanding her immediate future as "no more," Isabeau loosens from its shapeless form an occasion for political judgment. By understanding her exemplary past as "not yet," she releases from its decided grasp an inventory of historical models on which to base her translation of this judgment into political action. With these models for political action comes an attitude toward history reminiscent of Seneca's *Letters to Lucilius*. If the conduct of her predecessors is able to guide Isabeau through her catastrophic present and into her immediate future, it is because, in figuring this conduct as exemplary, Christine ties the present to the future through the past. Aristotle's discussion of historical paradigms, Cicero's insistence that *historia magistra vitae*, and Hegel's critique of "Pragmatical" history are all instructive on this point. But it is the Pauline conception of *typos*, meaning both "figure" and "prefiguration," that best captures the temporal politics of Christine's letter. For Paul, "each event of the past—once it becomes a figure—announces a future event and is fulfilled in it."[74] By citing the "earlier acts" of Isabeau's predecessors, then, Christine not only dislocates them from the continuum of history, empowering their "old gleam" to follow Isabeau wherever she flies. She also *typifies* or *figures* these acts as historical pronouncements of a future event in which their potential to serve as examples will be realized. If Christine's letter is the event in which this potential comes to legibility (the becoming-incomplete of the past), Isabeau's management or mishandling of the Orléans-Burgundy conflict is the event in which it comes to fruition (the becoming-complete of the future).

Dispersed Origins, Inexhaustible Potentialities

The origins of Christine's exemplary figures do not exceed her letter to the queen. They are located not in the continuum of history, but rather in its citation—the moment in which, to continue Benjamin's line of thought, "what has been" comes together with "the now" to form a constellation of time.[75] But Christine's letter is not the only text to identify Veturia, Esther, Bathsheba, Blanche, Jezebel, or Olympias as exemplary figures. Others include her *Book of the City of Ladies* and Boccaccio's *On Famous Women*, as well as texts written after the Orléans-Burgundy conflict, such as the book before you and a variety of discourses still to come. In this sense, the origins of these exemplary figures are not only dispersed across time and text but also fundamentally incomplete.

That events of the past—once they become figures—pronounce future events does not preclude their refiguration at a later date, and thus their pronouncement of alternate futures. Theoretically, refigurations of this sort will continue until the absent law of judgment for which Veturia, Esther, Bathsheba, Blanche, Jezebel, and Olympias all stand—that women are able, and even obliged, to engage in political activity—is revealed complete in the totality of the history of their circulation as exemplary figures.[76] In the meantime—the time it takes for this end-time to arrive—their origins await discovery not in the empirical flux of chronological time, but in the dialectical play of historical and contemporary citations, as well as citations still to come.

In this broader, theoretical context, the stakes involved in Christine's letter far exceed any impending conflict between the houses of Orléans and Burgundy. If *The Book of the City of Ladies* is "the first work by a woman in praise of women,"[77] her letter to the queen recapitulates this literary achievement as a historical pronouncement—a prefiguration—of the "feminine style" that would later rise to prominence in the electronic age. Moreover, her letter is a testament to the relevance of this political style to learned advocates in the age of academia, many of whom are still reliant on linear, abstract, and hyper-rational forms of argument, heedless of the fact that, although fitting for academic discussion and debate, this way of speaking is poorly suited for mass-mediated democratic culture, in which deliberation and decision-making thrive on inductive logic, associative reason, personal testimony, and historical narrative—in short, the rhetoric of exemplary figures.[78]

Christine's letter also calls our attention to an abiding feminist political program. Implicit in her appeal to the queen is a commitment to identifying, valorizing, and extending the contributions of women to public life. However else it may have functioned in late-medieval France, her letter continues to provide readers with an argument by example for the critical elaboration of female political actors. Of special import, Christine suggests, are judicious women such as Veturia, Esther, Bathsheba, and Blanche—all of whom, although they certainly belong to history, are rarely included in prominent historical narratives. In citing these women as exemplary figures, she uses her linguistic and cultural authority as a woman of letters to transform the sparsity of their historical representation into a powerful political resource. With origins dispersed and incomplete, they are unconfined by any one, fixed place in history, and thus able to circulate through a variety of times and texts. In this sense, they are *exempla*. And because none of these circumstances has the authority to insinuate itself as their "proper place," these women are free to represent qualities of leadership with which they were not initially inscribed, and in so doing to instate rules of political judgment that might not otherwise have found expression. In this sense, they also function as *paradeigmata*.

What distinguishes this commitment to the redemption of women political actors is not its extension to women past and present, but its anticipation of women still to come. For Christine, the achievements of Isabeau's predecessors are not actualities stranded in the continuum of history, but potentialities to be cited in rhetorics of exemplarity and realized in the future conduct of other women, be they political leaders or educated elites—or perhaps even both. And because these potentialities belong to women past, present, and future, they cannot be exhausted in any single actualization. In deciding whether to intervene in the Orléans-Burgundy conflict, then, Isabeau prepares herself for one among many future events in which the potential of her predecessors to function as exemplary figures will be realized. It is the inexhaustibility of this potential—its ability to preserve itself in actuality, to survive realization—that enables these and other notable women to guide past and present conduct, as well as conduct still to come.[79] Releasing this guidance from the continuum of history is the ultimate political stake in the rhetoric of exemplary figures.

4

PERFORMATIVE PUBLICITY:
THE CRITIQUE OF PRIVATE REASON

Socrates intended nothing less than a political revolution with his attempted transformation of religion.

—IMMANUEL KANT

The Interstices of Oppression and Enlightenment

The language of Seneca's Silver Age suffered in the centuries following the Hundred Years' War. By the 1780s, only one in eleven books published in the German states was written in Latin, down from roughly two out of every three books in the early sixteenth century. Enlightenment writers were completing the vernacular revolution begun centuries earlier by medieval authors such as Dante, Boccaccio, Chaucer, and Christine de Pizan. This preoccupation with the native tongue, especially when coupled with the eighteenth-century commercialization of cultural production, disrupted social hierarchy and allowed for the emergence of a bourgeois audience—"the civilized reader who inhabited the middle range of society, the man who would read Hobbes's English but not his Latin works and was less erudite than the scholar but more discriminating than the consumer of trash."[1] Much to the satisfaction of eighteenth-century men and women of letters, members of the general reading public were learned enough to handle complex topics but not so enlightened as to be uneducable.

Despite the teachability of bourgeois readers, religious orthodoxy and absolutist politics routinely frustrated efforts to enlighten them. Combating dogmatism, intolerance, and oppression without jeopardizing their physical and financial well-being was especially important to German *Aufklärer*, many of whom not only had close ties to the Protestant clergy but also served as government officials, university professors, pastors, pedagogues, and other middle-class administrative figures.[2] Between the dangers posed by absolutist power and the ideals of public discussion and debate, these educated elites found cunning and deception to be invaluable resources for political contention. As Peter Gay well notes, "They discovered that duplicity is inescapable in a society that denies criticism free range, especially if its literary men, lacking the missionary's taste for martyrdom, burn with the missionary's zeal for making converts."[3]

The result was an outpouring of cunning dissent. Consider, for instance, the professor and political journalist A. L. von Schlözer, who avoided censorship by infusing his political criticism with professions of obedience to public authorities. Or the Swabian publicist Christian Friedrich Daniel Schubart, who, longing to be the Schlözer of southern Germany, couched his complaints in indirect communication, casually discussing the freedoms of Englishmen in the periodical *Deutsche Chronik*. Or how about Schiller, who filtered his distaste for social restraint and princely tyranny through the protagonists of his early plays? Likewise, in her novel on *Fräulein von Sternheim*, Sophie von la Roche portrayed an English lord's unwitting attempt to seduce her middle-class heroine using what were then popular bourgeois reproaches to his own class. And even Lessing tried his hand at humor, likening freedom of thought in Prussia to a series of anticlerical jokes.

For too long, historians and philosophers alike have excluded Immanuel Kant from this pantheon of cunning *Aufklärer*. Nowhere is the error of this exclusion more apparent than in his 1794 correspondence with Friedrich Wilhelm II, where Kant cleverly manipulated his renowned philosophical distinction between "public" (freely critical) and "private" (duty bound) uses of reason in order to resist, without directly challenging, state-imposed conditions of academic censorship. Clarifying and conceptualizing this subtle mode of dissent is the primary task of this chapter. At stake in Kant's correspondence with the king is not only an argumentative resource for use in political cultures with similar limits on free expression, but also a unique opportunity to reconsider some of the basic tenets of Kantian political theory. In developing this resource and reevaluating these principles, I hope to redeem Kant as a role model for today's learned advocates—especially those housed in post-9/11 institutions of higher education, where they are occasionally subject to constraints like those he manipulated for purposes of social protest.

The Reign of Theo-Politics, 1786–1797

Scholarly comment on Kant's attitude toward public authority often confuses the intellectual climate in which he posed "An Answer to the Question: 'What Is Enlightenment?'" (1784) with the political exigencies that allowed him to publish *The Conflict of the Faculties* (1798).[4] The former was written in anticipation of the Prussian dictator in whose wake the latter would be published: Friedrich Wilhelm II (r. 1786–97). The relevance of his reign to Kant's later work cannot be overstated. And nowhere is this relevance more apparent than in their 1794 exchange of letters. In order to understand this lesser-known political correspondence, we must first excavate the religious, political, and professional circumstances in which it occurred.

Months before his 12 December 1784 essay on enlightenment, Kant learned from his former student F. V. L. Plessing of an approaching restriction on the freedom of thought and expression: "Fanaticism and superstition are now again threatening us with great restriction on freedom of thought [*Denk-Freiheit*], indeed, something even worse, and all men of integrity who love humanity are trembling." As the letter progresses, Plessing's fears spin out of control: "How great [Friedrich the Great] seems to me! And how grateful to him must human reason be! If only he could live another 20 years. It seems that despotism, fanaticism, and superstition are trying to conquer all of Europe. Catholicism and Jesuitism are reaching even England, Denmark, and Sweden. England will soon be overcome."[5] By 1785, rumors of this sort had become full-blown conspiracies. Groups of former Jesuits, after the church dissolved their order in 1773, were thought to have begun infiltrating Masonic lodges and secret societies in hopes of bringing about a counterreformation in Germany. Crypto-Catholicism, as the Illuminati called it, was on the make.[6]

The accuracy of these reports is surprising. With the death of Frederick the Great in 1786 came the ascendance of his nephew, Friedrich Wilhelm II. The new king had a history of religious fanaticism. In the 1770s, he was associated with the "strict observance" of Freemasons; around 1780 he converted to a mystical form of Christianity; and throughout the 1780s he was a member of the Rosicrucian Order, an esoteric and wildly conservative offshoot of Freemasonry renowned for its occult practices and elaborate hierarchies. By 1791, these earlier and ongoing sympathies were catching up with Friedrich Wilhelm's public image. "The king has already had several visions of Jesus," Kant learns from another former pupil, J. G. Kiesewetter. "They say he is going to build Jesus a church in Potsdam for his very own. He is weak in body and soul now, and he sits for hours, weeping."[7] Add to this the sexual escapades for which Friedrich Wilhelm was also well-known, and the whimsical ethos of his kingship begins to make sense.

The new king found solace in the strong will of his leading minister of domestic affairs, Johann Christoph Wöllner, an ambitious former clergyman whom Frederick the Great once described as "a scheming, swindling parson."[8] For Wöllner, also a member of the Rosicrucian Order, the Enlightenment was a threat to the religious and moral underpinnings of Prussian society. Even before Friedrich Wilhelm's coronation ceremony, Wöllner was actively stressing the importance of the Christian faith for maintaining the Prussian state. He even went so far as to draft a treatise denouncing such "apostles of disbelief" as Friedrich Gedike and Johann Erich Biester, whose *Berlinische Monatsschrift* was the periodical most responsible for advancing the Enlightenment in Germany. Also under fire was the "free thinker and the enemy of the name of Jesus" K. A. Zedlitz, one of the most distinguished—and most progressive—members of the previous regime, and the public official to whom Kant dedicated his 1781 *Critique of Pure Reason*.[9] More than anything, Wöllner longed to replace Zedlitz as head of the Prussian Ecclesiastical Department. On 3 July 1788, less than two years after the coronation of Friedrich Wilhelm II, Wöllner found his opportunity, using his position in court to seize a number of posts, including that of Zedlitz.

Six days later, Wöllner convinced the king to issue a "Special Edict by His Royal Prussian Majesty Concerning the Religious Constitution of the Prussian State." Also known as the Wöllner Edict, on account of its immediate author, this infamous decree attributed "the corruption of the fundamental truths of the belief of the Christians, and the dissolution of morals resulting from this," to "the exceedingly abused name: *Enlightenment.*" Henceforth, any educator or ecclesiastic caught engaging in speculative public discussions of religion would face "*inescapable dismissal,* and even harsher punishment and sanction at our discretion." Forestalling these public discussions was for Wöllner the surest way to protect "the poor people" from "the illusions of the new-fangled teachers." And yet, as his edict on religion was careful to insist, the state would respect its subjects' freedom of conscience: "*No one shall at any time suffer the least coercion of conscience,* as long as he fulfills his duties peaceably as a good citizen of the state, keeps his particular opinions to himself, and carefully refrains from disseminating them or persuading others to [adopt] them, and [avoids] making others erroneous or wavering in their faith." If the motto of Frederick the Great was "*Argue* as much as you like and about whatever you like, *but obey!,*" that of his nephew and his ministers was "*Think* as much as you like and about whatever you like, *but obey!*"

Some scholars read this emphasis on freedom of conscience as a sign that Wöllner was not entirely opposed to the Enlightenment. "Far from being the Enlightenment's antithesis, Woellner came from the same educational and social institutions that produced much of German's so-called enlightened elite," Michael J. Sauter contends. "He attended Halle, Prussia's leading enlightened university, where he studied philosophy and theology under enlightened professors. For fifteen years, he reviewed books for the *Allgemeine Deutsche Bibliothek* ('General German Reader'), Germany's most famous enlightened journal. In addition, he wrote several well-respected books on agriculture, one of which won a prize from the St. Petersburg Academy of Sciences.... In short, Woellner lived the Enlightenment."[10] Other scholars interpret it as proof that although Wöllner deeply loathed the Enlightenment, he was unable to escape its ideological grasp. "Even in the act of violating the principles, he continued nonetheless to invoke liberalism and toleration," Henri Brunschwig notes. "One of the most cogent testimonies to the strength of the Aufklärung and the hold it had acquired on all minds is the fact that even its enemies were totally unable to conceive of any different system."[11] Still others insist that Wöllner's defense of individual heterodoxy was in strict keeping with the Prussian tradition of multi-confessional religious toleration, which had been in place since the Peace of Westphalia in 1648. More than "the instrument of a reactionary state intended to suppress the free and enlightened use of reason," Ian Hunter argues, it attempted to maintain "a long-standing public-law balance of confessional religions, at the heart of which lay not the imposition of orthodoxy but the separation of public religion from private belief."[12]

Whether any or all of these interpretations are correct, it is difficult to ignore the persuasive artistry of Wöllner's edict. Prefiguring the conservative political agendas of many of today's private advocacy groups, the ordinance attempted to rally the support of uneducated Prussians by purporting to defend their private religious liberty as well as their public religious sentiment from the speculative pedagogies of overbearing educators and ecclesiastics: "What mattered was not the existence of theological speculation as such, but the fact that the 'poor masses of the population' were being led away from their accustomed faith in scriptural, clerical, and—by extension—sovereign authority."[13] Only by preventing spiritual and secular teachers from engaging in theological innovation and rationalist proselytism did Friedrich Wilhelm and his conservative ministers stand a chance of securing their control over the enlightened moral and political programs that had begun to emerge in Frederickian civil society. And only by rarifying their intolerance of progressive discussion and debate in a principled defense of private religious liberty did their *Religionspolitik* stand a chance of avoiding an immediate public backlash.

By September 1788, the failure of this rhetorical maneuver was apparent. Printed critiques of the Wöllner Edict had become so fierce that even the whimsical Friedrich Wilhelm could not look away: "freedom of the press" (*Presse-Freyheit*), the king remarked in one of his cabinet orders, has devolved into "impudence of the press" (*Presse-Frechheit*).[14] Wöllner immediately set to work on another, more aggressive ordinance. Issued on 19 December 1788, the "Renewed Censorship Edict for the Prussian States Exclusive of Silesia" demanded that all writings on moral and religious matters be submitted to a commission of seven censors for approval. Although preventative censorship had been in effect since 1749, when Frederick the Great established the Berlin Censorship Commission, this earlier ordinance afforded Prussian authors with considerable latitude. And when Frederick saw fit to renew it in 1772, he even went so far as to assure *Aufklärer* that the new edict would by no means inhibit their "seemly and serious investigation of truth."[15] If indeed the Berlin Commission was "a weapon ready at hand in case of need but in fact seldom to be used," as George Di Giovanni suggests, the Censorship Edict of 1788 encouraged public officials to begin wielding it, if only by replacing liberal members of the old commission with more pastoral censors—"men so zealous in their conservatism that even Wöllner looked askance at some of the actions they took."[16]

In addition to stricter and more nuanced penalties for authors and publishers, some of which involved exorbitant fines and even prison sentences, the Censorship Edict provided for the surveillance and regulation of Prussian lending libraries. From directors to delivery boys, any employees caught circulating "improper books" were now subject to prosecution.[17] Although the infamous "Business Records" section of the Patriot Act, which authorizes federal agents to obtain borrower records from libraries and purchase records from bookstores, certainly pales in comparison to this provision of the Censorship Edict of 1788, it is difficult to ignore their similarity. Both had a powerful impact on the learned public cultures in which they intervened. Just as the Patriot Act compromised the privacy protections and infringed on the civil liberties of American academics, effectively chilling their political rhetoric and moral protest, so also did the threat of state surveillance and fierce retribution outlined in the Censorship Edict drive two of the most venerable print organs of the German Enlightenment out of Berlin in fear. Soon after the edict appeared, Biester moved the *Berlinische Monatsschrift* to Jena and Friedrich Nicolai transferred production of the *Allgemeine Deutsche Bibliothek* to Kiel. Nevertheless, like American librarians in the wake of the Patriot Act, many Prussian educators and ecclesiastics continued to circulate controversial articles and pamphlets. To be sure, Wöllner's Censorship Edict was a threat to the Prussian Enlightenment. But it resulted in few trials, and even fewer prosecutions. In fact, its only significant effect, in addition to forcing Biester and Nicolai out of Berlin, seems to have been a sharpening of the political rhetoric and the conceptual terms of ongoing public discussion and debate.[18]

It was not until May 1791, when Friedrich Wilhelm established a Summary Commission of Inquiry (Immediat-Examinations-Kommission) to examine the fitness of spiritual and secular teachers, that outspoken *Aufklärer* began to fret. An eerie predecessor of the International Higher Education Board proposed in the International Studies in Higher Education Act of 2003, which would have overseen federally financed area-studies programs across the nation, the Summary Commission not only redoubled government censorship of all moral and religious writings in Prussia, but also began subjecting all theological students to a rigorous examination of their personal convictions in order to assess their exposure and vulnerability to "the damnable errors of contemporary neologists and the so-called *Aufklärer*."[19] Moreover, it required all theology candidates to pledge their allegiance to the theo-politics of the Prussian state—a distant yet distinct antecedent to the disclaimer oaths required of academics during the McCarthy era and, more recently, to state spinoffs of the Patriot Act like that of the 2006 Ohio General Assembly, which requires all new hires at public universities and community colleges to certify their loyalty to the United States.[20] As Kant was careful to point out in his September 1791 critique of this requirement, enlivening readers of the *Berlinische Monatsschrift* just months before Biester moved its production to Jena, these oaths of conformity did little more than encourage the next generation of Prussian educators, be they church officials or university professors, to undermine the government with acts of *"subtle deception."*[21]

Taken together, these three government initiatives—the Religious Edict of July 1788, the Censorship Edict of December 1788, and the establishment of a Summary Commission of Inquiry in May 1791—formed the theo-political backbone of the Wöllner regime. If the Religious Edict laid out its principles, and the Censorship Edict prohibited their critique, the Summary Commission translated them into a durable program of state surveillance.[22] Maintaining this *Religionspolitik* became especially important in the early 1790s, as the news from Paris became increasingly disturbing. "As long as the revolution in France appeared to be nothing more than an attempt to set constitutional limitations on the monarch, it could be viewed as little more than an effort to bring about a state of affairs that long existed in Prussia," James Schmidt explains. "It was only when it became clear that the institution of monarchy itself was under attack that the Revolution became something more troubling."[23] To be sure, public responses to the French Revolution were decidedly mixed, even among members of the German Enlightenment, and many learned men and women disapproved of its culmination in the Jacobin Terror.[24] But with revolution and regicide on everyone's lips, Friedrich Wilhelm did not want to take any chances: "The more restless Prussians became, the more necessary it was to keep them isolated from dangerous ideas."[25] Indeed, so dangerous were the ideas coming out of Jacobin France that the minister for Silesia, in response to protests among Breslau journeymen, ordered the immediate arrest of anyone who even mentioned that there was a revolution occurring across the border. Much to Kant's frustration, the age of enlightenment, and with it his rational theology, seemed destined to end in the conservative—and now counterterrorist—policies of a national security state.

From Religious Rationalism to Political Dissent

Months before Kant's critique of the Summary Commission's required oaths of conformity, the Wöllner regime had identified him as a learned political agent in need of state censorship. Again, Kiesewetter bore the news to Kant: "People around here are saying (though it must be their imagination) that Woltersdorf, the new *Oberconsistorialrat*, has managed to get the king to forbid you to write anymore."[26] But efforts to subdue Kant did not begin until 1 October 1794. In the years between Kiesewetter's report and his official indictment, Mendelssohn's "great destroyer" was engaged in a heated, albeit scholarly, conflict with the theo-politics of Friedrich Wilhelm II.

With Wöllner struggling to impose his edicts on the chief consistory of the Lutheran Church, which was then dominated by holdovers from the Zedlitz administration, Kant was free to continue the theological discussion he began in his third *Critique* (1790). His insults against the crown prince began to accumulate. Under the impression that "only deep thinkers read Kant's writings," one of Wöllner's appointed censors allowed "On the Radical Evil in Human Nature" to appear in the April 1791 issue of *Berlinische Monatsschrift*. In June of the same year, Kant submitted another essay for review, "Of the Struggle of the Good Principle with the Evil Principle for Sovereignty over Man." Though the censors saw "Radical Evil" as a work of philosophy, and thus unlikely to be read by the Prussian public, they read its successor as an assault on biblical theology and quickly prohibited its publication.

"The Struggle" found another outlet in the spring of 1793 when the theological faculty at Königsberg and the philosophical faculty of the University of

Jena allowed the essay to appear alongside "Radical Evil" and two new essays in a book-length study of *Religion Within the Limits of Reason Alone*. Arguably a fourth *Critique*, *Religion* explores "a possible union of Christianity with the purest practical reason."[27] Awaiting unconcealment in every individual, Kant argues, is the potential for a transition-through-deeds from partial ecclesiastical faiths to the universal church of religion. The moral solidarity produced by followers of this "pure religious faith," he thought, could unite the Prussian public, and perhaps even the world, beyond all ecclesiastical boundaries. The result would be a state of participatory rationality that, much like Seneca's "greater commonwealth," would require neither the idea of a being superior to the knower nor any motive for observing moral law beyond the law itself. Human reason, not public authority, would bind its constituents to unconditional law.

In publishing this argument, Kant opposed himself to the religious policies of Friedrich Wilhelm and his antechamber of power—much as his first *Critique* had positioned him in opposition to general metaphysics. So outraged was the king by the appearance of *Religion Within the Limits of Reason Alone* that he ordered Wöllner to silence Kant on all religious topics. The letter of indictment that arrived on 1 October 1794 was nothing if not explicit:

> Our most high person has long observed with great displeasure how you misuse your philosophy to distort and disparage many of the cardinal and foundational teachings of the Holy Scriptures and of Christianity; how you have done this specifically in your book, "Religion within the Limits of Reason Alone," and similarly in other shorter treatises. We expect better of you, since you yourself must see how irresponsibly you have acted against your duty as a teacher of youth and against our sovereign purposes, of which you are well aware [*wie unverantwortl(ich) Ihr dadurch gegen Eure Pflicht als Lehrer der Jugend, u. gegen Unsre Euch sehr wohl bekannte landesväterliche Absichten handelt*]. We demand that you immediately give a conscientious vindication of your actions, and we expect that in the future, to avoid our highest disfavor, you will be guilty of no such fault, but rather, in keeping with your duty [*Pflicht*], apply your authority and your talents to the progressive realization of our sovereign purpose. Failing this, you must expect unpleasant measures for your continuing obstinacy [*fortgesetzter Renitenz*].[28]

Kant wasted no time in crafting his response. Dated 12 October 1794, his letter of reply centers on two issues: the allegation that he had misused his philosophy and the king's insistence that nothing of the sort should occur in the future. Kant finesses the first issue by arguing that, in order to challenge "the highest purposes of the sovereign," especially those that "concern the state religion," he would have had "to write as a teacher of the general public, a task for which this book along with my other little essays is ill-suited." All are "scholarly discussions for specialists in theology and philosophy," he argues, which means that their discussion of religion is "one of which the general public takes no notice." And even if this were not the case, Kant goes on to explain, the king would have no cause for concern, for his philosophical theology is in no way opposed to religion. In fact, all his writings on this highly contentious subject seek "to determine how religion may be inculcated most clearly and forcefully in the hearts of men."

Nevertheless, Kant rightly inferred, a guarantee of his continued obedience was in order. More than a defense of his previous works, the king wanted some assurance of Kant's future restraint. On this point, Kant wasted no words: "I find that, as Your Majesty's loyal subject, in order not to fall under suspicion, it will be the surest course for me to abstain entirely from all public lectures on religious topics, whether on natural or revealed religion, and not only from lectures but also from publications. I hereby promise this."[29]

Secondary scholarship often reads this promise as a moment of cowardice, irresponsibility, or indifference.[30] When we consider the afterlife of Kant's promise to the king, however, it more closely resembles an act of *"subtle deception"*—the very mode of resistance on which he speculated in his 1791 critique of the loyalty oaths required of theology candidates. Nowhere is this more apparent than in the preface to *The Conflict of the Faculties* (1798), where Kant not only published his correspondence with the king, but also bolstered it with interpretive commentary and a carefully worded footnote, the purpose of which was to completely annul his promise to the king—and to do so performatively, in full view of government authorities as well as the Prussian reading public. Understanding the intellectual and cultural conditions of this maneuver, as well as its political consequences, is the task to which we now turn.

The Torch and the Train

Variously written between 1794 and 1796, the "minor essays" collected in Kant's *Conflict of the Faculties* argue for a division of the traditional university structure into three professional or "higher" faculties (theology, law, and medicine) and one philosophical or "lower" faculty.[31] Because clergymen, magistrates, and physicians "deal directly with the people, who are incompetent," and the government has a stake in "securing the strongest and most lasting influence on the people," these learned men and women "are not free to make public use of their learning as they see fit, but are subject to the censorship of the faculties." Philosophers, on the other hand, because they are concerned with "the truth" of the teachings of clergymen, magistrates, and physicians, require "the power to judge autonomously—that is, freely (according to the principles of thought in general)." As such, their activities should be regulated by "the laws of reason, not by the government."[32]

Shoring up this distinction between "higher" and "lower" faculties is the broader conceptual separation of "private" (restricted) from "public" (freely critical) uses of reason outlined in Kant's "Answer to the Question: What Is Enlightenment?" However tiny its initial audience, discourse that neither presupposes an external authority nor precludes the understanding of a generally educated public qualifies as a public use of reason. Recalling Seneca's description of the political rhetoric of the Stoic sage (*sapiens*), Kant insists that the public use of reason does not cater to the ethos of any given audience, but instead requires its practitioners to address the reasoning capacity of all humans. It is here, in this composite of personal autonomy and general communicability, that we find the condition of possibility for Kantian "publicity" (*Publicität*), a term that is not likely to have emerged until the early 1780s, probably in response to earlier British displacements of "world" and "mankind" with the word "public."[33]

If the public or freely critical use of reason is "that use which anyone may make of it as *a man of learning* addressing the entire *reading public*," the private or restricted use of reason is "that which a person may make of it in a particular *civil* post or office with which he is entrusted."[34] Military officers, medical doctors, clergymen, politicians, and the like—in their capacity as civil servants, all must defer to the powers that be. Unlike its freely critical counterpart, which presupposes the personal autonomy of those who wield it, the private use of reason presumes the institutional passivity of its practitioners, specifically their "need to be guided by others" or, as Kant is careful to specify, their "heteronomy of reason."[35] And unlike the public use of reason, which involves subjecting self- and state-imposed prejudices to public discussion and debate, the private use requires its practitioners to limit their discourse to an audience restricted and defined by some external authority. To reason privately, in other words, is to forgo addressing "the world at large."[36]

The roots of this distinction between "public" and "private" uses of reason stretch back to the *Critique of Pure Reason* (1781), in which Kant attempted to separate conviction (*Überzeugung*) from persuasion (*Überredung*):

> Persuasion is a mere illusion, because the ground of the judgment, which lies solely in the subject, is regarded as objective. Such a judgment has only private validity, and the holding of it to be true does not allow of being communicated. But truth depends upon agreement with the object, and in respect of it the judgments of each and every understanding must therefore be in agreement with each other (*consentientia uni tertio, consentiunt inter se*). The touchstone whereby we decide whether our holding a thing to be true is conviction or mere persuasion is therefore external, namely, the possibility of communicating it and of finding it to be valid for all human reason.[37]

It was atop this division of conviction from persuasion, universal from subjective modes of validity, that Kant went on to develop his often-overlooked distinction between rhetoric (*Rhetorik*) and oratory (*Rednerkunst*) in the *Critique of Judgment* (1790): "Rhetorical power and excellence of speech [*Beredtheit und Wohlredenheit*] (which together constitute rhetoric) belong to fine art; but oratory (*ars oratoria*), the art of using people's weaknesses for one's own aims (no matter how good these may be in intention or even in fact), is unworthy of any respect whatsoever."[38] Unlike the orator's effort to "win over people's minds for his own advantage before they judge for themselves, and so make their judgment unfree," it is the task of the rhetorician to minimize the use of "oratorical force [*rednerischer Stärke*]" in convincing an audience to "do what is right . . . on the ground that is right," a gesture that in turn opens the "logical rigor" of any given argument to philosophical examination.[39]

> For when civil laws or the rights of individual persons are at issue, or the enduring instruction and determination of minds to a correct knowledge and a conscientious observance of their duty [*Pflicht*] are at issue, then it is beneath the dignity of so important a task to display even a trace of extravagant wit and imagination, let alone any trace of the art of persuading people and of biasing them for the advantage of someone or other. . . . Moreover, the mere distinct concept of these kinds of human affairs has, even on its own, sufficient influence on human minds to obviate the need to bring in and apply the machinery

of persuasion [*die Maschinen der Überredung*] as well—it is enough if the concept is exhibited vividly in examples and if there is no offense against the rules of euphony of speech or the rules of propriety in the expression of ideas of reason (these two together constitute excellence of speech [*die Wohlredenheit*]).[40]

In this sense, oratory and persuasion, which adjust themselves to the satisfaction of political interest, "differ not merely in degree but also in kind" from rhetoric and conviction, which correspond to the illumination of lawful conduct.[41] What is at stake in this separation of oratory from rhetoric, then, is nothing less than an articulation of philosophical and rhetorical modes of reasoning, both of which can be shown to operate at the level of pure persuasion—radiant lawfulness unconfined by interest and reality.[42] Privacy and publicity, heteronomy and autonomy, persuasion and conviction, oratory and rhetoric—these are the conceptual distinctions on which Kant premised his division of the traditional university structure into "higher" and "lower" faculties.

If *The Conflict* allowed Kant to translate these distinctions into a defense of the autonomy of philosophical discourse, prefacing this collection of essays with his 1794 correspondence with the king allowed him to leverage this defense for purposes of moral protest. Although it had pleased the king to learn that *Religion* was "merely philosophical" and thus addressed to "only deep thinkers," the definition of philosophy contained in *The Conflict* reminded Prussian readers that, as a product of the "lower" faculty, this book should not have required approval from a theological faculty. Nor should Kant have had to defend it against the accusations of the state. Thus, although he had played by the king's rules in publishing *Religion*, it was a mistake to apply these rules to a product of the "lower" faculty. In addition to retheorizing the university system, then, *The Conflict* allowed Kant to publicize this mistake, transforming his letter into an act of political contention. What began as a personal assurance that his book on *Religion* was of no interest to a general readership, and thus of no threat to the Religious and Censorship Edicts—to say nothing of the Summary Commission of Inquiry—ended as a public objection to the conservative politics of Friedrich Wilhelm.

That Kant reenacted his correspondence with the king as a "public" document in 1798 does not mean their exchange of letters was a "private" affair in 1794. Even as early as 1787, he knew that correspondence with the king was anything but intimate. "The secret personal letters of people in the current regime are circulated openly at court and in town," J. C. Berens informed him.⁴³ And little had changed by 1794, as Kant learned from his friend J. E. Biester, who was then serving as secretary to the minister of education:

> I have had occasion to read your defense in answer to the department of spiritual affairs' claims against *Religion within the Boundaries of Reason*. It is noble, manly, virtuous, thorough. Only everyone regrets that you have voluntarily given your promise to say no more about either positive or natural [philosophy of] religion. You have thereby prepared the way for a great victory for the enemies of enlightenment and a damaging blow to the good cause. It seems to me also that you need not have done this. You could have continued to write in your customary philosophical and respectable way about these subjects, though of course you would have had to defend yourself on this or that point. Or you could have remained silent during your lifetime without giving people the satisfaction of being released from the fear of your speaking.⁴⁴

The implications of this note are twofold: not only was Kant aware that his letter to the king had been circulated at court and perhaps about town, but he also had reason to suspect that many of his fellow *Aufklärer* disapproved of his promise to the king. What is most striking about these implications is the way in which Kant defends against them in the preface of *The Conflict*. There, in a carefully worded footnote, he insists that his promise to obey was strictly limited to "*Your Majesty's*" paternal will: "This expression, too, I chose carefully, so that I would not renounce my freedom to judge in this religious suit *forever*, but only during His Majesty's lifetime."⁴⁵ Having patiently awaited the 1797 death of Friedrich Wilhelm II, Kant maintained, he was now free to resume his discussion of religious topics. And this is precisely what he did in *The Conflict*. If *Religion* demonstrated the authority of "pure" critical philosophy to interrogate the principles of church and confession, *The Conflict* developed the specifically "legal" and political consequences of this authority. Philosophy may be the handmaiden of theology, Kant explains, recalling his earlier treatise on "Perpetual Peace" (1795), but "the question remains, whether the servant *carries her lady's torch before or her train behind*."⁴⁶

Kant's privatization of "*Your Majesty*" was the condition of possibility for his reemergence as an author of religious texts. Before mid-eighteenth-century expansions of literary culture and the commercial press, privatization of this sort would have been difficult to achieve. In absolutist states such as Prussia, the king was a strictly public persona, the embodiment of an entire society of orders and estates. Moreover, he was the *only* public persona.

The public sphere was none other than the sphere of his public authority.[47] Consider, for instance, the December 1784 response of two ministers of the Prussian crown to criticisms made in the *Journal von und für Deutschland*: "A private individual does not possess the right to issue public judgments (let alone unfavorable judgments) upon the actions, procedures, laws, proclamations or decrees of sovereigns, their ministers, administrative boards or courts of justice."[48] In contrast to Kant's famous definition of enlightenment, which was published within days of this official rescript, Prussian authorities were convinced that public affairs—that is to say, affairs of state—were too complex and too sensitive to be considered by anyone other than themselves.

Denigrations of this sort were common and largely uncontested until the French Revolution. "With isolated exceptions," writes Norbert Elias, "one finds in Germany before 1789 no idea of concrete political action, nothing reminiscent of the formation of a political part or a political party program."[49] At most, scholars, publicists, civil servants, and other members of the German middle class proposed and pursued projects designed to enlighten monarchs. By the time *The Conflict* was ready for publication, however, an alternate, more recognizably political notion of "the public" had taken hold of Prussia, one that had been emerging for decades in and around the literature of Klopstock, Goethe, Schiller, Lessing, Herder, and Sophie de la Roche. Over and against the particularistic social order of the ancien régime, the public had become "an abstract category of authority, invoked by actors in a new kind of politics to secure the legitimacy of claims that could no longer be made binding in the terms (and within the traditional institutional circuit) of an absolutist political order."[50] Midway between the elites and the populace, this full-fledged public culture boasted a population upwards of two hundred thousand readers and writers, all of whom, in their devotion to pen and press, had begun to liberate themselves from the proximal constraints of oral communication and social class—and, by extension, monarchical rule.

Rather than standing in for public opinion, absolutist governments now had to compete for it with "private individuals" like Kant. "Pamphlets could be fought only with opposing pamphlets," Benjamin Nathans explains. "Appeals to public opinion against the monarchy required counter-appeals to public opinion in favor of the monarchy."[51] By competing with members of the *Publikum*, monarchs such as Friedrich Wilhelm II had unwittingly conspired with their opposition to enable what Keith Michael Baker aptly describes as "the transfer of ultimate authority from the public person of the sovereign to the sovereign person of the public."[52] Kant seems to have known as much: only with the public authority of the king in sharp decline and that of his royal subjects on the rise could Kant convince members of the reading public that the addressee of his promise was not the *persona publica* of the king (as Biester and other court officials initially thought), but the *privata voluntas* of Friedrich Wilhelm (as he insisted in *The Conflict*).

Submitting to one of the king's two bodies in 1794 was a necessary condition for Kant's resistance to both in 1798. But let's make no mistake: his rhetoric of personalization is an effect, not a harbinger, of his letter's publication. Like all origins, that of his preface to *The Conflict* is elective, belonging more to the interests of the present than the actualities of the past. Only by privatizing "*Your Majesty*" could Kant realize the death of Friedrich Wilhelm as an annulment of his earlier promise to abstain from religious discussion and debate. And only by doing so publicly, in the preface to a book on the freedom of philosophy from state censorship, could he show Biester and other *Aufklärer* that he remained committed to freedom of the pen.

More than a voluntary slackening of his public use of reason (writing for the general public being his right as an independent scholar), Kant argues, his promise to the king was a command performance requiring his private use of reason (compliance with the state being his duty as a teacher of youth). To have reemerged in 1798 as an author of religious texts without first clarifying this distinction would have been asking for trouble. Thus, as it turns out, Kant's preface to *The Conflict* brought with it a formal opportunity to publish his correspondence with the king—and, in so doing, to retroactively inscribe it as an intimate and obligatory exchange of letters that, when brought to the attention of an impersonal reading public, could at once justify and conclude a four-year period of silence in his philosophical theology.

Eighteenth-Century Epistolography

Kant could not have performed this retroactive inscription outside eighteenth-century epistolary culture, where the letter had become a medium in which to unfold oneself before an audience of addressees, auditors, witnesses, and eavesdroppers. Ostensibly, this Enlightenment attitude toward epistolography was a literary function of the intimate sphere of the conjugal family.[53] But it also borrowed from other, more established traditions of epistolography. Between ancient letter-writers like Seneca and the *ars dictaminis* of Christine's Middle Ages, the personalization of style and content became an epistolary ideal. In the eleventh and twelfth centuries, for instance, political feelings and personal experience began to find expression in written correspondence. Examining, rendering, and publishing one's opinions, feelings, and personal character quickly became the proper function of epistolary exchange. That love letters began to appear at this time is hardly surprising. Within a generation, they had acquired the aura of passion and suffering by which we continue to evaluate them. In subsequent centuries, the letter was not only a personal document designed to convey one's private opinions and intimate character, but also a reliable medium in which to discuss scholarly and philosophical topics. For fifteenth- and sixteenth-century humanists, epistolary exchange was integral to literary public culture, a privilege letter-writers had not enjoyed since the early Middle Ages.

That epistolography in the age of Kant modeled a kind of "audience-oriented subjectivity" (*publizitätsbezogene Subjektivität*, in Habermas's German) makes sense when we consider its ambidextrous history as a medium of private and public address. Nowhere was the influence of this history more apparent than in the eighteenth-century genre of epistolary fiction. Among its defining features was the use of epistolary exchange to portray the intimate thoughts and feelings of fictional characters, a literary device that allowed interpersonal narratives to develop apart from the interventions of an omniscient narrator. By offsetting their role as narrators with the written correspondence of their characters, authors were able to give their novels a heightened sense of reality, appealing to modern readers whose interest in travel narratives, public scandals, and pseudo-histories had left them with a taste for fiction loosely disguised as fact. This illusion of objectivity brought with it an occasion to advance, without overstating, a variety of moral and political agendas. From Rousseau's *La nouvelle Héloïse* (1761) to Goethe's *Leiden des jungen Werthers* (1774) to Hitchcock's *Memoirs of the Bloomsgrove Family* (1790), epistolary fiction was a forum for social commentary and public advocacy.

By presenting impersonal readerships with realistic displays of intimacy, the epistolary novel gave fiction the illusion of fact, didacticism the illusion of objectivity, and public discourse the illusion of private exchange. Kant replicated these illusions in his preface to *The Conflict*. Just as the epistolary novel encouraged its readers to mediate their lived experience through the literary actions of fictional characters, so, too, did Kant invite readers such as Biester—who had initially regretted his promise to the king—to substitute the historical correspondence in which this promise was made with the framed and footnoted version in which it was later annulled. What kept this correspondence-turned-preface from appearing contrived was also what kept it from appearing overly didactic. Although surrounded by moral and political commentary and shot through with a modifying footnote, Kant was careful to reproduce the entire correspondence in the opening pages of *The Conflict*. He even went so far as to include the superscriptions and salutations of each letter, formatting them to reflect late eighteenth-century conventions of letter-writing. That Kant included these personal details in the opening pages of a book whose readership was nothing if not impersonal further allowed him to replicate the "audience-oriented privacy" of epistolary fiction.[54] If the reading public was accustomed to books comprising private correspondence, reproducing his letter in the opening pages of *The Conflict* might bolster his argument for the intimacy of his correspondence with the king. In this sense, epistolary fiction was a discursive formation in which Kant could at once publicize and privatize his 1794 promise to the late Friedrich Wilhelm—and in so doing not only cancel this promise but also preserve it in a cancelled state, a sublation of sorts on which he could premise his return to religious discussion and debate.

Although the eighteenth century saw letter-writing flourish into an art form, Kant's letters (unlike his sprightly lectures and conversation) were often humorless and painful. Like many of today's e-mail-laden academics, he saw letter-writing as an unadorned distraction from more serious work. But he also saw it as a political resource. His letter to Friedrich Wilhelm bears this out. No fewer than three drafts preceded its departure for Berlin. Clearly, Kant felt that "keeping silence in a case like the present one is the duty of the subject," and that his promise to remain silent "must be true." However, as his use of "*Your Majesty's most loyal subject*" would later reveal, he was under no obligation to disclose the "whole truth" of this promise.[55] Though compelled to keep quiet on religious topics, Kant was not obliged to specify the duration of his silence. Only after the king had passed, in the preface to a book that might otherwise have broken his promise, did he need to explain this limitation. And only by affecting the literary genre of the epistolary novel could he do so persuasively, convincing Biester and other forlorn *Aufklärer* that this limitation was the untold "truth" of his correspondence with the king.

The Courage of Enlightenment

Whether Kant had withheld this "truth" for years or invented it after the death of Friedrich Wilhelm, his preface to *The Conflict* was not without consequence. If indeed a return to religious lectures and publications was implicit in his earlier promise to abstain from them entirely, it follows that the public use of reason is not entirely removed from the private use of reason—that the autonomy of public critique, which often results in open disputes with the state, is not completely extrinsic to heteronymous relations of power, which normally find expression in the performance of duty. In order to understand this imbricated line of conduct, especially as it intersects with the political potential of learned advocates in the academic era, we must first consider the relationship between the philosophy of religion for which Wöllner indicted Kant and the ethico-political theory in terms of which Kant framed his response.[56]

Just as the eighteenth-century language of learned men and women recast issues in a new, more universal way, giving public recognition to the backstage practices of a mass society, so also did the "participatory rationality" at work in Kant's universal religion propose the transformation of what might otherwise have remained "secret" or "subjective" (i.e., ecclesiastical networks of faith) into a shared concern capable of influencing public discussion and debate. The 1798 publication of his correspondence with the king politicized this maneuver by insinuating public controversy in the place of what was simultaneously reconfigured as an intimate exchange of letters. Not only were the latent practices and political motives of the state to be thrown into the light of public appearance. Moreover, the orthodox priorities and constraints of Prussian religious life were to be revealed as the limited, pragmatic struggle of government authorities for their own survival. As Kant envisioned it, the Enlightenment project of eroding provinciality, prejudice, and insensitivity was inseparable from the placement of conservative state officials under the supervision of a generally educated audience. Whatever else the kingdom of ends might entail, it would get its start in a democracy of performative publication.

Kant laid the foundation for this kingdom in the winter of 1783–84, when he was teaching his first university course on philosophical theology and drafting his famous "Answer to the Question: 'What Is Enlightenment?'" At that time, under the reign of Friedrich II, Kant could openly express his argument against political and religious dogma: "*Enlightenment is man's emergence from his self-incurred immaturity. Immaturity* is the inability to use one's own understanding without the guidance of another. This immaturity is self-incurred if its cause is not lack of understanding, but lack of resolution and courage to use it without the guidance of another. The motto of the enlightenment is therefore: *Sapere aude!* Have courage to use your *own* understanding."[57]

By 1794, courage of this sort was difficult to come by. But its relevance to Prussian civic life had grown exponentially. Kant's correspondence-turned-preface adapted "*Sapere aude!*" to these political circumstances, stretching this renowned Horatian tagline toward its archest translation. Although it was still important that members of the Prussian public "dare to be wise," the reign of Friedrich Wilhelm II also demanded that they "dare to be wise guys." By retroactively altering the exchange of letters it purported to represent, Kant's preface to *The Conflict* transformed a four-year period of silence in his philosophical theology into a cunning variation on the courage required by enlightenment, reinscribing his letter to the king as a lesson in the art of temporization. That 1794 saw Kant performing his duty as a royal subject, apparently committed to the private use of reason, was itself a condition of possibility for his subsequent revelation of this performance as just that—a *performance*. What initially appeared to Biester as "a great victory for the enemies of enlightenment" reemerged in 1798 as a strident critique of their public authority.

The motto of the previous regime—"argue but obey"—was no longer viable. If Friedrich Wilhelm was going to undermine public discussion and debate by silencing Kant on religious topics, Kant was going to revise his political philosophy by allowing subversive modes of reasoning (critique) to insinuate themselves in restricted codes of conduct (duty). After his *Conflict of the Faculties*, the politics of enlightenment would involve not only exposing the private, subjective understandings of oneself and one's superiors to the broad daylight of public appearance, but also concealing one's motives for overturning the law in its all-too-perfect adoption. Emerging from "ecclesiastical faiths" into the light of "pure religious faith," like emerging from self-incurred immaturity into the light of free thought and expression, would require a Senecan ability to remain both out of sight and unconcealed, depending on the occasion. Silence, cunning, exile—these were now among the available resources for participatory rationality.

Obedience and Autonomy, Passivity and Aggression

At issue here is not an ethics of meekness but a rhetoric of humility. Miss the ambiguity in *"Your Majesty's most loyal subject"* and we miss the mode of critique implicit in this phrase: it is easy to appear humble among intimates when we see ourselves as actors in a public performance. Humility, as Kant demonstrated in 1798, is a theatrical gesture.

Sermo humilis, the low or humble style: few modes of public address are better suited for the public advocacy of members of the "lower" faculty, if only because *humilis* and its political accompaniments—*pedester, trivialis, quotidianus*—seem so far removed from the linear, abstract, and hyperrational discourse of philosophy. "They seemed to me unworthy to be compared with the majesty of Cicero," Augustine remarks in his *Confessions*, reflecting on the humble stylings of biblical texts. "My conceit was repelled by their simplicity, and I had not the mind to penetrate into their depths. They were indeed of a nature to grow in Your little ones. But I could not bear to be a little one."[58]

Nevertheless, as Charles Dickens would later illustrate with his "so very 'umble" character of Uriah Heep, simplicity of this sort lends itself to subversive forms of empowerment: "'When I was quite a young boy,' said Uriah, 'I got to know what umbleness did, and I took to it. I ate umble pie with an appetite. I stopped at the umble point of my learning, and says I, "Hold hard!" When you offered to teach me Latin, I knew better. "People like to be above you," says father, "keep yourself down." I am very umble to the present moment, Master Copperfield, but I've got a little power!'"[59] Kant seems to have known as much. Consider, for instance, the *Critique of Practical Reason* (1788), in which he applauds Bernard de Fontenelle's remark that "I bow before an eminent man, but my spirit does not bow."[60] Is this not the rhetorical sensibility of his correspondence-turned-preface? At once recuperating and politicizing Fontenelle's insight, the opening pages of *The Conflict* reinscribe his deference to the king with motives befitting a political dissident, thereby offsetting the bow of his letter with its non-bowing spirit. For Kant, the time-honored moods of humility—"submission, prostration, and a feeling of our utter impotence"—were rhetorical devices for contesting abusive figures of authority without challenging them directly.[61] Where a simple act of humility was, a strategic mélange of obedience and duplicity became.

Through the looking glass of Kantian moral philosophy, this maneuver seems less like a cunning performance of duty than a finely spun lie. And mendacity does not fly in the kingdom of ends. Or does it? "If force is used to extort a confession from me, if my confession is improperly used against me, and if I cannot save myself by maintaining silence, then my lie is a weapon of defense," Kant argues in his *Lectures on Ethics*, prefiguring his September 1791 critique of the loyalty oaths required by Wöllner's Summary Commission. "The forcing of a statement from me under conditions which convince me that improper use would be made of it is the only case in which I can be justified in telling a white lie."[62] Was his vow of silence a forced statement? Wöllner's writ of indictment certainly suggests so: "We demand that you immediately give a conscientious vindication of your actions.... Failing this, you must expect unpleasant measures." In this sense, the false humility of Kant's reply was not a transgression of his moral philosophy but an exploitation of one of its often-ignored loopholes. Misleading the king was indeed an appropriate "weapon of defense."

Like most white lies uttered in the face of executive power, Kant's stopped short of insubordination, to which its telling was a cagey alternative. As a latent act of political contention, his promise to the king augmented, expanded, and added to the fullness of the Religion and Censorship Edicts of 1788 even as it intervened, interrupted, stood between, and deferred the public authority on which these edicts relied.[63] If Seneca's claim that philosophers "cherish" their rulers allowed him to subvert the authority of the principate to criminalize Stoicism, and Christine's use of exemplary figures allowed her to criticize the queen's political inaction without undermining her public authority, Kant's correspondence-turned-preface allowed him to radicalize his humility, performing without failing to obstruct his duty as a *"Your Majesty's most loyal subject."* How are we to understand this coincidence of legitimation and critique, the performance of duty and its subtle obstruction?

An answer comes to us in the opening pages of *Difference and Repetition*, where Gilles Deleuze insists that political actors can overturn the law by descending toward its consequences, submitting themselves to its public authority with an exacting attention to detail. "By adopting the law, a falsely submissive soul manages to evade it and to taste pleasures it was supposed to forbid," he explains. "We can see this in demonstration by absurdity and working to rule, but also in some forms of masochistic behavior which mock by submission."[64] Falsely submissive citizens at once publicly invite the consequences of their actions and secretly steal the freedom of response from established figures of authority. That Kant should be reproached for writing on religion was not completely within the ability of his highness to decide.

In the spirit of false submission, Kant flirted with the trappings of criminality, knowingly provoking the censors in Berlin, and then, when Friedrich Wilhelm was pressed into action, avoided incurring more "unpleasant measures" by dutifully submitting to this authority. That Biester and other *Aufklärer* saw his submission as unnecessary was crucial to its afterlife as a moment of public critique. Kant's willingness to remain silent on religious topics only strengthened his later critique of the king's demand that he do so. Indeed, he seems to have known what veterans of the civil rights movement continue to teach us: a scarred body lends more credibility to future acts of moral menacing than a dead one. For Kant, self-sacrifice was not the final testament to the intensity of his belief in enlightenment.[65] It was his endurance as a survivor, not his legacy as a victim, that allowed him to reveal the despotism of Friedrich Wilhelm and his ministers.

But we cannot limit our analysis to this insight. Indeed, to read Kant's letter as an act of civil disobedience is to misunderstand the mode of resistance for which it stands. Although certainly civil, his response to the king was hardly disobedient. Neither Wöllner nor the king nor Biester nor any eavesdropping *Aufklärer* doubted the sincerity of Kant's promise. Nor did any of them suspect that it was limited to the king's lifetime. In fact, if Biester's response is any indication of how his letter was received at court, it was the death of the seventy-year-old Kant, not that of the fifty-year-old king, that many thought to be the outer limit of his compliance. Only later, when a new king had claimed the throne, was Kant willing to claim that the duration of his obedience, and thus the meaning of his promise, was completely undecidable. Neither an explicit act of contention nor definitive proof of his compliance, Kant's vow of silence became a primal scene in which readers of *The Conflict* could insinuate a previously illegible offense in the space organized by his letter's capacity for allowing multiple interpretations.

Undecidability of this sort is not a feature of civil disobedience. Nor are multiplicities of interpretation. Civil disobedience begins with a nonviolent but unmistakable act of transgression, often in the name of a higher law, leaving little doubt about the mind-set of its practitioners or the meaning of their conduct. Like intellectuals in the wake of Zola and the Dreyfusards, civil disobedients are conscientious, outspoken, and steadfastly public in their opposition to abusive figures of authority. Kant could have acted similarly, as Biester points out: "You could have continued to write in your customary philosophical and respectable way about these subjects, though of course you would have had to defend yourself on this or that point." But he did not. Instead of civilly disobeying the conservative religious policies of the Prussian state, all of which were in direct opposition to his ethico-political philosophy, Kant adhered to them. And when this was not enough—when even his adherence to these policies incurred the king's wrath—he complied again, willingly submitting himself and his scholarship to an obvious abuse of power.

How, then, are we to interpret the preface to *The Conflict*? One thing is certain: although Kant suggests that *"Your Majesty's most loyal subject"* was a phrase designed to deceive the king or, at the very least, to provide him with a partial truth, we are unable to verify his intentions. It is impossible for readers of *The Conflict* to prove, in a strict sense, anything for or against the argument on which his return to religious scholarship depends. Like any meaning-to-say, the truthfulness of Kant's claim that he chose his words "carefully," in anticipation of the king's death, is radically indeterminate. Politicizing this indeterminacy was the basic rhetorical achievement of his preface to *The Conflict*. Unlike civil disobedience, the efficacy of which hinges on the clarity, consistency, and openness of its intentional structure, his correspondence-turned-preface derives its convincingness from a displacement of clarity with ambiguity, consistency with changeability, and openness with obscurity. With a cagey footnote, some interpretive commentary, and the conceptual apparatus of *The Conflict*, Kant was able to offset Biester's initial interpretation, transforming his promise to the king from a missed opportunity for civil disobedience into a clever act of passive aggression.

With the addition of this final term—"passive aggression"—we can bring some conceptual clarity to the resistant function of Kant's rhetoric of obedience. Although civil disobedience privileges the coincidence of passivity and aggression, there is nothing passive-aggressive about its practitioners. None "swing back and forth between a struggle for autonomy and a desire for external appreciation."[66] Nor are they known for their inability to decide "whether to adhere to the desires of others as a means of gaining comfort and security *or* to turn to themselves for these gains, whether to be obediently dependent on others *or* defiantly resistant and independent of them."[67] Regardless of whether he was torn between the absolutist demand for civic duty and the Enlightenment imperative to public critique, Kant performed this ambivalence marvelously, allowing *both* motives to find expression in "*Your Majesty's most loyal subject.*"

Although suitably ambivalent, the concepts of "false submission" and "civil disobedience" are unable to account for this Janus-faced persuasive technique. Kant's promise to the king is at once more contentious than "false submission" and more compliant than "civil disobedience." And the foregoing definitions of passive aggression fare no better. Although both accurately depict the tensions between obedience and autonomy, dependence and dissent, private and public uses of reason in Kant's letter of reply, neither is able to specify how the letter functions as a mode of resistance. In order to do so, we must shift our attention from the intentional structure of Kant's promise to its rhetorical and political effects. In service to this task, let us consider another, more ordinary characterization of passive aggression, this one from the op-ed section of a regional newspaper:

> Of all the workplace's misdemeanors, from the CC:list demotion to intellectual-property theft, passive aggression is among the most untraceable infractions. The assaulter, who appears to comply with a request but actually resists it, quietly commits not one crime but two.
>
> After the initial injury, it doubly torments the victim by making him look like a twit for complaining about something as slippery as the aggressor's tone or attitude. At its worst, the victim can seem so paranoid—"You did that on purpose!"—that it's best to nod and slowly back away.[68]

The salient feature of this description is its running metaphor: criminality. Passive aggression is a slight, yet significant, infraction of the law—more transgressive than the Deleuzian concept false submission but less transgressive than modern practice of civil disobedience. What distinguishes it as a "crime" is its quiet, untraceable nature. Like most criminals, passive aggressors seek to benefit from their infractions, and the surest way to do so is to leave no evidence of their transgressions—or, more accurately, to present their transgressions as too minor to warrant punishment. At once public and unpunishable, their criminality, like their motivation, is twofold: passive aggressors add the insult of embarrassment to anyone in search of retribution for their initial injuries.

Menacing of this sort is not likely to shift distributions of status, wealth, and power, but it can lead to more adversarial forms of dissent. Like weapons of the weak, acts of passive aggression are "the stubborn bedrock upon which other forms of resistance may grow, and they are likely to persist after such other forms have failed or produced, in turn, a new pattern of inequity."[69] In this sense, conduct like that of Kant can hold the place and occasionally pave the way for collective acts of insurgency. On this point, James C. Scott is adamant: "Declarations of open war, with their mortal risks, normally come only after a protracted struggle on different terrain."[70] But how does this happen? How, exactly, does passive aggression—or any other ambivalent mode of resistance—facilitate more adversarial and collective forms of political contention?

In order to begin answering this question, we must understand the importance of publicity to passive aggressors. As a mode of resistance, passive aggression requires at least three audiences. First, passive aggressors must be noticeable to the authorities. This much is obvious. Second, passive aggressors require a witness other than authority, specifically an audience capable of rendering the aggression of their passivity apparent to others. Without this second audience, their dissent is likely to go unnoticed—not only by those who were there for the performance but failed to pick up on its aggressive undertones, but also those who missed the performance but, with a testimonial or two, could imagine how contentious it was. These imaginative individuals form a third audience, without which passive aggressors would be unable to hold the place, much less to pave the way, for more adversarial and collective forms of dissent.

To this extent, passive aggressors must keep their enemies close and their allies even closer. Because the line of conduct between passivity and aggression is remarkably thin, if noticeable at all, established figures of authority must be close enough to perceive and feel menaced by their behavior, and bystanders must be close enough to notice in their conduct something other than passivity. Together, these intimate and impersonal relationships constitute a public sphere. Although it looks nothing like "the world at large" described in Kant's essay on the German Enlightenment, this public sphere does resemble the epistolary culture in which he transformed his deferential response to the king into the defiant preface of his *Conflict of the Faculties*. Only by manipulating the participation framework of his correspondence, interchanging addressees, auditors, witnesses, and eavesdroppers, could Kant trouble the boundaries between "private" and "public" uses of reason enough to redeem himself as an author and an advocate of rationalist religious texts.

Where passivity and aggression go hand in hand, and everyone knows it, all submissions to power, be they cunning or sincere, appear suspicious. No longer can the powers that be confidently distinguish reliable underlings from passive aggressors. The result is a kind of executive paranoia in which established authorities, now doubtful of their minions, and their minions, now suspected for their compliance, both become others to themselves. To this extent, we might say that passive aggression tills the soil for social protest by assimilating and radicalizing other forms of compliance. Where submission is an offense to power, subordinates who might otherwise defer to their superiors are likely to consider alternate, maybe even more aggressive, lines of conduct. In this sense, passive aggressors not only radicalize other modes of compliance, insinuating moments of critique into even genuine acts of obedience. They also introduce a moment of doubt into every habitually compliant political subject. It is precisely here, where passivity has become a sign of aggression and the performance of duty an occasion for public critique, that passive aggressors till the soil for more adversarial forms of dissent.

As a protracted instance of passive aggression, Kant's correspondence-turned-preface not only presented readers with an alternate, more cunning version of the courage required by enlightenment, insinuating a moment of opposition in what might otherwise have remained a gesture of obedience. Moreover, by allowing everyone, including the distrustful and notoriously indecisive son of Friedrich Wilhelm II—who had only recently succeeded to the throne—to witness the cunning subversion implicit in Kant's promise, the preface to *The Conflict* encouraged members of the Prussian reading public to consider other, more outspoken critiques of power. As Kant well knew, even an apparently private use of reason could result in fuller standards of public discussion and debate, thereby advancing Enlightenment-era assaults on abusive figures of authority.[71] Publicizing this insight was one of his greatest political achievements.

Sustine et abstine

Like Socrates, Kant was charged with corrupting the youth and offending religious orthodoxy. Unlike Socrates, however, who would "much rather die" in defense of his philosophy than "stoop to servility" in hopes of spending the rest of his days in silence, Kant decided to heed the accusations of the state, humbly agreeing to abstain from religious discussion and debate.[72] The result was a four-year period of silence in his philosophical theology. Physical and financial well-being—neither of which Socrates seems to have possessed at the time of his defense—were more important to Kant than the persistence and unstifled publicity of his critique of religious dogma.

Many of today's learned advocates would have chosen similarly, subordinating themselves and their scholarship to the dictates of the state. And by joining the academy, many of them already have—or so the argument goes. As critics of the American academy often lament, today's professors have relinquished the political autonomy and resistant potential of yesterday's intellectuals, selfishly swapping them out for the financial security and social stability of academic careers. "The once-proud outsiders joined faculties," Anthony Grafton writes, satirizing this common complaint of late-modern academics. "The voice of dissent was drowned out by the louder, jargon-clotted voices of tenure-seeking scholars."[73] In his preface to *The Conflict*, Kant adds political traction to this satire, transforming his complex political philosophy into a resource for what Bruce Robbins aptly describes as "professional oppositionality." Anticipating the political potential of contemporary academics, Kant was among the first professors to demonstrate that oppositional political cultures are not only imaginable but also realizable within the professional framework of the university.[74]

And like many of today's learned advocates, especially those who occupy the university's massive lower tiers of contingent employment, Kant tempered his political rhetoric with a simple and thoroughly Stoic code of conduct: *sustine et abstine*, "endure and do without." Consider, for instance, this message to Biester, written months before his 1 October indictment: "If new laws command what is not contrary to my principles, I will obey them at once; I shall do that even if they should merely forbid that one's principles be made public, as I have done heretofore (and which in no sense do I regret). Life is short, especially what is left of it after one has lived through 70 years; some corner of the earth can surely be found in which to bring it to an untroubled close."[75]

This lust for life reappears in the final part of *The Conflict:* "Death always arrives too soon for us, and we are inexhaustible in thinking up excuses for making it wait."[76] For Socrates, nothing could be further from the truth: "The difficulty is not so much to escape death; the real difficulty is to escape from doing wrong, which is far more fleet of foot." It is misconduct, not mortality, that must be avoided. From this perspective, Kant's response to the king was deplorable. In service to his professional well-being, he gave Prussian authorities what Socrates refused to grant his accusers: "You would have liked to hear me weep and wail, doing and saying all sorts of things which I regard as unworthy of myself, but which you are used to hearing from other people." More than a prelude to moral protest, Socrates would have us believe, Kant's vow of silence was an immoral excuse to avoid it.

For Socrates, avoidance of this sort was akin to surrender on the battlefield. "In battle it is often obvious that you could escape being killed by giving up your arms and throwing yourself upon the mercy of your pursuers," he explained to the Athenians, further belittling their hopes for his plea by reminding them that "in every kind of danger there are plenty of devices for avoiding death if you are unscrupulous enough to stick at nothing."[77] We could do worse than understand *"Your Majesty's most loyal subject"* as one of these devices. But we might also do better. Between the Kantian imperative to live by the law and the Socratic willingness to die for it is the Stoic obligation to *live as though dead*. As Seneca notes in his letters to Lucilius, surrendering our weapons to our opponents and ourselves to their mercy is not the only way to avoid danger. Nor is it the most effective, especially if we remain committed to our cause. Playing dead is another, sometimes more effective, option: "Even in battle, prostrate soldiers are neglected: men fight with those who stand their ground."[78] We need only wait for the battlefield to clear before resuming our antagonism.

Kant was willing to wait. Indeed, he seems to have known of his king what the Athenian jury failed to realize about their convict. "If you had waited just a little while," Socrates explains, "you would have had your way in the course of nature. You can see that I am well on in life and near to death."[79] During his four years of *sustine et abstine*, patience had proven to be Kant's greatest ally. By forbearance, he was able to become his own exemplary figure, offsetting the martyr's need to suffer before others with the philosopher's ability to behold his own conduct—an ability that time alone could afford him. Only in the twilight of his unquestioning obedience, when Socratic tragedy had given way to Senecan farce, could the tyranny of Friedrich Wilhelm be drawn into the realm of unconcealment.

5

HIDDEN BEHIND THE DASH:
TECHNIQUES OF UNRECOGNIZABILITY

I regard this as precisely my task, always to be capable of what the vanity and secular-mindedness of the world hanker after as supreme.

—SØREN KIERKEGAARD

A Defense Turned Crisis

Like most oral defenses in Golden Age Denmark, that of Søren Kierkegaard's 1841 dissertation "On the Concept of Irony" was performed in Latin. Unlike other mid-nineteenth-century defenses, however, it attracted a remarkably large and hostile audience. In addition to two official opponents, a handful of educated elites came forward to challenge the young Kierkegaard. Among them were two of Denmark's leading Hegelians: Andreas Frederik Beck and Johan Ludvig Heiberg. Kierkegaard parried their critiques with ease. But Beck refused to accept defeat. Soon after the defense, his side of their argument appeared in *The Fatherland*, a liberal Copenhagen newspaper. It was the language of Kierkegaard's dissertation that bothered Beck. Although happily stripped of "narrow-minded scholastic terminology," it too closely resembled "an informal chat," sounding more like "a conversation while walking in the street" than something fit for "the printed page."[1] Kierkegaard bit back with a response so ironic in tone that his dissertation immediately dropped from public discussion. Prudently, Heiberg let his end of the argument slide. But Kierkegaard never forgot the initial attack of this "half-educated Hegelian robber."[2]

Seven years after his widely discussed oral defense, Kierkegaard published his own critical essay in *The Fatherland*. A brief article with a wordy title, "The Crisis and a Crisis in the Life of an Actress" appeared in the summer of 1848 as an encomium to Denmark's leading actress, Johanne Luise Heiberg, who just so happened to be married to Johan Ludvig Heiberg. Although "The Crisis" appeared under the pseudonym "Inter et Inter" and nowhere mentions the name of its "admired artist," readers were quick to identify Kierkegaard as its author, Fru Heiberg as its subject, and themselves as its addressees. Many read this feuilleton article as a celebration of her recent portrayal of Shakespeare's Juliet, a role to which she had returned after eighteen years, and with noticeably less applause from Danish audiences. But praising Luise Heiberg was not the only reason Kierkegaard published "The Crisis." When situated in his broader philosophical project and the historical circumstances to which its publication was a response, this "little esthetic essay" can be shown to function as a highly wrought political critique of her husband, J. L. Heiberg.[3]

By celebrating Luise Heiberg, who was still enormously popular among Danish citizens, and simultaneously attacking her husband, who was then notorious for his intellectual and cultural elitism, Kierkegaard hoped to appeal to middle- and lower-middle-class readers, at once distinguishing himself from previous generations of educated elites and identifying himself (and his work) with the populist, egalitarian ideals of an emerging democratic public culture. In this sense, the addressee of his article was neither a crowned prince nor a cultured elite, but instead a mass society. And the rhetoric with which he engaged its constituents was not simply one of praise and blame. Nor was it in service to a politics of representation, in which Kierkegaard purported to speak for them. On the contrary, his was a rhetoric of courtship. As we shall see, "The Crisis" was among the first—and certainly among the most cunning—subversions of the modern system of power that continues to position educated elites as spokespersons for "the people." That this subversion also took place in a public culture defined by its anti-intellectualism makes it even more interesting—and even more worthy of our careful consideration.

The Public and Its Problems, 1830–1849

The first edition of *The Fatherland* appeared in 1834—the same year in which Denmark held its first democratic elections. Its mission was singularly political: "responsible representative government with popular control in particular over financial matters."[4] And its first major victory came in 1837, when King Frederick VI allowed his royal subjects to elect town councils. A second came in 1841, when the range of representative government was extended to include counties and parishes. From the urban middle classes to the smallest agrarian communities, political consciousness was everywhere on the rise. A more fully "national" Denmark was visibly emerging.

But it was not until 1846—when farmers in search of land reforms and social equality joined forces with urban liberals in search of a national constitution—that absolutism finally began to lose its grip on Denmark. The catalyst came two years later, when King Frederick's successor, Christian VIII, suddenly died of blood poisoning, allowing for the ascension of his son, Frederick VII. No sooner had the new king settled onto his throne than a throng of Danish liberals, inspired by the European revolutions of 1848, marched to Christiansborg Palace and petitioned him for a constitution. Sensing the gravity of his situation, Frederick quickly acquiesced: "If you, gentlemen, will have the same trust in your king as he has in his people, he will lead you honestly along the path of honor and liberty."[5] By the summer of 1849, Denmark had its constitution, and with it the most inclusive franchise in the modern world.

While its farmers and politicos were hacking away at absolutism, Denmark's literati were clinging to the aristocratic standards of the ancien régime. In the half century leading up to the constitution of 1849—an era of lavish creativity known as "Golden Age Denmark"—learned and artistic cultures were limited to a narrow but influential group of educated elites, many of whom ranked highly in the absolutist bureaucracy, which was safely encompassed by the walls of Copenhagen. With little incentive to challenge royal authorities, and even less cause to leave the city, students, professors, priests, and upper-level civil servants were largely removed from the sociopolitical transformations of their time.

Bordering these well-educated urbanites were two other literate classes. Above them on the social scale was a smaller aristocracy comprising high nobles, owners of great estates, and wealthy merchant families. And below them was a larger, uneducated distribution of bourgeois readers, ranging from prosperous shopkeepers to thriving craftsmen. Both classes looked to academically educated elites in matters of literary taste.

No one garnered more attention from these two social groups than the poet, philosopher, and playwright Johan Ludvig Heiberg. Although his writings would eventually come to typify the urbane, aristocratic conservatism of Golden Age Denmark, they were not always opposed to mass society. In fact, Heiberg began his literary career with a series of vaudevilles, all of which were designed to appeal to "individuals with very diverse educational backgrounds and personal inclinations . . . not just the lowest classes, but also the highest, not just the uneducated rabble but also the most educated individuals, plus everyone in-between." Professors and peasants, artisans and apprentices, civil and domestic servants—all found their way to Heiberg's vaudevilles in the 1820s and 1830s.

In addition to entertaining "the well-educated," Heiberg sought to "address the lesser educated in a manner that would cultivate their taste for things that they formerly could not appreciate." Like many of today's progressive academics, who also remain committed to Enlightenment pedagogies, he saw it as his task "to guide thought from everyday reason—representation—to the point where ideas—and therefore philosophy—begins."[6] And like many of their partisan lectures, which are increasingly attracting negative publicity from conservative advocacy groups, Heiberg's attempt to uplift the masses soon met with considerable resistance. By the late 1830s, it was obvious that middle- and lower-middle-class Danes were not adjusting their artistic and cultural sensibilities to his academically educated standards. Much to Heiberg's frustration, they seemed mired in a populist, anti-intellectual ideology.

Rather than adjusting his work to uneducated Danes, Heiberg began to ridicule their aesthetic and political preferences, and, more precipitously, to narrow his addressees to academic burghers (*studenter*). Among his most emphatic statements was an 1840 collection of essays titled *On the Theater*, in which he drew a sharp conceptual distinction between "good" and "bad" public cultures:

> In a good public it is the best who set the tone and represent the whole as if by tacit agreement. The good public is not, as the bad, an atomistic juxtaposition of the most different sorts of individuals who are all, nevertheless, equal in rights, . . . but is an aristocracy of those who do have rights, whose tutelage is accepted by those who do not have rights, who have not attained the age of majority, and who then cultivate themselves until they achieve the same sort of mastery, instead of instantly and immediately asserting the atom of opinion.[7]

In opposition to mounting demands for freedom of speech and the liberty of the individual, Heiberg was now calling for a society in which "the public" would attend to Golden Age elites in quiet, collective deference. More than constitutional guarantees, he argued, uneducated audiences were in need of stricter aesthetic and philosophical imperatives. And who better to formulate these imperatives than members of the Golden Age mainstream—"individuals in whom consciousness is aroused to the higher clarity while in the mass of people it is still more or less slumbering"?[8] Thus, with increasing bitterness, and a pronounced sense of entitlement, Heiberg came to see the enforcement of his academically educated standards as a "responsibility to the less-endowed."[9]

If Heiberg saw the democratization of Denmark as an occasion to replace absolutist bureaucrats with intellectual pedagogues, Kierkegaard saw it as a chance to transfer public authority from the monarch to the masses. More so even than their elected officials, it would be the people who held the reins of power: "One need not be a big politician to see that all over Europe the governments, instead of possessing too much power, are weakened; one need not be a great politician to see what a major poet in Paris said: *that in Europe the 'crowd' is the dangerous power*." Unlike Heiberg, who openly chastised this "dangerous power" for its populist, anti-intellectual sentiments, Kierkegaard respected and in many ways feared its ability to enable or oppress learned political action. "The danger involved in attacking a government when one has the support of public opinion is not very great," he realized in 1847, just two years before the constitution of democratic Denmark, "but it is indeed dangerous to expose oneself to the persecution of a confused and in some measure corrupt public opinion."[10]

Nevertheless, Kierkegaard was often outspoken in his critique of public opinion. But he was not an unwavering critic of nineteenth-century democratic culture. Indeed, his attitude toward "the public" is far more complicated than commentators often suggest. And it differed vastly from that of Heiberg. Where Heiberg saw an "atomistic juxtaposition of the most different sorts of individuals," Kierkegaard saw a rabble devoid of character, distinction, and independent judgment. The problem with "the public" (*Publikum*), he complained in his 1846 *Literary Review*, is that it "annihilates all the relative concretions of individuality," leaving in their stead "a deathly stillness in which nothing can rise up but everything sinks down into it, impotent." Thus, if Heiberg ridiculed Danish citizens for "asserting the atom of opinion" against prominent men and women of letters, Kierkegaard accused them of aspiring to be "nobodies"—impersonal members of a "sluggish crowd which understands nothing itself and is unwilling to do anything."

With neither ideas to inspire them nor opinions of their own, members of this "sluggish crowd" often turn to others for guidance. More than a political force, they constitute a "gallery-public" (*Gallerie-Publikum*), in which everyone simply "waits for someone to come along who wills something—so that they may place bets on him." "This public likes to transform all actuality into a theater," he goes on to note, "to have nothing to do itself but imagine that everything anyone does happens in order for it to have something to chatter about." As Kierkegaard saw it, the submissive mass audience for which Heiberg longed was already thriving in Denmark as an "abstract aggregate ridiculously formed by the participant's becoming a third party."

Given their divergent conceptions of the public and its problems, it is not surprising that Heiberg and Kierkegaard also disagreed on how best to handle them. Heiberg called for a rigid social hierarchy in which Golden Age elites could regiment and refine the opinions of atomized individuals. In exchange for their deferent attention, he offered intellectual and cultural tutelage. Kierkegaard was less nostalgic for the ancien régime. Rather than returning to an aristocratic order of learned and popular cultures, he encouraged Danish citizens to amplify their demand for equal rights by transforming it from "a quiet, mathematical, abstract enterprise" into the experiential and religious basis for an egalitarian community of individuals. "The bleakness of antiquity was that the man of distinction was what *others could not be*," he concluded in the mid-1840s. "The inspiring aspect [of the modern era] will be that the person who has gained himself religiously is only what *all can be*."[11]

At issue here is not only a comparative evaluation of antiquity and modernity, but also a polemical statement against intellectual and cultural elitism. As Bruce H. Kirmmse explains, Kierkegaard is "throwing down the gauntlet to all 'educated' political and cultural opinion, espousing a sort of divine egalitarianism in which existing notions of Dannelse [character-forming education] are worthless and in which only the simple integrity of the individual before God—which is available to everyone—has any worth."[12] Without a radical disavowal of aristocratic conservatism, members of "the public" would be unable to realize their ecumenical promise as modern individuals: "apprehension of the universal in equality before God."[13]

In this sense, "the public" is not simply an "abstract aggregate" that blocks the formation of individuals. Moreover, it is a testing ground for individuality itself, an *"examen rigorsum"* in which every "single individual [*enkelte Individ*]" has the potential to redeem the "alienating, abstract equality [*abstrakte Ligelighed*]" of mass society as an opportunity structure in which to "make up his own mind instead of agreeing with the public," and in so doing to "find rest within himself, at ease before God." For Kierkegaard, everything depended on this redemptive potential of mass society: "The public is the cruel abstraction by which individuals will be religiously educated—or be destroyed." Indeed, without these religiously educated and universally equal individuals, mature forms of communal life would be unable to develop.

"Not until the single individual has established an ethical stance despite the whole world, not until then can there be any question of genuinely uniting," he concludes. To stop short of this goal would be to limit modern democratic culture to "a union of people who separately are weak, a union as unbeautiful and depraved as a child-marriage."

Taken together, these arguments against the cultural elitism of the Golden Age mainstream and the "mathematical equality" of its uneducated mass audience form the basis for Kierkegaard's social and political thought. No longer can individuals "look to the nearest eminence for orientation," he argues. "That time is now past. They either must be lost in the dizziness of abstract infinity or be saved infinitely in the essentiality of the religious life." In other words, "individuals have to help themselves, each one individually." It is precisely here, in this triangulation of freedom, equality, and responsibility—individual freedom from established figures of authority (be they ruling monarchs or educated elites), unconditional equality before God, and personal responsibility for the development of moral values—that Kierkegaard made his most decisive break with Heiberg and his lettered sympathizers. No one—not even Kierkegaard—had the right to regiment and magisterially refine modern Danish citizens. The days of intellectual and cultural elitism, like those of monarchical power, were at an end. Populist individualism was the spirit of the times.

In keeping with this insight, Kierkegaard encourages academically educated authors to develop alternate modes of public address. Without inhibiting or curtailing "the proper development of individuality," they must help members of the reading public to realize "the weight of moral and social responsibility that lies on each individual."[14] And because "what counts is to work as an individual, to stand as a single individual," they must bring their readers to this realization without at the same time "acquiring status and importance as authorities."[15] To establish themselves as "men of excellence," Kierkegaard claims—all but indicting Heiberg and the Golden Age mainstream by name—would be to violate the "law of their existence" as modern democratic pedagogues, which is "not to rule, to guide, to lead, but in suffering to serve, to help indirectly." If all citizens are to experience their universal equality before God, learned advocates must not "give direct help, speak plainly, teach openly, assume decisive leadership of the crowd." Instead, they must render their assistance "*unrecognizable* [*ukjendelige*]," "concealing their respective distinctions and giving support only negatively." Remaining concealed, advising others indirectly, embracing the rhetoric of humility—the very techniques on which Seneca, Christine, and Kant relied—these were for Kierkegaard the ways in which learned political actors could help ordinary citizen-subjects to the "same decisiveness" that they themselves possess.[16]

"The Crisis and a Crisis in the Life of an Actress" is a polemical extension of this attitude toward modern democratic authors and audiences. More than an encomium to the acting abilities of Johanne Luise Heiberg, it is an encrypted attempt to undermine the intellectual and cultural elitism of her husband, and in so doing to reorient Danish readers to Kierkegaard's work, at the center of which, as we have seen, is a radical restatement of the principle of equality and a pointed insistence on the responsibility of single individuals. In this sense, "The Crisis" is more than "a little article in a newspaper," as Kierkegaard often referred to it.[17] It is a political expression of his stance on modern democratic authorship, his frustration with the Golden Age mainstream, and his commitment to populist individualism. In order to understand these historical, political, and philosophical dimensions of "The Crisis," especially as they lend themselves to learned advocacy in late modernity, we must first consider the biographical event that inspired Kierkegaard to publish this missive to literate Denmark in the first place: the *Corsair* affair.

The People Versus Its Patricians

On 27 December 1845, just three months before his discussion of the public and its problems, Kierkegaard, writing under the pseudonym "Frater Taciturnus," published a two-pronged critique of the Danish press, specifically its use of character assassinations to undermine the public authority of learned men and women. His first target was Peder Ludvig Møller, a Danish critic who had recently published a scandalous and completely superficial review of Kierkegaard's *Stages on Life's Way*. His second and more important target was *The Corsair*, a satirical and often libelous newspaper with which Møller was affiliated, and which was then enjoying the largest circulation of any paper in and around Copenhagen.

As Kierkegaard saw it, *The Corsair* was "an instrument of rabble-barbarism" designed to incite uneducated members of the public against prominent men and women of letters.[18] And its editors completely agreed, as the first line of their masthead motto well indicates: "His hand shall be against all, and the hands of all against him."[19] Despite its revolutionary theme, the paper resulted in little more than yellow journalism. Like many of today's well-funded private advocacy groups, which also resort to denigrating, sensationalist character assassinations of learned men and women, *The Corsair* made no qualms about its effort to "tear down" any and all pedagogues who challenged the anti-intellectual status quo on which it capitalized—whether they were outspoken critics of Danish popular culture or, as Kierkegaard would eventually find out, guilty of little more than "the crime of having different buttons on one's coat than other men have."[20] Indeed, long before David Horowitz's best-selling book *The Professors: The 101 Most Dangerous Academics in America* and the American Council of Trustees and Alumni's renowned indictment of 117 "un-American professors," not to mention the various "take back the campus" campaigns that circulated these infamous lists on websites, e-mail lists, and online message boards, *The Corsair* and its talented anonymous writers—the "Demolition and Defamation Institute," as Kierkegaard referred to them—had mastered the propaganda technique of courting public opinion in order to censor radical thought.

Leaving Møller to fend for himself, *The Corsair* countered Kierkegaard's attack on 9 January 1846, inaugurating a smear campaign that would eventually become the "most renowned controversy in Danish literary history."[21] Breaking with established codes of pseudonymous authorship, the paper teased him for thinking of himself as "an eccentric brilliant light that appears at irregular times to us mortals." It even went so far as to beleaguer the length of his pant legs, one of which was apparently shorter than the other, insisting that he wore them this way "in order to look like a genius." The next day, again disguised as "Frater Taciturnus," Kierkegaard published an article likening *The Corsair* and its editors to "public prostitutes" and begging them to continue deploying their "corrupt cleverness" against him.[22] And deploy they did. Over the next two years, *The Corsair* published more than a dozen derogatory pieces on Kierkegaard, nearly all of which were coupled with demeaning cartoons of his physical appearance.

The incessant ridicule took its toll on Kierkegaard. Before his dispute with *The Corsair*, contemporaries saw him as "a complete peripatetic who wanders around the streets of Copenhagen without any goal at all, from morning until late at night, in all weather and all seasons."[23] As Frederik Nielson recalls, "The thin little man, whom you could meet one moment at Østerport and the next on the entirely opposite side of town, apparently a carefree peripatetic, was recognized by everyone."[24] Kierkegaard was completely aware of this public image: "If Copenhagen was ever of one single opinion about someone, I dare say it has been of one opinion about me: I was a street-corner loafer, an idler, a *flâneur*, a frivolous bird, a good, perhaps even brilliant pate, witty, etc.—but I completely lacked 'earnestness.'" Moreover, he went out of his way to cultivate it:

> When I was reading proof pages of *Either/Or*, I was so busy that it was impossible for me to spend the usual time strolling up and down the street. I did not finish until late in the evening—and then in the evening I hurried to the theater, where I literally was present only five to ten minutes. And why did I do that? Because I was afraid that the big book would bring me too much esteem. And why did I do that? Because I know people, especially in Copenhagen; to be seen every night for five minutes by several hundred people was enough to sustain the opinion: So he doesn't do a single thing; he is nothing but a street-corner loafer.[25]

As long as Denmark could see him "gadding about on the streets and being a nobody," Kierkegaard thought he would be able to ward off, without in turn subverting, the authority of his pseudonymous writings. More importantly, he notes in *The Point of View*, "appearing irresponsible" was a sure way to combat Golden Age elitism: "By weakening myself in this way I was on the whole contributing to weakening [their] power and esteem."[26]

The Corsair shattered this literary-political agenda. Not only did its editors refuse to abide by Kierkegaard's use of pseudonyms, but by continuously mocking him in a newspaper famous for the second line of its masthead motto—"les aristocrats à la lanterne," or "hang the aristocrats"—they also identified Kierkegaard as a cloak-and-dagger elitist. No longer could he stroll the streets of Copenhagen in peace, playing the part of a street-corner loafer. "Now this is all upset," he realized during the *Corsair* affair. "The rabble, the apprentices, the butcher boys, the schoolboys, and all such are egged on."[27] Ridicule followed him everywhere. On the thoroughfare, people greeted him with shouts of "Either/Or!" And Sunday services were no better: "To sit in church where a couple of louts have the impudence to sit down beside one in order to gawk at one's trousers and insult one so loudly that every word is audible." Not even the countryside allowed Kierkegaard to escape: "I drive thirty-five miles to my beloved forest looking for simple solitude. Alas, curiosity everywhere. These tiresome people are like flies, living off others." Whether he was within or beyond the walls of Copenhagen, every public appearance met with the same reception: "a smirking, grinning crowd, and some of those present are even nice enough to call me names."

Even "Søren" became a term of abuse. As *The Corsair* sharpened its critiques, "the signal was given to the rabble to call me by my first name only, making it a nickname to be shouted at me." "My first name is now a nickname every schoolboy knows," Kierkegaard lamented in 1848, the same year he decided to publish "The Crisis."[28] This nominal abuse even made its way into everyday talk, as Georg Brandes observed in 1877, more than thirty years after the *Corsair* affair: "My earliest recollection of Kierkegaard is that when, as a child, I failed to pull my trousers down carefully and evenly over my boots, which in those days were serviceably long, the nurse would admonish me, saying: 'Søren Kierkegaard!'"[29]

What began as a biting response to "Frater Taciturnus" quickly became a widespread attack on Kierkegaard himself. And not only among members of the public. Golden Age elites also left him to twist in the wind. When it was not being shouted at him in street, his name was often being batted about preposterously onstage: "It is very rare these days to see a new Danish play without a character in it named Søren. Hostrup has one in every one of his plays; Carit Etlar, too, has gotten himself a similar character; so also—Professor Heiberg." Thus, as Kierkegaard saw it, responsibility for his public humiliation was distributed across the social scale: "Coarseness and brutality are just as glaring in the prominent people as they are in the rudest man." And each group has a specific role to play: "The law of persecution I am suffering is quite simple: the rabble are the ones who do it, while the elite are silent out of envy." Both social classes seemed to have rejected him and his work.

More than he was disappointed with members of the public, Kierkegaard was resentful of the Golden Age mainstream. "What pains me most," he remarks in his private journal, "is not the vulgarity of the rabble but the secret participation in it by the better people." Among these "better people," it was "Heiberg and his whole gang" who most offended him: "Heiberg, for whom I openly did the greatest service possible by throwing myself at P. L. Møller and *The Corsair*—he not only remains silent, no, secretly he also literally joins in with the rabble."[30] Breaking up this hidden alliance was among the primary tasks of "The Crisis." As we shall see, Kierkegaard used this serialized newspaper article to position himself between the public and its would-be patricians, at once identifying himself with "the common people" and distinguishing himself from "Heiberg and his kind."[31] How he did so without presenting himself an academically educated elite remains to be seen.

Religious Aesthetics

Kierkegaard's initial response to the *Corsair* affair came in 1847 with the publication of two signed religious works: *Upbuilding Discourses in Various Spirits* and *Works of Love*. In April 1848, he followed them with *Christian*

Discourses, an extensive critique of established church politics, notably the invocation of "Christianity" to support "the politics of liberal, of democratic-demagogic, and of snobbish conservative circles."[32] Given the revolutionary events preceding it, the most recent of which was the March 1848 petition for constitutional monarchy, Kierkegaard feared that *Christian Discourses* might plunge him into "personal danger." But nothing of the sort occurred. Its public reception was at best quiet. No one even took the time to write a review.

"The Crisis and a Crisis in the Life of an Actress" had to be different. "That little article," Kierkegaard argues to himself in a journal entry, must confuse anyone who has grown "lazy and pompous in the habit of thinking that I was the earnest one—perhaps an apostle, something I am a very long way from being." Avoiding this public image is precisely what he had tried to do in *Upbuilding Discourses*, *Works of Love*, and *Christian Discourses*. Indeed, he even went so far as to avoid using the term "sermon" in connection with these works, insisting that, unlike a "discourse," which "can be by a layman," "a sermon operates absolutely and solely on the basis of authority, that of Scripture and of Christ's apostles." More than an apostle, he was a layman. And more than an earnest author, he was a frivolous bird. Or so the argument went.

Literate Denmark was not convinced. In fact, as Kierkegaard rightly surmised, his return to religious writing was having the opposite effect. Instead of healing the wounds inflicted by *The Corsair*, his religious discourse was now threatening to deepen them. "I have been occupied now for such a long time exclusively with the religious, and yet people will perhaps try to make out that I have changed, have become earnest (which I was not previously), that the literary attack has made me sanctimonious," Kierkegaard remarks in his journal. "This is a heresy I consider extremely essential to counteract."

With "The Crisis," Kierkegaard hoped to prove beyond a doubt that he was not a sanctimonious religious author. In service to this task, he shifted his authorship from signed to pseudonymous, his mode of communication from direct to indirect, and, most important, his topic of discussion from religion to aesthetics. "Those who live esthetically here at home have no doubt given up reading me, since I 'have gone religious and do not write anything but sermon books,'" he realized in 1848. After reading a "little article about an actress," however, they might be willing to "peek into the next book, hoping to find something for them[selves]." The logic was simple: "An article in a newspaper, particularly about Mrs. Heiberg, creates much more of a sensation than big books. . . . Yes, it could easily become a firecracker." If Kierkegaard was ever going to recover from the *Corsair* affair and regain the support of popular opinion, he would have to publish this "little esthetic essay."

And there were other reasons for its publication. "I believe I owe it to Mrs. Heiberg," he explains in another journal entry. Moreover, "I would like to poke Heiberg a little again." And what better way to realize both ambitions than by embedding an assault on J. L. Heiberg in an encomium to his wife? "This way certain things can be said that I could not say so lightly and conversationally."[33] That Luise Heiberg was "a child of the common people" made this dissimulation even more appealing.[34] Not only would it allow Kierkegaard to renew his mastery of indirect communication and, in so doing, to resume his critique of the Golden Age mainstream. Because the Royal Danish Theater was a widely popular source of entertainment, and Luise Heiberg was among its most esteemed actresses, publishing "The Crisis" would also help him regain the approval of Danish audiences.[35]

On its surface, the article proceeds aesthetically, directly praising Luise Heiberg. But in keeping with Kierkegaard's desire to ridicule her husband, it also serves a political purpose, offering an indirect yet scathing critique of the intellectual and cultural elitism for which he stands. Embedded in the article are two additional layers of significance. The first is religious and, like the aesthetic and political dimensions of "The Crisis," did not elude Kierkegaard: "Perhaps someone will be made aware of the essentially Christian simply by avidly reading that little serialized article."[36] The second is theoretical and coincides with his critique of Heiberg. In addition to challenging his opponent's aristocratic conservatism, Kierkegaard reveals Heiberg's political agenda, at once theorizing and deploring it as a form of mass deception.

Although the aesthetic and religious contours of "The Crisis" have received adequate scholarly attention, its political and theoretical dimensions have been largely ignored.[37] In order to correct for these analytic blind spots, we must begin where Kierkegaard and most of his commentators leave off: the religious potential of "The Crisis." For it is atop his conception of "the essentially Christian," which is itself grounded in his notion of modern democratic authorship, that Kierkegaard builds his critique of Heiberg.

As we have seen, modern democratic culture was for Kierkegaard a forum in which to liberate members of "the public" from the tutelage of established authorities, enabling the people to "help themselves, each one individually." Likewise, the essentially Christian pivots on a notion of free will. "Christianity is indeed the religion of freedom, and precisely the voluntary is essentially Christian," Kierkegaard notes in *Christian Discourses*. "There is something that God cannot take away from a human being, namely, the voluntary, and it is precisely this that Christianity requires."[38]

As we also have seen, modern democratic authors have a duty to facilitate the autonomy of their readers without, in turn, "acquiring status and importance as authorities." In much the same way, representatives of the essentially Christian are obliged to instruct the "individual self-becoming" of others without appearing to be "on the market with a new teaching."[39] The trick is to remember that Christianity is "not a doctrine but an existence, that what is needed is not professors but witnesses," Kierkegaard explains. "If Christ did not need scholars but was satisfied with fisherman, what is needed now is more fishermen." In this sense, the distinction afforded by the essentially Christian, like that of modern democratic authorship, is actually "a distinction turned around."[40]

What, then, is the relationship between practitioners of the essentially Christian and their mass audiences? Although it is neither one of discipleship nor interdependence, it remains one of instruction. For Kierkegaard, theirs is a maieutic relationship, the purpose of which is to help members of the public realize their sovereignty as individuals, while simultaneously concealing their indebtedness to those who provide this "greatest beneficence." Of central importance here is *the way* this assistance occurs: "the greatest beneficence, to help another stand alone, cannot be done directly," he argues, again recalling his earlier discussion of democratic authorship. There must be no sign of help, "no awkward bungler's hand," in the assistance provided by representatives of the essentially Christian. Instead, they must "deceive the other into the truth."[41] Thus, like modern democratic authors, they are "obliged to keep on working—and at the same time work to conceal their working."[42]

At issue here is a form of learned advocacy that refuses to play the part of learned advocacy. Kierkegaard theorizes this curious mode of persuasion in his undelivered 1847 lecture on "The Dialectic of Ethical and Ethical-Religious Communication," the model for which seems to have been Aristotle's *Rhetoric*.[43] There are two ways "to help another stand on his own," he claims, but only one of them is premised on a maieutic relationship: "To stand—by another's help alone" or "To stand alone—by another's help." In the first instance, the stander's indebtedness to another's support is apparent: "There is therefore no reason to use a dash."[44] In the second instance, however, all debts and supports are "hidden behind the dash."[45] "To stand alone is not to stand by another's help," Kierkegaard concludes, for the maieutic technique consists in "having been able to do everything for a person and to appear to have done nothing at all."[46]

Maintaining this appearance requires not only the concealment of assistance, but also the "unrecognizability" of the assistant.[47] The freestanding individual "must by no means have any conception of this other as advantageous."[48] Here, Kierkegaard is drawing on Socrates's discussion of the "just man," who "does not wish to seem but to be good."[49] But he also has Jesus in mind, "a man who himself was aware of being the extraordinary—but whom his contemporaries failed to notice."[50] As both of these unrecognizable leaders well knew, helping others to stand alone requires "a self-disciplined act of maieutic disappearance."[51] And this disappearing act is just that—an act. Like any performance, its success depends on its publicity. To remain "hidden behind the dash" is not to remove oneself from the world of appearances, but to remain "incognito in such a way that one seems much lowlier than one is."[52] Insofar as the unrecognizable leader has a public image, then, it is one of abasement, not aloofness.

By courting abjection, unrecognizable leaders are able to stand "infinitely close" to "the common people," especially those who are "poor, abandoned, despised, abased."[53] They are, to borrow Kierkegaard's description of himself in *The Point of View*, leaders "with whom any poor person could without ceremony speak and associate on the street."[54] Although lowly leadership of this sort is essential to the maieutic development of others, it is also a source of great personal suffering: "It is always painful to have to conceal an inwardness and have to seem to be other than one is," Kierkegaard comments, especially when one plays the part of "a zero, a nonperson, an objective something."[55] It is a willingness to identify with ordinary people and to suffer on their behalf that ultimately ties the modern democratic author to the representative of the essentially Christian. Both "magnanimously will to annihilate [themselves]" in order to strengthen the autonomy of others.[56]

Kierkegaard's critique of Heiberg in "The Crisis" is premised on this interface between modern democratic authorship and the essentially Christian. Free will, subtracted authority, indirect assistance, unrecognizability, public abasement, personal suffering—and all in service to "the single individual" (*den Enkelte*)—these are the conceptual building blocks of his critique. With cultural aristocrats like Heiberg as his foil, Kierkegaard argues that, in order to cultivate the autonomy and decisiveness of others, one must avoid all "self-important scholarliness" (*Videnskabelighed*), an imperative that in turn requires the concealment of one's assistance and the unrecognizability of oneself.[57] That Heiberg and his learned coterie refuse to undertake this maieutic project, choosing instead to play the part of elitist pedagogues, is precisely what distinguishes them from Kierkegaard. And clarifying this distinction is precisely what "The Crisis" set out to do.

The Sophistries of Time and Habit

In July 1848, Kierkegaard divided "The Crisis and a Crisis in the Life of an Actress" into four sections and published it in as many editions of *The Fatherland*. Each of the first three segments was a testament to the emptiness and monotony of what often passes as praise for Fru Heiberg. Over the past fourteen years, he writes, "it has actually become a habit for her contemporaries to admire her." And in becoming a habit, their admiration has become "very weak, very mechanical, very flat." To be sure, audiences continue to adore Luise Heiberg, but they now do so only "very weakly, very powerlessly, very devoid of soul." To illustrate the danger of this idle admiration, section three of "The Crisis" provides the following example:

> If a king were to visit a humble family—yes, the family would feel honored, proud, almost overwhelmed by their good fortune. But if his majesty were to keep on visiting the same family every day, how long would it be before the king would almost have to make an effort to find a little meaning in his visiting the family, who out of habit went on saying without change: We thank you for the great honor. Of all sophists, time is the most dangerous, and of all dangerous sophists, habit is the most cunning.[58]

Here, Kierkegaard likens the public to a family, Luise Heiberg to a king, and her acting career to a series of familial visits. Over time, the family grows accustomed to these visits, so much so that its gratitude begins to lose significance—and not only for the family, but also for the king, who in turn feels compelled to help its members "find a little meaning" in his visits. Habit has deceived them both, Kierkegaard suggests, allowing a humble family to forget the grandeur of its king, and a sovereign king to convince himself of the need to impress a humble family.

What bothers Kierkegaard about the sophistries of time and habit is not their disruption of existing power relationships. On the contrary, as we have seen, the leveling of established social hierarchies is a precondition for the development of modern individuals, all of whom must pass through the "alienating, abstract equality" of democratic life in order to begin thinking for themselves, "each one individually." Rather, it is the king's attempt to counteract these sophistries by reminding the family of his regal status that bothers Kierkegaard. Instead of privileging the political autonomy of his political subjects, the king attempts to circumscribe it in their collective acknowledgment of his sovereign status.

In stark contrast to modern democratic authors and representatives of the essentially Christian, all of whom deny themselves in order to help others, the king is guilty of denying others in order to help himself.

It is at this point in "The Crisis" that Kierkegaard resumes his critique of J. L. Heiberg. He begins by distinguishing between those who share the democratic and essentially Christian impulse to assist others and those who share the kingly desire to help themselves: "All truly unworthy, that is, unselfish servants of truth, whose life is sheer struggle with the sophisms of existence, whose concern is not how one can best come out of it oneself but how one can most truly serve the truth and in truth benefit people—they have known how to use illusions in order to test people." In this sense, the king had a choice. Instead of attempting to valorize his repeated visits, an effort that merely compounded the illusion of familiarity with an illusion of his eminence as king, he could have used his intimate acquaintance with the family to determine how best to benefit its individual members.

And these were not his only options. He also could have undermined the illusion of familiarity by scaling back his interactions with the family, thereby reversing the effects of time and habit. And had he done so from the start, the king might not have allowed these effects to occur in the first place. But even these alternatives are not without their illusions, as Kierkegaard is careful to indicate in the example with which he follows his allegory of the king: "When, for example, a distinguished man lives very secluded, when he only seldom makes an appearance, people are not spoiled by seeing him. There develops, however, a splendid, an expedient, *si placet* [if you please], illusion that this distinguished man must be somebody altogether extraordinary. Why? Is it because people know how to evaluate his splendid qualities? Alas, no—it is because they see him so seldom that the rare sight produces a fantastic effect."[59]

It is difficult to read this passage apart from Kierkegaard's private indictment of "Heiberg and his whole gang" for remaining silent during his persecution by *The Corsair*: "no one dared to do anything publicly," he painfully reminded himself in 1848, "for each one feared the tyranny of the rabble."[60] More generally, this passage alludes to Heiberg's ridicule of uneducated readers in the early 1840s, the hallmark of which was his characterization of them as members of a "public that has walked on its own for so long that it must be guided back from the morass it inevitably finds itself in when left to its own devices."[61] In the years leading up to "The Crisis," Heiberg's bitterness toward this wayward public increased, as did his seclusion from its middle- and lower-middle-class constituents. "He became increasingly isolated," Kirmmse notes, withdrawing with his work to a kind of "lofty pessimism."[62] By the time "The Crisis" appeared, Heiberg had excluded all but "the educated reading-world" from his audience.[63]

That Kierkegaard meant to index and berate this elitism is readily apparent in an earlier, more explicit draft of the sentence with which his second illustration begins: "When, for example, a distinguished man lives very secluded, *at the exclusive circle's aristocratic distance from daily life and the human crowd*, when he seldom makes an appearance, people are not spoilt by seeing him." With the addition of this sentence's first draft, we are several steps removed from the acting abilities of Luise Heiberg. If Kierkegaard's first illustration refigures her as a visiting king and her public as a humble family, his second illustration refigures this king as "a distinguished man" and this family as an indefinite group of "people." And the omitted portion of this second example further refines both parties, transforming the distinguished man into an exclusive aristocrat and this group of people into "the human crowd." What began as "a little esthetic essay" in praise of Luise Heiberg has now begun to function as an indirect political critique of the elitism for which her husband was famous.

Another Pale-Fac'd Moon

In addition to criticizing "Heiberg and his kind," this pointed assault on the "distinguished man" allows Kierkegaard to make a broader theoretical statement against the use of seclusion to deceive mass audiences, especially when deception of this sort results in the advancement of narrow self-interest. Without relenting his attack on Heiberg, Kierkegaard goes on to consider and critique the tendency of established figures of authority—be they sovereign kings or literary-political elites—to seclude themselves from mass audiences in order to better manipulate them:

> Past experience shows that this can be done. The method, masterfully described by Shakespeare in Henry IV's charge to Prince Henry, has been used successfully by a great number of kings and emperors and ecclesiastics and Jesuits and diplomats and schemers etc., among whom there no doubt were many excellent people, some of whom also wanted to serve the truth, but all of whom were nevertheless united in wanting to influence with the aid of an illusion, whether it was merely to profit from it themselves by making sure of the stupor of the crowd, or whether they devoutly, perhaps also sagaciously, thought they were securing for the truth a more universal propagation with the aid of—an illusion.[64]

In order to understand this theory of deception, which is at once opposed to the illusion of familiarity and entirely separate from the illusion of unrecognizability, we must begin with Kierkegaard's reference to *1 Henry IV*, for it is in terms of this play that the relationship between his first two exemplary figures—the king and the distinguished man—becomes fully legible.

Set in early fifteenth-century England, *1 Henry IV* traces the slow and ultimately successful efforts of Henry of Bolingbroke to usurp the throne of Richard II. In the scene to which Kierkegaard refers, the newly crowned Henry is advising his son, Hal—or, as "The Crisis" refers to him, "Prince Henry"— on the use of personal seclusion to secure and maintain political power:

> Had I so lavish of my presence been,
> So common-hackney'd in the eyes of men,
> So stale and cheap to vulgar company,
> Opinion, that did help me to the crown,
> Had still kept loyal to possession,
> And left me in reputeless banishment,
> A fellow of no mark nor likelihood.
> By being seldom seen, I could not stir
> But like a comet I was wond'red at,
> That men would tell their children, "There is he";
> Others would say, "Where, which is Bullingbrook?"
> And then I stole all courtesy from heaven,
> And dress'd myself in such humility
> That I did pluck allegiance from men's hearts,
> Loud shouts and salutations from their mouths,
> Even in the presence of the crowned King.
> Thus did I keep my person fresh and new,
> My presence, like a robe pontifical,
> Ne'er seen but wond'red at, and so my state,
> Seldom but sumptuous, show'd like a feast,
> And wan by rareness such solemnity.[65]

In his opening statement, Henry encourages Hal to imagine what would have happened if he had begun his political ascent by associating with "vulgar company." Rather than helping him to the crown, public opinion would have "kept loyal" to its current possessor, Richard II, thereby leaving Henry in "reputeless banishment." Just as the visiting king became perilously familiar to the humble family, so also would he have become "common-hackney'd in the eyes of men." Only by remaining "seldom seen" was he able to avoid this cheapened appearance, forestalling it with the illusion that he was "a comet" to be "wond'red at." Clearly, Henry's image of himself mirrors that of the "distinguished man." Building on the Machiavellian insight that public performance is the basis for political power, both figures manufacture an illusion of "rareness" in order to achieve "a fantastic effect" on public opinion.[66]

That Heiberg spent much of the mid-1840s secluded in his private observatory makes Henry's astronomical rhetoric all the more intriguing. For Heiberg, "contemplation of the starry heavens" was a way to distance himself from middle- and lower-middle-class public culture and, by preserving this distance, to make sweeping judgments of its constituency.[67] His poem "Charlottenlund" was a case in point, inviting readers to adopt—or at the very least to admire—Heiberg's telescopic view of human togetherness: "I think you become dizzy in the head / If you do not stand above the whole thing. / The observer ought to stand at a distance, / At a point outside the throng." In another poem from this period, "The Starry Heaven," Heiberg invites readers to join him in the celestial sphere, all along the way scorning their daily lives: "The mass crawls about, blind, / Amongst its low and narrow business. / My ceaseless motion is the judgment of time / Upon everyone who mucks about and fusses. / But you who wish to dwell in peace, / Undisturbed by planless dither, / Lift yourself to me and sample the calm / Provided by my tranquil rhythm."[68]

Another outlet for this cosmic propaganda was Heiberg's yearbook, *Urania*, named for Uranienborg, the main building on the island of Hven, where Tycho Brahe, a famous sixteenth-century nobleman and observational astronomer, conducted his research. In addition to preparing astrological charts and interpretations, Brahe predicted worldly events such as births and storm fronts, as well as celestial phenomena like the supernova of 1572 and the comet of 1577. Like Brahe, Heiberg fancied himself an interpreter and forecaster of astronomical events, especially as they pertained to "the aesthetically cultivated public." To this end, he included a "Star Calendar for 1844" and an article on the upcoming "Astronomical Year" in the first edition of *Urania*, both of which were designed not only to prepare his academically educated audience for the upcoming year, but also to provide them with a "New Year's gift" to purchase and exchange with one another.[69]

Kierkegaard was not the only one to ridicule Heiberg for his astronomical elitism. In January 1846, *The Corsair* published "The New Planet," a fictional dialogue between Heiberg, Kierkegaard, *The Corsair*, and Christian F. R. Olufsen, who was then a professor of astronomy and the director of the

Copenhagen observatory. When asked to discuss the recent emergence of a "new planet" (a metonym for Møller's December 1845 review of *Stages on Life's Way*, the same review that embroiled Kierkegaard in the *Corsair* affair), Heiberg responds:

> It proves my astronomical prophetic power. Two years ago I predicted in my *Urania* that within a month two large, bright stars would appear. But only one appeared. Whatever happened to the other one has been beyond me until now. This year I predicted no stars at all, and one has made its appearance. A mathematical calculation—mathematics is of utmost importance. Astronomy now shows:
>
>   a. Predicted: 2 stars. Appeared: 1.
>   b. <u>Predicted: 0"</u>   <u>Appeared: 1.</u>
>   Total: Predicted: 2"   Appeared: 2.
>
> The honor of astronomy is saved; I congratulate myself.

When asked the same question, Olufsen begins by claiming that the new planet is actually a comet, at which point Kierkegaard interrupts: "Yes, but it has no tail, Mr. Professor!" To which Olufsen responds, "It has no tail? Well, who says so? You have no tail either, and yet you are a comet." With only a hint of embarrassment, Kierkegaard acquiesces: "What, am I comet? Well, then—Oh, I almost—" "Don't get excited!," Olufsen interjects. "You fly off the handle so fast! Now I'll probably be in *Fæderlandet* [*The Fatherland*] tomorrow. But it is true just the same. What, then, is a comet?" "It is an eccentric brilliant light that appears at irregular times to us mortals," Kierkegaard replies. "Well," Olufsen concludes, "aren't you a comet then? Are you not a brilliant body, a light?" "Yes," Kierkegaard proudly admits, "I am a light, that is correct."[70]

This caricature of Kierkegaard resonated with literate Denmark. And it was not the first time someone described him and his work in this way: "A new literary comet (I think it looks like I wrote 'camel,' but I mean a comet) has soared in the heavens here—a harbinger and a bringer of bad fortune," wrote Signe Læssøe in her 1843 commentary on *Either/Or*.[71] By publishing "The New Planet," *The Corsair* added teeth to comments of this sort, encouraging literate Denmark to see Kierkegaard's peripatetic lifestyle as little more than a cryptic form of egocentrism. "He himself roared his way into becoming 'the rocket,'" wrote one contemporary, presumably referring to Kierkegaard's portrayal in "The New Planet." "This was the only thing he achieved in his mighty efforts to show himself everywhere, now at Gammel Strand among the fishmongers, now at Holmensgade. He places great emphasis on this in his writings, as if people were really supposed to care about where he showed himself."[72] The effects of these cosmic caricatures were as lasting as they were widespread, as Gilles Deleuze well indicated in his 1968 characterization of Kierkegaard as a "thinker-comet."[73]

Of all the parodies published in *The Corsair*, "The New Planet" was the most devastating. How could anyone confuse Kierkegaard's street-corner lifestyle with Heiberg's cosmic seclusion? It was Heiberg, not him, who spent his time communing with the comets. It was Heiberg, not him, who purported to be "somebody altogether extraordinary." It was Heiberg, not him, who accepted Henry's advice to Hal. Publishing "The Crisis" was an attempt to clarify these distinctions. Like kings, emperors, ecclesiastics, Jesuits, diplomats, and other schemers before him, Heiberg was a self-interested practitioner of mass deception. Given the caricature of Heiberg in "The New Planet," it is not surprising that, of all these cunning predecessors, Kierkegaard likens him to Henry IV, for both envisioned themselves as otherworldly figures of authority. Theirs was not the "low and narrow business" of mass society, but a solemn and tranquil correspondence with the heavens. Only the "greater" commonwealth was worthy of their attention—and only insofar as it allowed others to recognize them as undisputed leaders of the "lesser" commonwealth.

Given the enormous popularity of Shakespeare among middle- and lower-middle-class Danes, Kierkegaard could rest assured that readers of "The Crisis" would grasp his critique of Heiberg. And given the widespread commitment to liberalism in late-1840s Denmark, which brought with it a public disdain for social privilege and personal privacy (the same disdain on which tabloids like *The Corsair* capitalized), he also could rest assured of their endorsement. But he did not want to take any chances. Although 1 *Henry IV* had been available in translation for decades, and several of the Falstaff scenes had already appeared at the Royal Theater, the play had yet to be performed in its entirety. If Kierkegaard was going to distinguish himself from Heiberg, and in so doing restore his previous allegiance with the people, he would have to sharpen his argument. Thus, immediately following his rebuke of self-interested deception, he presents his readers with an alternate, more admirable line of conduct:

> The unconditionally unselfish servants of truth, however, have always had the practice of associating considerably with the people; they have never played hide-and-seek with the crowd in order to play in turn the wonder game when, on the rare occasion, they appear in public as the

surprising object of wonder. On the contrary, they have always appeared regularly in everyday clothes, have lived with the common man, have talked on the highways and byways, thus relinquishing all esteem—for when the crowd sees a man every day, then the crowd thinks something like this: Is that all? Alas, yes, "*mundus vult decipi* [the world wants to be deceived]," but the unselfish witnesses to the truth have never wanted to enter into this illusion, they have never wanted to go halves with the crowd on the next part: "*decipiatur ergo* [therefore let it be deceived]." They have, on the contrary, deceived by doing the opposite, that is, they have judged the world by appearing unimportant.[74]

Over and against the aristocratic conservatism of Golden Age Denmark, which aimed to enforce the public authority of academically educated elites, Kierkegaard celebrates the populist political activities of those who, instead of fabricating illusions of grandeur, immerse themselves in mass society. At issue here is not a politics of representation, but instead a "rhetoric of identification."[75] In contrast to his Marxist contemporaries and their twentieth-century successors—many of whom, like Heiberg, saw themselves as the clear, conscious, vanguard leaders of a mass society whose obscure, unconscious, and subordinate status was embodied in "the people"—Kierkegaard saw himself as a member of this anonymous collectivity whose leadership consisted in his unrecognizable service to the transformation of its equally nondescript members into a community of freestanding individuals. If indeed he is a role model for today's learned political advocates, especially those housed in American institutions of higher education, it is because he found a way to reconcile his status as an educated elite with the anti-intellectual sentiments of Danish popular culture.

To further illustrate this public persona, let us consider the similarity between the above-mentioned excerpt from "The Crisis" and Kierkegaard's unpublished "Self-Defense," both of which were written in the first few months of 1847:

> In our endeavor we have honestly renounced working with the aid of any illusion. We are well aware, knew it before we began, knew it from our acquaintance with antiquity, and with the most profound poet who someplace has a king impart this knowledge to the prince; we were well aware that to live concealed, secluded, exclusive, seldom seen in public, creates a splendid illusion that helps one enjoy esteem. But deliberately and with our eyes on those noble ones, whom we regard as teachers of the human race, we have renounced and scorned securing esteem for the truth by means of illusion or, more correctly, securing

esteem for ourselves at the expense of truth. On the contrary, we have striven in every way to annihilate ourselves in order to serve the truth. We did not think that our cause would truly gain by our becoming honored and glorified—and then perhaps becoming weary of working for it; on the contrary, we have thought that our cause, like any good cause, shows up to best advantage when we stand with our good cause regarded with low esteem, laughed at, insulted, mistreated.[76]

Again, Kierkegaard recalls Henry's advice to his son in *I Henry IV*. And again he contrasts the use of illusion to advance self-interests with its unselfish disavowal in service to the truth. How are we to understand these repeated juxtapositions? If Henry IV stands in for Heiberg, who stands in for Kierkegaard? And if Henry's seizure of political power prefigures Heiberg's struggle for intellectual and cultural authority, whose behavior anticipates Kierkegaard's courtship of the uneducated public? Another look at Henry's advice to Hal provides an answer. Immediately after recounting his rise to power, Henry cautions his son against the populist political agenda of his predecessor, Richard II. It is here, in Henry's description of Richard II, that Kierkegaard's self-image becomes apparent:

> The skipping King, he ambled up and down,
> With shallow jesters, and rash bavin wits,
> Soon kindled and soon burnt, carded his state,
> Mingled his royalty with cap'ring fools,
> Had his great name profaned with their scorns,
> And gave his countenance, against his name,
> To laugh at gibing boys, and stand the push
> Of every beardless vain comparative,
> Grew a companion to the common streets,
> Enfeoff'd himself to popularity,
> That, being daily swallowed by men's eyes,
> They surfeited with honey and began
> To loathe the taste of sweetness, whereof a little
> More than a little is by much too much.
> So when he had occasion to be seen,
> He was but as the cuckoo is in June,
> Heard, not regarded; seen, but with such eyes
> As, sick and blunted with community,
> Afford no extraordinary gaze.[77]

If Luise Heiberg has taken the path from which Henry veered, resulting in an illusion of familiarity ("Had I so lavish of my presence been, / So common-hackney'd in the eyes of men"), and her husband has followed in Henry's footsteps, resulting in an illusion of grandeur ("Ne'er seen but wond'red at, and so my state, / Seldom but sumptuous, show'd like a feast"), Kierkegaard's self-characterization as a frequenter of "the highways and byways" of everyday life allows him to affect and redeem Henry's portrayal of Richard II as "a companion of the common streets," transforming their similarly "carded" states from illusions of unimportance into evidence of their unrecognizable leadership.

Shoring up this identification are several historical parallels. Like Richard, Kierkegaard has had his "name profaned" by everyone from nannies to playwrights. Like Richard, Kierkegaard has endured the irreverent laughter of "gibing boys." Like Richard, Kierkegaard has been "daily swallowed by men's eyes" and thus afforded "no extraordinary gaze." And like Richard, Kierkegaard has suffered at the hands of a usurper. With this final likeness, the critique of Heiberg implicit in Kierkegaard's identification with Richard becomes readily apparent. Regardless of any public abuse he suffered, Richard II was a divinely anointed monarch, and regardless of the public opinion he manufactured, Henry IV was a usurper of this sacramental kingship.

This distinction would have been obvious to Elizabethan audiences, for whom traditional forms of political identity had already given way to theatrical conceptions of the self and the state.[78] Nevertheless, Shakespeare chose to emphasize it in 1 *Henry IV*. And much to Kierkegaard's amusement, he did so by turning Henry's cosmic rhetoric against him, allowing Hotspur to liken the self-fashioned king to a "pale-fac'd moon."[79] Much as the moon steals light from the sun, Henry has usurped the God-given authority of Richard. And in much the same way, Heiberg has attempted to secure for himself the public authority and personal advantage that Kierkegaard has willfully foregone in service to others.

From Monarchical Power to Modern Profiteering

But again, not everyone reading "The Crisis" may have known 1 *Henry IV* well enough to discern this added jab at Heiberg. To compensate for this potential blind spot, Kierkegaard concludes his critique by amplifying the distinction between Heiberg's attempt to "profit from" the deception of mass audiences and his own "unconditionally unselfish" service to the truth and to others:

> If an author who neither has a considerable fund of ideas nor is very industrious were to publish at long intervals an elegant copybook that is especially ornate [*nitid*] and is resplendently provided with many blank pages—the crowd gazes at this elegant phenomenon with amazement and admiration and thinks that if he has been such a long time in writing it and if there is so little on the page it really must be something extraordinary. If, on the other hand, an idea-rich author who has something else to think about than elegance and making a profit from an illusion, exerting himself with ever great diligence, finds himself able to work at an unusual speed, the crowd soon becomes accustomed to it and thinks: It must be slovenly stuff. The crowd, of course, cannot judge whether something is well worked out or not; it sticks to—the illusion.[80]

In this final flourish, Kierkegaard invites his readers to recall Heiberg's recent publication history. From his 1841 edition of *New Poems* to his mid-1840s editions of *Urania*—all were famous for their glazed covers, meticulous typefaces, and richly ornamented borders. And all were equally well-known for their appearance in the month of December—just in time to meet the demand of holiday shoppers. Moreover, by calling attention to the "long intervals" between these "especially ornate" works (*nitid* being a term he often used to allude to Heiberg), Kierkegaard also points to his own publication history, reminding readers of the rapidity with which his own works have appeared.

Among the speediest, and certainly the most memorable, moments in this history was his publication of four books in half as many weeks in June 1844. And among the most popular of these books was a satirical collection of *Prefaces*, in which Kierkegaard repeatedly lashed out against Heiberg. In fact, his collection of *Prefaces* was renowned for its derision of "Prof. Heiberg." "We have spoken with various people who immediately seemed to betray a certain acquaintance with Nicolaus Notabene's *Prefaces* as well as with Vigilius Haufniensis's book *The Concept of Anxiety* and S. Kierkegaard's *Philosophical Fragments* and his new *Upbuilding Discourses*," wrote one reviewer of the four books Kierkegaard published in the summer of 1844. "But, strangely enough, every time we wanted to go into one or another of these works a little, they always reverted to comments about Prof. Heiberg."[81] Even P. L. Møller, one of Kierkegaard's opponents in the *Corsair* affair, was willing to acknowledge that *Prefaces* was "some of the wittiest but unconditionally the most elegant of what has been written against Heiberg."[82]

Not coincidentally, *Prefaces* coupled its most scathing critiques of Heiberg with several broader, more sweeping statements against the publication, promotion, and purchase of lavish "New Year's" books during the holiday season. "As is well known, the literary New Year's rush of commercial scriveners begins in the month of December," Kierkegaard writes. "Several sleek and elegant [*nitid*] books intended for children and Christmas trees, but especially useful as gifts in good taste, chase past each other in *Adresseavisen* [a Danish advertising paper]." Although many authors capitalized on this holiday tradition, only Heiberg is identified by name: "Oh you great Chinese god! I would have sworn to it; is not Prof. Heiberg along in the parade this year? Yes, quite right, it is Prof. Heiberg. Yes, when one is decked out in this fashion, one can easily put in an appearance before the astonished crowd. Not even Salomon Goldkalb in all his glory was thus clothed."[83]

This parting reference to Salomon Goldkalb, the merchant who is mistaken for a baron in Heiberg's popular 1825 vaudeville *King Solomon and George the Hatter*, allowed Kierkegaard to drive home his critique with middle- and lower-middle class Danes, many of whom, although poorly educated, where avid fans of Heiberg's vaudevilles. Like a common salesman masquerading as a noble lord, Kierkegaard suggests, Heiberg has learned to conceal his financial motives behind the illusion that he is "somebody altogether extraordinary." Add to this the nominative overlap between Salomon Goldkalb and the biblical figure of King Solomon, and the popular resonance of this 1844 critique begins to make sense. "Observe how the lilies of the field grow," Jesus implores his apostles in one of his well-known parables (also one of Kierkegaard's favorites): "They do not toil nor do they spin, yet I say to you that even Solomon in all his glory did not clothe himself like one of these."[84] Not even the famously wealthy King Solomon was as "decked out" as Heiberg and his elegant copybooks, Kierkegaard suggests.

And what of King Solomon's renowned wisdom? Just as he authored works on medicine, mineralogy, and magic, Kierkegaard goes on to jest, so also is "Herr Prof." conducting "astronomical, astrological, chiromantical, necromantical, horoscopical, metoscopical, chronological studies." With so many sources of wisdom from which to chose, it is interesting that Kierkegaard, once again, directs his readers to Heiberg's astronomical studies: "Let the results be what they may, it is already glorious to envisage

Herr Prof. when he stands there and prophetically gazes far away until he catches a glimpse of the system and the realization of long contemplated plans; or when as in these later days, he fixes his eyes on heavenly things, counts the stars, reckons their courses, and watches for the heavenly inhabitants of those distant planets, forgetting the earth and earthly life."[85]

Given the memorability of this 1844 polemic, readers of "The Crisis" would have easily pegged Heiberg as the author of the "elegant copybook" under scrutiny. And they would have easily grasped the argument against him: underpinning the illusion of intellectual and cultural authority on which "Herr Prof." thrives is little more than a collection of fancy books, all of which are designed to astonish readers and enrich their author. To "profit from an illusion," Kierkegaard laments, is not only to manipulate public opinion, but also to line one's pockets.

Which brings us to the basic rhetorical wager of "The Crisis." Would readers who recalled the critique of Heiberg in *Prefaces* also have identified Kierkegaard as his opponent? Were there enough clues in this "little esthetic essay" for them to realize that, behind the facade of "Inter et Inter," there was "an idea-rich author who has something else to think about than elegance and making a profit"? If readers could recall his previous attack on Heiberg's lavish New Year's books, might they also recall its accompanying praise of the author who chooses to write prefaces instead? "He moves in and out among the people like a dupe in winter and a fool in summer," Kierkegaard notes. He is "always joyful and nonchalant, contented with himself, really a light-minded ne'er-do-well," someone who "does not go to the stock exchange to feather his nest but only strolls through it."[86] More than a profit seeker, the author of *Prefaces* is a frivolous flaneur, a carefree peripatetic, a street-corner loafer—in short, everything from which *The Corsair* would eventually dissociate Kierkegaard, and everything with which "The Crisis" would later attempt to identify him.

That his assault on Heiberg begins with a discussion of time and habit, the subtext of which is a disruption of monarchical relations of power, and ends with an argument against the commercialization of literary public culture was crucial to Kierkegaard's recovery from the *Corsair* affair. Unlike Heiberg, who had rarefied his public appearances as well as his publications in order to profit from "the stupor of the crowd," thereby adding a modern capitalist twist to the theatrical politics of Henry IV, Kierkegaard had disavowed financial gain in order to better serve "the common man," a renunciation that promised to locate him in a lineage of divinely anointed populists ranging from Jesus to Richard II. "For seven years now we have been an author in the Danish language," Kierkegaard wrote of himself in 1847, hearkening back to the days of his dissertation. "We have worked on a scale that is seldom seen. With all this work we have not earned a penny."[87]

The primacy of this economic argument cannot be understated. Not only did it inform Kierkegaard's religious and political writings in the mid- to late 1840s. As we have seen, it also fueled his critique of Heiberg during this period. Consider, for instance, one of the passages that Kierkegaard eventually decided to omit from "The Crisis," the original location of which, not surprisingly, immediately preceded his attack on the profiteering author of "an elegant copybook": "Some years ago a ram was on exhibition on Vesterbro; the price of entry was eight shillings. It was exhibited only in the afternoon; in the morning the same ram grazed in a field out on Gammel Kongevej—there was not a soul who paid any attention to it, but in the afternoon when it cost eight shillings and the exhibition lasted only a few hours—then they gazed at the ram with amazement."[88] Had this passage appeared in "The Crisis," it would have crystallized the article's basic social critique: rarity is not only a source of political power in monarchical society, as Henry IV well knew, but also the basis for financial gain in modern democratic culture, as Heiberg's publication record indicates.

Only at this point in "The Crisis," when public authority, populist propaganda, and shameless profiteering have begun to overlap, does Kierkegaard resume his discussion of Luise Heiberg. Echoing the tribute Jesus gave to John, Kierkegaard concludes that most of her audience members are little more than "children in the marketplace." Like passersby of the ram grazing in the field on Gammel Kongevej, they "perceive that they have something and are permitted to keep it," and subsequently "become ungrateful, and if not plainly ungrateful, then at least lazy in the habit of admiration." How are we to interpret this parting analogy between the theater and the marketplace? At issue here, Kierkegaard suggests, is the insidious mercantile truth of the allegory of the king with which he began his critique of her husband: "The actress's stock stands unchanged at the quoted price, yet not at all so firmly."[89] In a tragic twist of fate, the aesthetic economy on which her reviled elitist husband had long prospered was the same in which this actress of the people now showed signs of perishing.

Authors and Addressees of "That Little Serialized Article"

Kierkegaard's choice of the pseudonym "Inter et Inter" has long mystified readers. Some suggest that given the stated topic of "The Crisis," the phrase refers to intermissions in a theatrical performance.[90] Others insist that it marks a partition in Kierkegaard's work as an author.[91] Given the polemical nature of "The Crisis," I would like to offer an alternate explanation. More than a theatrical reference or the quilting point for his work as an author, "Inter et Inter" is a contracted, highly abridged reminder of the distinctions between Luise Heiberg, J. L. Heiberg, and Kierkegaard.

Recalling the Latin proverb *Distinguendum est inter et inter*—"It is necessary to distinguish between notions that need to be distinguished"—Kierkegaard's pseudonym entails two analogous distinctions. If the first "Inter" marks a distinction between the wildly popular Luise Heiberg and her increasingly maligned husband, the second marks a parallel distinction between her husband and Kierkegaard. Implicit in these analogous distinctions is a "congregation by segregation," in which Kierkegaard at once affects the celebrity status of Fru Heiberg and dissociates himself from the reviled elitism of her husband, thereby redeeming his public persona from the humiliating aftermath of the *Corsair* affair.[92]

Democratic Denmark may have been through with social distinctions, but Kierkegaard was not, especially when it came to matters of public opinion. With articles like "The New Planet" in circulation, it was crucial for him to distinguish his allegiance to "the common man" from Heiberg's allegiance to himself and "his kind." And it was especially important that he do so publicly, before all of literate Denmark—not only Luise Heiberg, whom he intended to flatter, and her husband, whom he hoped to insult, but also middle- and lower-middle-class members of the Danish citizenry, with whom he hoped to identify.

The newspaper form of *The Fatherland* was crucial to Kierkegaard's effort. But this is not to suggest that "The Crisis" was an ordinary nineteenth-century newspaper article. Unlike Seneca, Christine, and Kant before him, all of whom inscribed their personal correspondence with flourishes of public discourse, Kierkegaard infused his anonymous article about an anonymous actress addressed to an anonymous audience with moments of intimate, private address. Recalling the epistolary origins of modern democratic newspapers—namely, their prehistory as newsletters, which were often personally addressed, written for publication, and semi-anonymous—Kierkegaard obscures his authorship in a pseudonym and divides his readership into an epistolary network of addressees, auditors, and witnesses.[93]

It is precisely here, in this authorship and audience design framework, that the function of "The Crisis" as a letter to power becomes apparent. For better and for worse, its addressee was neither an emperor nor a queen nor a king, but instead a mass society. As Kierkegaard well knew, the site of political power in democratic Denmark was not a single, identifiable figure of authority but instead a reticulate public sphere comprising ordinary citizens and unofficial collectivities.[94] Rather than attempting to represent these individuals and groups, as Christine did in her tearful petition to the queen, Kierkegaard sought to identify with them. Anticipating the post-representational politics of Foucault and Deleuze, in which educated elites no longer purport to speak for the masses but instead struggle against the systems of power that position them as spokespersons, Kierkegaard refused to characterize himself as a representative of "the people," opting instead for a lateral affiliation with those subsumed in this social category.[95]

His strategy was premised on what Kenneth Burke would later call "the rhetoric of identification." In addition to stripping "The Crisis" of all second-person collective pronouns, choosing instead to address the Danish citizenry using the first-person collective terms "we" and "us," Kierkegaard embedded these terms in a rhetoric of sympathy and antipathy. In their admiration of Luise Heiberg's stage acting and abhorrence of her husband's cultural elitism, Kierkegaard and "the common man" were united. No longer was "the public" an object to be overcome by the persuasive force of vanguard educators and their opponents in the popular press. Preempting the anti-intellectual pundits and right-wing advocacy groups of contemporary democratic culture, as well as the "tenured radicals" from whom they claim to protect "the public," Kierkegaard found a way to resist both of these identity formations, transforming the public into a diffuse ensemble of individuals and himself into their unrecognizable leader. In their struggle for control over the reading public, neither Heiberg nor *The Corsair* could make sense of this political program. Like many of today's would-be intellectuals, Heiberg was blinded by the prescience of his effort to uplift the masses. And like many of their sensationalist adversaries, those at *The Corsair* were too busy profiting from the ignorance of this collectivity. Mired in rhetorics of combat, both failed to see that, in modern democratic Denmark, nothing was more disarming than a rhetoric of courtship.

That praising Luise Heiberg was an occasion to critique her husband, and this critique an opportunity to court public opinion, was utterly lost on the Heibergs. In response to "The Crisis," Fru Heiberg thanked Kierkegaard for expressing his appreciation of her art so "clearly and unambiguously." His remarks were "altogether correct," she wrote in her autobiography. "I have many times felt precisely as it is described here."[96] In all fairness, though, Kierkegaard had gone out of his way to enable this interpretation. In an 1851 letter to the actress, which he appended to a copy of *On My Works as an Author*—the book in which he acknowledges his authorship of "The Crisis"—Kierkegaard claims that although he published the article in a newspaper, it was designed to be read as a letter, and that although it had many addressees, it was destined to be read by one auditor alone. "Whether it was read at that time by many or only by a few—if you did not read it, then it is the author's opinion that it has not reached its destination," Kierkegaard explains to Fru Heiberg. "But on the other hand, if you have read it—if it was then found to be, if not in perfect, yet in happy accord with your thoughts on that subject, then it is the author's opinion that it has indeed reached its destination."[97]

Interestingly, this epistolary confession went through two drafts, neither of which was addressed to Luise Heiberg. Instead, Kierkegaard was writing to her husband. And although both drafts were designed to accompany a copy of *On My Work as an Author*, only one of them mentions this famed actress. Curiously, the other draft of Kierkegaard's letter resumes his indirect critique of Heiberg in "The Crisis." In addition to reminding him of their different publication rates, Kierkegaard mocks the commercialism of what little Heiberg produces, especially the literary "gifts" from which he continues to profit during the holiday season.

> Dear Sir:
> Although I almost have no reason to fear that receiving this little pamphlet [*On My Work as an Author*] may once again cause you some discomfort by letting you sink deeper into a debt that you have repeatedly assured me that you hoped soon to rid yourself of by returning the favor, surely you will easily be able to understand that I, who know how insignificant my gifts are and how insignificant the giver is in comparison with the recipient, cannot in this case give in to such an unreal fear; I must instead reverse the relationship and consider this a new debt I owe to you or as an old debt to you into which I am sinking more deeply because once more you have the kindness to be willing to accept such an insignificant little gift from the insignificant author of all these insignificant gifts.
> Yours respectfully, S. K.[98]

Had Kierkegaard attached this letter to *On My Work as an Author* and mailed both texts to J. L. Heiberg, the polemical thrust of "The Crisis" would have been obvious. But he did not. Heiberg had no idea that the article was a critique of his intellectual and cultural elitism designed to rally public opinion to Kierkegaard. If literate Denmark was its anonymous addressee and Fru Heiberg was its intimate auditor, her husband was the article's ignorant witness. This became painfully apparent in January 1856, when

Heiberg published Kierkegaard's letter to his wife in a liberal Copenhagen newspaper—and with it a letter of his own, written just weeks after his antagonist's death, in which he recommends "The Crisis" to all of literate Denmark, insisting that the article "deserves to be read anew, if for nothing else, then for the contempt with which it dismisses current incompetent theater criticism in all its esthetic thinness and moral baseness."[99] Clearly, Heiberg was referring to the public's habitual admiration of his wife. In praising "The Crisis" for its critique of "esthetic thinness and moral baseness," however, was he not also referring to himself, unwittingly deriding the "especially ornate" copybooks with "many blank pages" on which he had been capitalizing for years? Had Kierkegaard lived to see this hilarious turn of events, he probably would have written a letter of thanks to Heiberg. And with any amount of luck, Heiberg would have published this one, too.

6

OPPOSITIONAL POLITICS IN THE AGE OF ACADEMIA

The troublemaker is precisely the one who tries to force sovereign power to translate itself into actuality.

—GIORGIO AGAMBEN

Dilemmas of Learned Advocacy

Imperial Rome, feudal France, Enlightenment Prussia, and Golden Age Denmark have little in common with one another. Nor do any of these historical periods bear a striking resemblance to our own. Nevertheless, as we have seen, the specific rhetorical situations in which Seneca, Christine, Kant, and Kierkegaard intervened have a secret affinity with the relations of power in which many of today's learned advocates now find themselves. The disempowerment of the Roman Senate and the concentration of executive power during Nero's reign parallels the circumvention of shared governance by centralized college administrations; the ducal attempt to privatize and profit from the king's public authority in late-medieval France compares to the privatization and exploitation of the university's traditionally public services (knowledge production and dissemination) by powerful corporate sponsors; the acceleration of state censorship in conservative Prussia during the French Revolution accords with the post-9/11 effort to regulate and monitor outspoken scholars by the national security state; and the outburst of populist reason and anti-intellectual sentiment in mid-nineteenth-century Denmark mirrors the incitement of public opinion against progressive academics by today's right-wing advocacy groups.

And how about the rhetorics of withdrawal, exemplarity, obedience, and identification? Are these strategies, like the situations for which they were geared, analogous to those of contemporary academics? Not quite. In fact, the persuasive techniques and resistant practices of Seneca, Christine, Kant, and Kierkegaard are largely antithetical to those of their academic successors—and, as I argued in chapter 1, this is precisely why they are worthy of recuperation. Each is an antidote to one of four basic obstacles to learned advocacy in the age of academia. Seneca's rhetoric of withdrawal counteracts the politics of desertion implicit in the specialized, disciplinary language of late-modern academics; Christine's rhetoric of exemplarity challenges their tendency to rely on linear, abstract, and hyperrational forms of argument; Kant's rhetoric of obedience offsets their Dreyfusard inheritance of overt dissent and radical opposition to public authority; and Kierkegaard's rhetoric of identification short-circuits the prevailing Marxist standards of vanguard leadership to which many of them continually aspire. Neither obscure eggheads nor rationalist debaters nor radical dissidents nor revolutionary pedagogues, the learned political agents envisioned by this book occupy a zone of indiscernibility between academic professionalism and the tradition of the intellectual.

In order to understand the political potential of this liminal position, we must first clarify the dilemmas of learned advocacy from which the rhetorics of withdrawal, exemplarity, obedience, and identification offer an escape. As Seneca well knew, the political abstention of Thrasea Paetus posed a serious threat to imperial control. And as Marxist scholars continue to remind us, desertion remains a viable mode of dissent. "Battles against the Empire might be won through subtraction and defection," Michael Hardt and Antonio Negri insist. "This desertion does not have a place; it is the evacuation of the places of power."[1] Although certainly relevant to public officials like Thrasea, the politics of desertion has little to offer today's educated elites, many of whom are already struggling to overcome "ivory tower" estrangements from "the real world." And history is not on their side. From Epicurus to Thoreau, learned practitioners of desertion have done little more than reinforce the classical belief that, whatever else it involves, the life of the mind is fundamentally subtracted from the realm of public affairs, its only outward appearance being a state of absentmindedness or, as Hannah Arendt sharply notes, "an obvious disregard for the surrounding world."[2]

Nowhere is this disregard more apparent than in the specialized, professional language of contemporary academics. Like that of Cicero's philosopher, their discourse "has no equipment of words or phrases that catch the popular fancy."[3] And like that of Plato's philosopher, it limits their audience to "the very few," all but completely secluding their principles and their politics from "the general run of men."[4] On this point, critics of American academic culture have a history of outspokenness. "It leads the individual, if he follows it unreservedly, into bypaths still further off from the highway where men, struggling together, develop strength," John Dewey warned in 1902.[5] "Campuses are their homes; colleagues are their audience; monographs and specialized journals their media," Russell Jacoby went on to explain later in the century. "Unlike past intellectuals they situate themselves within fields and disciplines—and for good reason. Their jobs, advancement, and salaries depend on the evaluation of specialists, and this dependence affects the issues broached and the language employed."[6] Make no mistake: from Plato's Academy to our own, the desertion of popular culture has been a condition of possibility for scholarly discussion and debate. Recovering the Senecan art of withdrawal, which derives its strength from an enfoldment rather than an evasion of publicity, can offset this academic tradition, allowing absentminded professors to remain safely concealed and actively engaged in rhetorical cultures that have little tolerance, and even less respect, for the arcane language on which their livelihoods depend.

In addition to trading in specialized, jargon-clotted vocabularies, learned advocates in the age of academia have a tendency to deploy them in linear, abstract, and hyperrational forms of argument. In keeping with the substance of their scholarly debates, the style of their public advocacy is often devoid of rhetorical flourish and personal identity, more closely resembling claims in a quasi-logical demonstration than passionate interventions in the world around them. Christine's rhetoric of exemplarity challenges this form of public discourse. Consistent with the "feminine style" that would later rise to prominence in the electronic age, her appeal to the queen is "inductive, even circuitous, moving from example to example," without regard for "deductive forms of organization."[7] By replacing syllogisms with enthymemes and enthymemes with exemplary figures, her letter upended the arcane, scholastic prose of earlier generations, supplanting formal logic with associative reason, arid debate with personal testimony, hypothetical claims with historical narratives, and combative tones with themes of reconciliation. Indeed, long before Jacoby realized "the danger of yielding to a new Latin, a new scholasticism insulated from larger public life," Christine was arguing by example against the old Latin, the old scholasticism—and encouraging other learned advocates to do the same.[8]

For Kant, the rhetoric of obedience was a cunning alternative to the radical politics of his French contemporaries—the same politics that would later find expression in Zola's open letter to the president of France and its attendant "Manifesto of the Intellectuals." As we have seen, it was the radical political rhetoric of these educated elites, more than their artistic, literary, and scholarly achievements, that crystallized the social category of "the intellectual." And it was in tribute to this radicalism that postwar academics and activists would later mourn the migration of intellectual life into institutions of higher education, where, in exchange for financial security and social stability, men and women of letters were accused of relinquishing their former authority as public advocates. Kant's correspondence with the king troubles this hackneyed narrative, reminding us that learned political rhetoric can and often does emerge from within the firewalls of academic jargon, though rarely in the form of radical dissent. Anticipating Michel Foucault's image of the "specific intellectual" and, more recently, Bruce Robbins's theory of "professional oppositionality," Kant manipulated his renowned conceptual distinction between "public" (freely critical) and "private" (duty bound) uses of reason in order to contest, without directly challenging, Prussian government officials. That he did so in the preface of a book designed to radicalize the university system only enhanced his political opposition, reminding readers then and now that acts of *"subtle deception"* are not only legitimate but also sometimes required in professional academic systems.

If Kant troubles the ideology of dissent in terms of which many academics understand their relation to power, Kierkegaard questions the politics of representation in terms of which they regularly understand their relation to the people. Preempting classical Marxist conceptions of vanguard leadership, he refuses to speak for the masses, much less to rally their anonymous constituents against abusive figures of authority. Instead, Kierkegaard invites his readership to interrogate the systems of power that continually position educated elites as the conscious spokespersons for diffuse ensembles of presumably unconscious individuals and groups. The test of learned advocacy in the academic era, he suggests, is not our willingness to represent "the people" but our ability to identify with its anonymous elements. Thus, if Kant's rhetoric of obedience allows us to deconstruct the false oppositions between deference and dissent, academic professionalism and public intellectualism, Kierkegaard's rhetoric of identification encourages us to dislocate the question of learned activism from the ongoing "culture war" between populist, right-wing advocacy groups and the "tenured radicals" from whom they claim to protect "the people."

Where are we, then? At the risk of putting too fine a point on this summary, we might say that the rhetoric of withdrawal challenges our attitude toward *publicity*, the rhetoric of exemplarity challenges our attitude toward *persuasion*, the rhetoric of obedience challenges our attitude toward *power*, and the rhetoric of identification challenges our attitude toward *the people*.

Publicity, persuasion, power, and the people—few issues are more in need of consideration by today's learned advocates. And like many dilemmas of contemporary academic culture, these issues are difficult to untangle and nearly impossible to address all at once. Nevertheless, in keeping with the critical-historical method of this book, we can begin both tasks by drawing these issues into alignment with one of the historical texts in which their interrelationship first became intelligible. Thus, by way of conclusion, I would like to consider one more instance of learned advocacy and, in so doing, to offer a tentative answer to one of the basic questions of this book: How can educated elites in the academic era, when the tradition of "the intellectual" has been reduced to ruins, pose a meaningful challenge to abusive figures of authority?

After Strauss

In the second half of the 1920s, just as the American university was rising to international prominence, Bertolt Brecht began a series of short stories about a "thinking man" named Mr. Keuner. Among the first stories he published was "Measures Against Power" (*Maßnahmen gegen die Gewalt*), the opening passage of which warrants close scrutiny:

> As Mr. Keuner, the thinking man [*der Denkende*], was speaking out against power in front of a large audience in a hall, he noticed the people [*die Leute*] in front of him shrinking back and leaving. He looked around and saw standing behind him—Power [*die Gewalt*].
> "What were you saying," Power asked him.
> "I was speaking out in favor of Power," replied Mr. Keuner.
> After Mr. Keuner had left the hall, his students inquired about his backbone. Mr. Keuner replied: "I don't have a backbone to be broken. I'm the one who has to live longer than Power [*Gerade ich muß länger leben als die Gewalt*]."[9]

Clearly, Mr. Keuner is no Cynic. Unlike Diogenes, who famously ordered Alexander the Great to step aside and then openly rebuked his authority as king, Mr. Keuner refuses to play the part of the *parrhesiastes*. His conduct more closely resembles that of a Stoic sage. Recall, for instance, Seneca's seventy-third letter to Lucilius, in which he cleverly subverts the authority of the principate to criminalize Stoicism: "It seems to me erroneous to believe that those who have loyally dedicated themselves to philosophy are stubborn and rebellious, scorners of magistrates or kings or of those who control the administration of public affairs. For, on the contrary, no class of man is so popular with the philosopher as the ruler is."[10] Given this attitude toward power, we might also recall the Straussian practice of "philosophic politics," a persuasive technique that, as we saw in chapter 1, involves "satisfying the city that the philosophers are not atheists, that they do not desecrate everything sacred to the city, that they reverence what the city reverences, that they are not subversives, in short, that they are not irresponsible adventurers but good citizens and even the best of citizens."

To be sure, Mr. Keuner is intent on appeasing Power. However, the conduct of this "thinking man" differs from philosophic politics in three fundamental ways, each of which indexes a central theme of this book. First, the proper site of philosophic politics is not the political activity of thinking men and women but rather their philosophical tracts and treatises. Thus, in searching for the philosophic politics of Mr. Keuner, Strauss and his successors would have us focus not on his interaction with Power, but instead on the writings for which he has come to be known as a "thinking man." As we saw in chapter 1, this emphasis on the rhetorical and political undercurrents of philosophical discourse brings with it a tendency to ignore the overt political rhetoric of key figures in the history of ideas. Second only to Marxist and deconstructionist critiques of philosophy, the Straussian hunt for philosophic politics has enabled this trained incapacity to persist. As a "thinking man" engaged in his political culture, and without reference to an overarching philosophical corpus, Mr. Keuner enables us to correct this methodological blind spot further, suggesting that learned advocacy in the age of academia need not index a scholarly corpus, even if it remains closely tied to the identity of "the scholar."

Second, the Straussian practice of philosophic politics consists in defending the discipline of philosophy, not advocating for political or social change. For Strauss, "there is no necessary connection between the philosopher's indispensible philosophic politics and the efforts which he might or might not make to contribute toward the establishment of the best regime."[11] For Mr. Keuner, on the other hand, the profession of thought—and with it his identity as a "thinking man"—is neither in need of defense nor distinct from his political activity, but instead available for use as a persuasive resource in his interaction with Power. Like Seneca, Christine, Kant, and Kierkegaard, he affects the discipline of philosophy but refuses to subtract himself and his thoughts from the realm of public affairs. Over and against the politics of desertion, Mr. Keuner sees the life of the mind as an occasion for learned advocacy, and learned advocacy as a mode of dissent that avoids all-or-nothing confrontation with public authority.

Finally, even when philosophic politicians do commit themselves to advocating for political or social change, they do not proceed as Mr. Keuner does, openly expressing and then immediately recanting their opposition to established figures of authority. Rather, they rely on what Strauss describes as "a peculiar technique of writing, and therewith to a particular type of literature, in which the truth about all crucial things is presented exclusively between the lines."[12] At the center of philosophic politics, then, is not a willingness to contradict oneself, depending on the occasion, but an effort to craft and circulate polysemous texts, in which unorthodox views are at once conveyed to potential sympathizers and concealed from established figures of authority. Although Seneca, Christine, Kant, and Kierkegaard relied on polysemy in their interactions with power, Mr. Keuner does not. For better and for worse, there is little ambiguity in his discourse. He simply contracts himself. As a "thinking man" heedless of the law of noncontradiction, Mr. Keuner marks the outer limit of strategic ambiguity, and thus the outer limit of the political agency discussed in this book.

What happens at this outer limit? Is this the point at which learned advocacy gives way to craven accommodation, as the response of his students suggests? And if not, how are we to understand Mr. Keuner's claim that he "has to live longer than Power"? Is there more at stake here than his personal and professional well-being? As we shall see, this "thinking man" does more than outlive power, and he does more than preserve his personal and professional well-being along the way. Like many of today's learned advocates, he toggles inconclusively between rhetorics of deference and dissent, obedience and opposition, resulting in a fractious and seemingly inconsistent articulation of personal, professional, and public interests. What we have here, I would like to suggest, is not a craven act of accommodation but an undecidable form of political contention—specifically one that allows "thinking" men and women to occupy and undermine existing systems of authority, tactfully yet effectively mobilizing certain power relationships in order to oppose others. Theorizing this undecidable form of political contention, especially as it relates to other modes of dissent, is the challenge now before us.

Parrhesia, Protest, and Deliberative Democracy

When asked to imagine political dissidence, many of us envision one of three activities: revolt, protest, or resistance. By *revolt*, I mean the irregular, extraconstitutional, and/or violent overthrow of established authorities by a popular movement.[13] By *protest*, I mean the activity of coordinated social movements, specifically the open, organized, collective, and sustained effort by ordinary citizens to challenge prevailing systems of power. And by *resistance*, I mean the oblique yet constant struggle of relatively powerless individuals and groups against ruling elites who expect little more from them than submission and compliance.[14]

Revolts and protests are *overt acts of dissent*. Their agents pose a direct, public challenge to established figures of authority. Practitioners of resistance, on the other hand, are rarely so open with their contention. Their disputes with power usually find expression in *covert acts of dissent*. Nevertheless, when we consider the sociopolitical landscapes in which these three activities tend to occur, the kinship between resistance and revolt becomes apparent. Both are characteristic of *closed political orders*, where state censorship often prevails. Protests, on the other hand, are characteristic of *open political orders*, where freedom of expression is thought to reign supreme.

Like most typologies, this one is interesting for what it excludes. When positioned alongside one another, these descriptions of revolt, resistance, and protest reveal a curious gap in our understanding of political contention. Although we have a name for overt acts of dissent in closed political orders (revolt), a name for overt acts of dissent in open political orders (protest), and a name for covert acts of dissent in closed political orders (resistance), we have no name for *covert acts of dissent in open political orders*. Why not? Is it because covert dissent never occurs in free society? Certainly not. At issue here is not its occurrence but its legitimacy: It is not that covert acts of dissent never take place in open political orders, but that many of us believe they *have no place* in these orders. For academics and activists alike, they are the part of free society that has no part to play in its transformation.

If covert acts of dissent often go unnamed in open political orders, it is because they call into question the basic principle of deliberative democracy: freedom of expression. That "freedom of expression" was itself a trademarked term until the fall of 2004, making its circulation anything but "free," should give us pause.[15] But ironies of this sort rarely do. From ancient Athens to late capitalism, an unfettered logos has been the centerpiece of democratic thought and the lifeblood of its heroic practitioners. "In the heart of every democrat," John Durham Peters quips, "beats the pulse of Athens envy, a desire to put on a toga and speak swelling oratory."[16] And not just any kind of swelling oratory: underpinning our appreciation for democratic discussion and debate is the Greek tradition of "frank speech" (*parrhesia*), which continues to goad us with openly critical, personally risky, and (thus) conventionally courageous forms of public address—in short, ways of speaking that look nothing like covert dissent.[17]

More than swelling orators in the age of Athens, however, today's deliberative democrats resemble Roman senators in the age of Nero or, put a bit more archly, faculty senators in the age of the academy. Many of us would rather revel in the aura of free speech than grapple with any evidence of its decline, be it a cleverly trademarked phrase like "freedom of expression" or a covert act of dissent like that of Mr. Keuner. This is partly because we have allowed our fascination with persuasion, which presupposes an egalitarian order of discussion and debate, to obscure the fact that much of today's democratic deliberation occurs in subtly authoritarian orders of collective life, where the principle of hierarchy can be shown to underwrite all claims of egalitarianism. In these arenas, the crucial question is not "How might things be otherwise?" but instead, as Kenneth Burke reminds us, "Just how does the hierarchic principle work in this particular scheme of equality?"[18]

Parrhesia is part and parcel to this misrecognition. "All speech is subject to the problems of power inequalities and deception," Elizabeth Markovits explains, cautioning us against any idealist inattention to "the threat of power and intimidation" in contemporary democratic public culture. "The problem with *parrhesia* is that it claims exemption from such human constraints."[19] Much like its modern outlet, the bourgeois public sphere, *parrhesia* is at once a utopian ideal and an exclusionary norm of deliberative democracy.[20] This does not mean that "frank speech" cannot be heard in democratic discussion and debate. Nor is it to suggest that this valiant way of speaking is limited to members of the ruling class. But it is to remind us that the personal risks and political impediments of "frank speech," and thus the courage and the strength required of its practitioners, are unevenly distributed among today's democratic citizen-subjects. Indeed, not everyone can afford to play the part of the *parrhesiastes*. And for those who cannot, cunning dissent remains an available mode of political contention.

Parrhesia is not the only figure of deliberative democracy to militate against this cunning alternative. Another is the modern nation-state. With the development of centralized, relatively democratic states in North America and western Europe came unprecedented resources and opportunities for disadvantaged political subjects—often at the behest of radical pedagogues—to mount, coordinate, and sustain direct confrontations with powerful opponents.[21] And with these confrontations came an abiding democratic romance with forms of dissent that are *organized, collective,* and *sustained* instead of uncoordinated, individualized, and opportunistic—and not only organized, collective, and sustained, but also *oppositional* and *openly antagonistic*. To be sure, it was coordinated social protest, not the practice of covert dissent, that captured and continues to inspire the modern democratic imagination, allowing relatively disempowered individuals and groups to channel their limited political resources into collective outbursts of *parrhesia*.

Given this historico-political kinship, it is no surprise that coordinated social protests are often thought to index the health and vibrancy of democratic public culture. "The rise and fall of social movements mark the expansion and contraction of democratic opportunities," Charles Tilly explains. "If social movements begin to disappear, their disappearance will tell us that a major vehicle for ordinary people's participation in public politics is waning."[22] In this sense, our penchant for coordinated social protest, and with it our aversion to covert acts of dissent, is bound up with our commitment to the modern democratic state.

Nor is it surprising that coordinated social movements and modern democratic states share many of the same threats. Governmental decentralization, extensive privatization of state functions, the eclipse of the national state by transnational powers—all are common dangers. That these dangers have never loomed larger than they do today makes it especially important to reflect on our inherited notions of political contention. Must our dissent be unreserved, openly confrontational, and personally risky in order to pose a meaningful challenge to established figures of authority? And must it be organized, collective, and sustained in order to effect lasting social change? Or is there room in deliberative democracy for something different, something more akin to resistance, something more closely resembling the conduct of Mr. Keuner?

A New Line of Inquiry: Resistance and Relative Power

If indeed Mr. Keuner is engaged in an act of dissent, but his behavior looks nothing like a protest, and even less like a revolt, what are its salient features? As I see it, his conduct has four basic characteristics: (1) it requires little or no coordination or planning, (2) it relies on implicit understandings and information networks, (3) it resembles a kind of individual self-help, and (4) it avoids direct confrontation with the powers that be.[23] In short, Mr. Keuner's conduct is *opportunistic, appropriative, individualized,* and *noticeably evasive*.

In this sense, it is tempting to identify his speech and action with the resistant practices of marginalized individuals and groups. Consider, for instance, the accommodation techniques of immigrant groups, or the "counter-school" culture of lower-class youths, or the passing practices of queered identities, or everyday forms of workplace dissent such as foot shuffling, dissimulation, false compliance, and feigned ignorance.[24] Mr. Keuner's speech and action also recall persuasive techniques characteristic of ordinary public discussion and debate, such as the request, negative politeness, and the tag question, as well as discourse particles such as "yeah-no" and "I don't know," both of which work wonders in conversational transitions from subordinate to dominant speakers.[25]

However, as James C. Scott is keen to remind us, these are all "weapons of the weak." What distinguishes the oppositional politics of Mr. Keuner is the relative power with which he wields it. Clearly, he is a teacher. That he presides over a lecture hall full of students further suggests that he is a university professor. Although the political potential of his professional identity remains to be seen, it is obvious at this point in our analysis that Mr. Keuner has enough linguistic authority to address and influence a mass audience. Indeed, he already possesses what many marginalized individuals and groups still struggle to achieve: institutionalized access to a prevailing medium of mass communication. Add to this the likelihood that the "Power" against which he positions himself is also that which allows him to do so before a mass audience, and the extent of his privilege becomes even more apparent.

In this sense, Mr. Keuner's conduct presents us with a curious line of inquiry: How can people in positions of relative power, notably educated elites in late-modern democratic culture, work against the very systems that give them privilege? In order to begin answering this question, we must be willing to widen the gyre of "dissent" to include not only conduct occurring in the margins of society, but also speech and action located at the very center of power, resulting in another, more pointed line of inquiry: How can academics like Mr. Keuner position themselves in and against established relations of power, mobilizing certain systems of authority in order to oppose others? At issue here, as Jean-François Lyotard notes, is "a strategy which can dispense with exteriority, which, as far as language is concerned, would not place itself outside the rules of the discourse of Truth, that is of the discourse of power, but inside those rules." By using "what is said" to pronounce and withstand "what allows one to say it," strategies of this sort can "tap the strength of power to neutralize it."[26]

That learned advocates can infiltrate public authority and render it inoperative does not mean they can alter its function as a repressive apparatus. On the contrary, as Alain Badiou notes in his consideration of state power, "it cannot change, save hands."[27] To this extent, it is not enough to widen our understanding of dissent to include opposition occurring at the center of power. We also must be willing to subtract this understanding, and perhaps even the question of social change itself, from the politics of emancipation, notably the classical Marxist call for a revolutionary suppression of the state. Scholarship on the resistant practices of marginalized individuals and groups has already begun this task, showing how relatively powerless citizen-subjects can manipulate prevailing systems of authority to their minimum disadvantage.[28] The speech and action of Mr. Keuner calls us in a similar direction, allowing us to refine our line of inquiry even further: How can learned advocates in the academic era confound and defy these same systems, without in turn forfeiting the linguistic and cultural authority that allows them to do so?

The Philosopher, the People, and the Powers That Be

Despite his authority to address and influence a mass audience of students, Mr. Keuner is unable to baulk Power without jeopardizing his personal and professional well-being. He is, to borrow Pierre Bourdieu's apt description of late-modern academics, a *dominated member of the dominating class*—an authority in the field of cultural production but a subordinate in the overarching field of political power.[29] That his speech and action resemble "weapons of weak" and his reliance on these weapons invite students to question his "backbone" is in keeping with this liminal subject position. Like many of today's would-be intellectuals, Mr. Keuner feels solidarity with any and all dominated political subjects, even though the linguistic authority with which he discloses this solidarity identifies him with dominating systems of power.

This awkward political identity is integral to his status as a "thinking man." In fact, cultivating this liminal position has often been the basic political task of major Western thinkers. From Seneca to Christine to Kant to Kierkegaard, the history of Western thought is riddled with efforts to occupy the borderlands between sovereignty and subordination, membership in dominating groups and subservience to most of its members. In order to specify the political agency of Mr. Keuner and its relevance to educated elites in the academic era, when dilemmas of publicity, persuasion, power, and the people continue to inhibit their activism, we must consider the kinship between this "thinking man" and his sociohistorical predecessor, "the philosopher."

Few aspects of "philosophy" are more venerable than its relation of alterity to ordinary and official public cultures. Since Greek antiquity, the profession of thought has struggled to subtract itself from the intellectual pursuits of ordinary people and the ideological interests of public officials. This first relation of alterity finds its representative anecdote in the sixth book of the *Republic*, where Plato tries to insulate *philosophia* from the "multitude of pretenders unfit by nature, whose souls are bowed and mutilated by their vulgar occupations even as their bodies are marred by their arts and crafts."[30] At issue here, as Jacques Rancière rightly notes, is at once the subordination of "those dedicated to labor to those endowed with the privilege of thought," and the authority of these privileged thinkers to determine who, among the totality of thinking men and women, has the right to practice "philosophy."[31]

By relegating the thoughts of ordinary people to "non-philosophy," Plato established the authority of the philosopher to legislate intellectual life. In so doing, he also positioned the philosopher as a censorious spokesman for the inferior class to which these "bowed" and "mutilated" non-philosophers belong. With the advent of Marxism, this spokesmanship took on a new form, reemerging as an intense commitment to the purity of *the people, the plebeians, the masses*, or, reversing Plato's indictment of "vulgar occupations," *the proletariat*. Instead of censoring the thoughts of ordinary citizen-subjects, as Heiberg and other nineteenth-century elites did, Marx and his successors celebrated the anonymous inclusion of these individuals in specific social categories, suggesting that "people like that are the more to be admired the more they adhere strictly to their collective identity, and that they become suspect, indeed, the moment they want to live as anything other than legions and legionaries." "Solemn admiration for the unknown soldiers of the proletarian army," "tender-hearted curiosity about their anonymous lives," "nostalgic passion for the practiced movements of the craftsman"—all were freely offered by philosophers after Marx.[32]

The strength of this relationship between the philosopher and the people was contingent on their mutual opposition to established figures of authority. If there was a discrepancy between the consciousness of vanguard philosophers and the unconsciousness of their non-philosophical legions, it was because an evil third party—*the ideologist, the master thinker, the ruling class*, or, as Brecht puts it, *Power*—kept it this way. Consider, for instance, Gramsci's indictment of "the Church" for maintaining a hierarchical split between "intellectual" and "simple" communities of the faithful. Instead of "raising the simple to the level of the intellectuals," the Catholic Church leaves them in "their primitive philosophy of common sense." And it does this "by imposing an iron discipline on the intellectuals so that they do not exceed certain limits of differentiation." Only in defiance of this third party can the intellectual and the simple, the philosopher and the people, "destroy the widespread prejudice that philosophy is a strange and difficult thing just because it is the specific intellectual activity of a particular category of specialists or of professional and systematic philosophers."[33] Or so the argument goes.

In their mutual exclusion from the profession of thought, power and the people became its negative conditions of possibility. By exaggerating the positivity of the masses as an active subject and pitting this anonymous collectivity against the interests of an overarching ideological apparatus, Marxist philosophers were able to establish a political identity apart from their professional lives—or, as Rancière sarcastically remarks, "a dignity independent of their occupational status alone."[34] It was in keeping with this independent dignity that Zola and the Dreyfusards transformed themselves from academics, artists, and writers into "intellectuals." And it is in pursuit of this independent dignity that many of today's learned advocates often proceed, descending from the "ivory tower" in moments of public crisis in order to demonstrate their "reverence for non-philosophy and denunciation of ideological vanities."[35]

Although it is tempting to align Mr. Keuner with this tradition, we cannot ignore the fact that his interaction with Power takes place in a lecture hall, presumably on a college campus and in all likelihood during a class session. Nor can we ignore his students' abhorrence of this interaction. Like his Marxist predecessors and their intellectual siblings, he is a dominated member of the dominating class. But unlike these learned political agents, his subordination to Power does not lend itself to solidarity with his students. Publicity, persuasion, and the people—all seem out of reach to Mr. Keuner. Nevertheless, as we shall see, his conduct manages to render Power mute and inoperative, and all before a captive, albeit frustrated, mass audience. How this happens and what it means for learned advocacy in the age of academe are the questions to which we now turn.

Neither Demagogues, nor Show-Offs, nor Strongmen

Given their marginal status as "dominated parties within the field of power," it is not uncommon to see thinkers like Mr. Keuner wielding weapons of the weak against abusive figures of authority.[36] Seneca, Christine, Kant, and Kierkegaard all accessed this arsenal in their letters to power. But this is not the only way that educated elites have made use of their marginal status. The history of Western thought suggests two additional applications, both of which are implicit in the foregoing discussion, and both of which differ significantly from Mr. Keuner's "measure against power."

The first is Straussian and provides a counterpart to the practice of "philosophic politics." In addition to guarding themselves against established figures of authority, philosophers often seek their protection from what Plato called "the madness of the multitude."[37] "I do not believe in the possibility of a conversation of Socrates with the *people*," Strauss explains in a letter to Alexandre Kojève. Rather, "the relation of the philosopher to the people is mediated by a certain kind of rhetoricians who arouse fear of punishment after death; the philosophers can guide these rhetoricians but can not do their work."[38] Trapped between the depravity of the masses and the persecution of the ideologist, the philosopher seeks to avoid both hazards by counseling power on how best to pacify the people.

The second use to which their marginal status has often been put is Marxist and originates in the relation of alterity between working, learned, and ruling classes. Over and against Straussian political agendas, Marxist thinkers have a tendency to use their membership in the dominating class to advance the interests of dominated individuals and groups. "The philosophy of praxis does not tend to leave the 'simple' in their primitive philosophy of common sense," Gramsci reminds his fellow intellectuals, "but rather to lead them to a higher conception of life."[39] With this leadership comes a political program that transforms the philosopher "from a supplier of the productive apparatus into an engineer who sees it as his task to adapt this apparatus to the purposes of the proletarian revolution."[40] Thus, for "dominated dominators" in the Marxist tradition, the profession of thought consists in a decisive betrayal of their class origins.

If Straussian thinkers use the ideologist to subdue the masses, which in turn enables them to protect their occupational status, Marxist thinkers use their occupational status to rally the masses against the ideologist. If the former strategy originates in the conservatism of Plato and culminates in the academic expertise of "the technocrat"—or, as is more often the case, "the pundit"—the later strategy originates in the cosmopolitanism of Diogenes and culminates in the late nineteenth- and quintessentially twentieth-century tradition of "the intellectual." Learned advocates in the academic era often align themselves with one of these political traditions, either capitalizing on their likeness to established figures of authority or disavowing this likeness entirely. Interestingly, Mr. Keuner avoids both options. Unlike Straussian propagandists, who mediate their relation to "the many" through an alliance with "the few," Mr. Keuner refuses to allow Power to seclude him from his mass audience. But neither does he use his interaction with Power as an occasion to establish a vanguard relation to his students, as a classical Marxist pedagogue would. Instead, Mr. Keuner allows them to *observe* his interaction with Power, thereby transforming his students from addressees into auditors. No longer are they the passive recipients of his public discourse; when Power enters the lecture hall, they become its judging spectators.

How are we to understand this unique triangulation of the philosopher, the people, and the powers that be? We could do worse than recall the epistolary rhetorics of Seneca, Christine, Kant, and Kierkegaard. What separates their letters from those of other figures in the history of ideas is their function as dialogues with power staged for an array of third parties. Anticipating much of today's e-mail advocacy—in which Listservs, forwarded notes, replies to all, and blind carbon copies regularly blur the line between private and public address—their correspondence suggests that the art of lettered dissent, like letter-writing itself, requires a synchronization of intimate and impersonal audiences. Mr. Keuner seems to know as much. His response to Power is at once narrowly addressed and open to the judgments of his students. And like the wider reading public of witnesses and eavesdroppers for which Brecht published "Measures Against Power," Mr. Keuner's judging spectators are neither directly involved nor entirely remote from his interaction with Power. Instead, by "shrinking back" from this interaction, they become a physical assembly of auditors that, much like the virtual assembly of witnesses and eavesdroppers implicit in Brecht's written narrative, is uniquely poised to assess the speech and action of this "thinking man."

But we might also do better. Although its rhetorical function is epistolary, the material form of his interaction with Power is not. As Brecht is careful to indicate, the medium in which Mr. Keuner interacts with his students and Power is speech, not writing. Like that of many contemporary academics, his activism begins in the lecture hall, not on the printed page. Indeed, he seems to have realized what critical social theorists have been suggesting for decades: the resistant potential of intellectual labor in the academic era consists in the fact that, although most professors have little control over the apparatus of higher education as a whole, many exercise considerable authority in their individual classrooms; and this relative autonomy in the social field of educational production is a condition of possibility for their subversion of power relationships in the political field of bourgeois ideology. On this point, Erik Olin Wright is characteristically pointed: "The internal social relations within the university facilitate the penetration and consolidation of antibourgeois ideology."[41]

But that was the late 1970s. Since then, the social relations of educational production have shifted considerably. Most college instructors are now mired in economies of contingent labor, where freedom of expression in and beyond the classroom is less a right than a risk.[42] And even their tenured and tenure-track colleagues are less autonomous than they used to be, largely on account of private advocacy groups like Campus Watch, Students for Academic Freedom, NoIndoctrination.org, and the American Council of Trustees and Alumni, all of which continue to recruit undergraduate students in their ongoing effort to monitor and avenge "classroom abuses" in the American academy. According to Ellen Schrecker, this is precisely why today's right-wing assault on academic culture is more dangerous than that of the McCarthy era: "it reaches directly into the classroom."[43] Indeed, as Brecht reminds us in "Measures Against Power," lecture halls are the contested sites of learned advocacy in the age of the academy.

This is not to suggest that populist right-wing attacks on American academic culture are confined to the college classroom. On the contrary, most indictments of "liberal bias," "political correctness," "reverse discrimination," "multicultural relativism," and the like occur online, where student accusers usually go unnamed, leaving accused professors with few, if any, legal protections. Unlike print publishers, who are liable for every text they release, owners of passive websites are not responsible for the comments of their online visitors. Only those who post these comments are liable for them, and only when their identities are known can they be held to account. Thus, as long as their student accusers remain anonymous, libeled college instructors have no avenues of legal redress. Add to this the serious likelihood that any professor who is visible enough to incur online scrutiny would be deemed a "public figure," and thus obliged to demonstrate the "actual malice" of his or her accusers, and the possibility of a libel suit seems even more remote.[44]

In an era of smart phones, digital recorders, and nonstop Internet access, outspoken academics also run the risk of encountering their lectures online, or at least incriminating snippets of them. And as right-wing activist Andrew Jones recently demonstrated, private advocacy groups are more than willing to compensate offended students for making this possible: $100 for recorded lectures and handwritten notes from a left-leaning course, $50 for the notes alone, and $10 for the course handouts. Backing this bounty hunt was the Bruin Alumni Association, a conservative group of UCLA graduates dedicated to combating their alma mater's "continued slide into political partisanship and indoctrination."[45] Although Jones later rescinded his cash offer—largely in response to university officials, who warned him that recording faculty lectures and posting them online was a violation of copyright law, and one for which his "newsgathering" students would be legally liable—he continues to insist that classroom surveillance of this sort is protected by the First Amendment.

And, in a sense, he is correct. "Under existing copyright law, a professor's lectures are clearly protected against publication and distribution without the author's permission," Robert O'Neil explains. "However, it is equally clear that students enrolled in the course are free to take even verbatim notes for their own needs and are presumably just as free to share those notes with fellow students."[46] Moreover, as long as they limit themselves to excerpts, fragments, and summaries of these lectures and notes, students are free to disseminate them online, even if this means posting them on websites owned by private advocacy groups like the Bruin Alumni Association.

How, then, are outspoken academics to defend themselves? Although their prospects of legal remedy are severely limited, their resources and opportunities for public rebuke are not. One option is to defend themselves and their courses on the same websites where conservative students routinely post their frustrations. Take NoIndoctrination.org. In addition to inviting students to report on bias and imbalance in the college classroom, the website allows vilified professors to respond to their anonymous accusers. Although responses of this sort can do a good job of setting the record straight, they often leave untouched the broader, more intractable issue of classroom surveillance. Moreover, they do little to improve the public authority of progressive academics, thus allowing the conservative advocacy groups that manage these websites to maintain their anti-intellectual stranglehold on public discussion and debate.

Another, more cunning, and certainly more counterintuitive maneuver would be for left-leaning academics to ambiguate or, better still, to sublimate the partisanship of their lectures and in-class discussions, artfully encrypting without ever abandoning their political agendas. Doing so would deprive conservative activists like Andrew Jones of the "radical professors" on whom their right-wing populist appeals depend. Indeed, not even David Horowitz, who accounts for his rise to stardom with "two words: Ward Churchill," would be able to withstand this assault.[47] But at what cost to learned advocacy would the sublimation of "radical professors" come? Many left-leaning college instructors would rather endure the scattered attacks of David Horowitz than do without the exemplary figure of Ward Churchill. And for good reason: In addition to highlighting one of the key dilemmas of learned advocacy in deliberative democracy, namely, the reciprocally constitutive relationship between academic radicalism and right-wing populism, the polemic between Horowitz, Churchill, and their various supports has reinvigorated public deliberation on the problems and the prospects of intellectual politics in the age of academia.

Nevertheless, just as the social relations of educational production have shifted since the late 1970s, limiting the ability of most college instructors to articulate and defend "antibourgeois ideology" in the classroom, so, too, have these social relations shifted since the attacks of 9/11, making it equally difficult for college instructors to play the part of public intellectuals. One notable shift, which continues to receive vast amounts of scholarly attention, is the increase—and the increasing imbrication—of administrative, corporate, populist, and governmental abuses of power. Another important shift in the social relations of educational production, which has only begun to catch the attention of learned advocates, is the "open educational resources" movement. Since 2001, when MIT launched its OpenCourseWare initiative, faculty members around the world have been recording their undergraduate lectures and posting them online, resulting in thousands of new educational offerings, the vast majority of which are open to anyone with an Internet connection. Indeed, thanks to distributors like iTunes U, which has now garnered more than 100 million downloads, many academics are expanding their lecture halls to include not only students enrolled in their classes but also members of the general public. Consider, for instance, the MIT collection. Nearly half of its 1.2 million visitors per month are neither educators nor undergraduates, but instead "self-learners"—ordinary men and women who are not enrolled in a formal education program.[48] And the ratio is even more stunning at Yale: 69 percent of those who view its online lectures are independent learners.[49]

We could go on listing statistics, but the point seems clear enough. Implicit in the open educational resources movement is a unique, and as yet unrealized, opportunity for left-leaning instructors at all academic ranks to rival in publicity and popular appeal the conservative advocacy groups that continue to surveil their classrooms. By sublimating their political agendas in lectures fit to become open educational resources, they can begin to transform themselves from ivory tower malcontents into what the *New York Times* recently described as "the tweedy celebrities of cyberspace."[50] And we need look no further than the rhetorics of withdrawal, exemplarity, obedience, and identification for the political resources needed to initiate this transformation. If the rhetorics of withdrawal and obedience allow tenured professors and contingent instructors alike to protect themselves from abusive figures of authority in and beyond the American academy, the rhetorics of exemplarity and identification enable them to strengthen their appeals to mass audiences in and beyond its established network of college campuses.

If only this were enough. Truth be told, these resources are no match for the reluctance of "tenured radicals" to play the part of "tweedy celebrities." Much of this has to do with their fear of Pyrrhic victories. That the convincingness of their social and political critiques might come to depend less on compelling analyses and revolutionary insights than on totalizing and completely tenuous agreements with public opinion is a prospect that few engaged professors are willing to consider.[51] But it has more to do with their fixation on the written word. Many learned advocates in the academic era cling to the aura of print culture, heedless of the fact that, as Foucault realized decades ago, "the threshold of *writing*, as the sacralizing mark of the intellectual, has disappeared."[52] On top of this, many of them, like Henry A. Giroux, are suspicious of online forums of collective life, where they see little more than "a dumbed-down cultural apparatus" at work, allowing "a generation of young people hooked on the immediacy and high interactivity of an audio and visual culture" to hasten the development of "a new kind of society of the spectacle," and with it "a new kind of thoughtlessness."[53] Fear of Pyrrhic victories, fixation on print culture, antipathy for online communities—all mitigate against the political potential of the open educational resources movement, isolating learned advocates in the academic era from a vast and truly public culture of "independent learners," most of whom, unlike traditional undergraduates, are eager to attend and abide by their lectures.

Which brings us back to "Measures Against Power." As we have seen, Mr. Keuner's interaction with Power transforms his students from the passive recipients of his discourse (addressees) into its judging spectators (auditors), and in so doing aligns them with the wider public of witnesses and eavesdroppers for which Brecht published this story. Is this not a literary-political version of the participation framework characteristic of the open educational resource movement, in which the spatiotemporal remoteness of enrolled and independent learners gives way to imagined communities of deliberation and decision-making? And are these imagined communities not, in turn, newer, more media-savvy versions of the discerning citizenries for which public intellectuals before the age of academia once wrote?

Maybe so. But what of Mr. Keuner? Does this make him an academic intellectual in the tradition of Zola and the Dreyfusards? Certainly not, especially when we consider how little he does to mobilize his students. Indeed, our "thinking man" refuses to play the part of a radical pedagogue. Nevertheless, as Walter Benjamin points out, he is still the "leader" of his students—but not in the usual sense of this word. "He is in no way a public speaker, a demagogue; nor is he a show-off or a strongman."[54] What separates Mr. Keuner from these familiar figures of leadership is his lack of distinction. Like the "unrecognizable ones" of which Kierkegaard wrote, he refuses to "give direct help, speak plainly, teach openly, assume decisive leadership of the crowd."⁵⁵ Indeed, as Benjamin goes on to explain, his concerns and commitments are "light-years away from what people nowadays understand to be those of a leader." Like the Greek *koinos* from which his name derives, Mr. Keuner—or, as Brecht occasionally referred to him, "Keunos"—is a figure of the commons, every part of which belongs to "the people." And like this anonymous collectivity, he is no one in particular, a German *keiner*, a "nobody." In this sense he is also like Odysseus, who made his escape as "Noman" from the cave of Polyphemus. Both are men of "many devices," Benjamin notes— "infinitely cunning, infinitely discreet, infinitely polite, infinitely old, and infinitely adaptable." And both are "much enduring."⁵⁶

In this sense, Mr. Keuner is less a political leader than one of Brecht's "political models." His arguments and his attitudes are not only "quotable" but also objects of political judgment. Thus, if Mr. Keuner is a political model, it is because he provides his students with an exemplary figure. And it is the *subjective purposiveness* of this exemplary figure—namely, its *being-for* their power of judgment—that allows us to specify their relationship with Mr. Keuner. As a "thinking man" who is willing to speak out against Power but unwilling to do so consistently, he is at once a part of and apart from the tradition of "the intellectual" in terms of which his students, like many of Brecht's readers, attempt to understand his conduct. In addition to exhibiting the intelligibility of this tradition (this being his function as a *paradeigma*), Mr. Keuner steps out from it, establishing himself as a singular exclusion (this being his function as an *exemplum*). In so doing, he encourages his students-turned-spectators to question this tradition, if only by insinuating a moment of *krisis* in its attendant conception of "leadership." To be sure, Mr. Keuner's interaction with Power is difficult to admire. But it is also difficult to ignore the way in which it brings his students "to the point where they become clear about the assumptions that have led them to the so-called leaders, the thinkers or politicians, their books or speeches," thereby enabling them "to subject these assumptions to as thorough a criticism as possible."⁵⁷

How effective is this political maneuver? Clearly, Mr. Keuner's students are critical of his response to Power. And given their query about his "backbone," it seems they are also critical of the assumptions that led them into his lecture hall. But what of their relation to Power? Are they also critical of the assumptions that made them shrink back, and even to flee the room, when Power appeared? To what extent does Mr. Keuner encourage them to doubt, and perhaps even to contest, this abusive figure of authority? Might their frustration with his conduct inspire them to pursue alternate, more assertive forms of learned advocacy? Maybe even to recuperate the tradition of the intellectual? Or does his interaction with Power, like Seneca's soliloquy on death, leave them in the throes of deliberation, with little inclination and even less ability to engage in political contention? Which is another way of posing the question with which Benjamin concludes his analysis of Mr. Keuner's conduct: "What is it good for?"

The Revelation and Seizure of Executive Potential

Although his influence is difficult to determine, we know enough about Mr. Keuner to indicate how his speech and action function as dissent. Like the subjects of this book and many of today's educated elites, he is able to address and affect mass audiences but is not invulnerable to the powers that be. His conduct in the classroom reflects this liminal position. One minute he is speaking out against Power, and the next he is disavowing this critique. As he shifts between rhetorics of dissent and deference, Mr. Keuner reminds us that the radicalism of "the intellectual" and the professionalism of "the academic" are no longer mutually exclusive forms of political intelligence, one of which aims to contest and the other of which serves to legitimate established figures of authority. In the age of academia, learned advocates can and should be both at once—"leading spokespersons, diffident supporters and reactionaries at one and the same time—that is, legitimists in some areas of political discourse and action, and contesters in others."[58]

At issue here is a form of "professional oppositionality" that looks much like resistance. For learned advocates in late modernity, "conformity is often a self-conscious strategy and resistance is a carefully hedged affair that avoids all-or-nothing confrontations."[59] More strident than the "philosophic politics" of Platonists, Straussians, and technocrats but also more subtle than the "frank speech" of Cynics, Marxists, and orthodox intellectuals, this line of conduct neither challenges Power directly nor facilitates its unrestrained operation. Instead, it goads Power into an executive posture and then, when a direct conflict seems imminent, uses techniques of submission and compliance to delegitimize the use of force. The display of Power is in this way denied access to the exercise of violence, be it physical, financial, or, as is often the case, professional. "How provoking it can be to have nothing justifiable to be provoked about, to find oneself sputtering with rage while the object sits there sweetly," Peters comments, adding captions to this curious form of provocation. "Aggressiveness is instantly exposed as illegitimate."[60]

By ruling out aggression, Mr. Keuner manages to escape the grasp of Power. Here, I am not referring the impalpable concept of "public authority" but instead to one of its innumerable centers—a specific locus of authority in and through which discernible acts of control, supervision, prohibition, and constraint take place. Willful college administrators, avid corporate sponsors, overzealous advocacy groups, paranoid government agencies—all are centers of authority in the academic era, and all are implicit in Brecht's use of the term "Power." Instead of *Kraft* or *Stärke* or *Wucht*, each of which suggests a kind of physical strength, Brecht uses the term *Gewalt* to describe Mr. Keuner's superior. Like *Herrschaft*, *Macht*, and *Machtbefugnis*, *Gewalt* is another word for "lordship." But unlike these sibling terms, all of which imply forms of sovereignty and coercion, *Gewalt* brings with it a distinct sense of "public authority" (*öffentliche Gewalt*), specifically one in which power is distributed across a network of separate agencies (*Gewaltentrennung*), each of which in turn is invested with a specific, localized form of "administrative authority" (*Verwaltungsgewalt*). In addition to executive power (*vollziehende Gewalt*), legislative power (*gesetzgebende Gewalt*), and judicial power (*richterliche Gewalt*), all of which are presumably equalized by a system of "checks and balances" (*Gewaltenteilung*), *Gewalt* lends itself to asymmetrical relations of power, in which varying degrees of "operating potential" (*ausführende Gewalt*) can be shown to exist.

Thus, what enters Mr. Keuner's lecture hall and begins to interrogate him is neither a tyrant nor a sovereign, but instead *a figure of public authority whose operating potential exceeds his own*. And what he manages to escape is not his general subordination to "public authority" but instead the *specific surplus potential of Gewalt*. Moreover—and this is the crucial point—he does so without contesting this surplus potential, and yet in such a way that renders its possessor mute and inoperative. How is this possible?

By speaking out against Power before a mass audience, Mr. Keuner compels Power to reveal itself as a repressive apparatus, thereby depriving it of all mystical advantage. If being powerful means not having to act, Mr. Keuner revokes this privilege. No longer does Power have the ability to conceal its operating potential.[61] But neither does it have the ability to actualize this potential. By inverting his critique with an all-too-perfect attention to detail—"I was speaking out in favor of Power"—Mr. Keuner arrests Power in its passage from a state of executive potential to one of executive action. It is precisely here, in the revelation and the seizure of this potential to control, supervise, prohibit, and constrain his conduct, that the speech and action of Mr. Keuner become legible as modes of dissent.

Contingency Beyond Contradiction

As we have seen, Mr. Keuner's interaction with Power presents us with a curious line of inquiry: How can people in positions of relative power, specifically late-modern academics, confound and defy the very systems of authority on which their privileged status depends? At issue here, I suggested, is the degree to which we are willing to subtract our understanding of dissent, and perhaps even the question of social change itself, from the politics of emancipation. In the last few pages of this book, I would like to return to this topic. In particular, I would like to consider some of its political and theoretical entailments, especially as they find expression in Mr. Keuner's parting comment: "I'm the one who has to live longer than Power."

One way to interpret this comment is in terms of Hegelian political philosophy. I have in mind here Hegel's use of the word *Eigensinn*, meaning "stubbornness" or "obstinacy" or, as it is often translated, "self-will." Subordinates who have not "experienced the fear of death," he tells us in his famous analysis of "Lordship and Bondage," can achieve little more than tactical prowess—a narrow cleverness in the service of petty, finite self-interests. Theirs is what Hegel describes as "freedom which is still enmeshed in servitude," where "enmeshed" translates the German *stehenbleibt*, meaning "paused," "standing still," and "arrested."[62] Through the optics of Hegelian *Eigensinn*, it is Mr. Keuner, not Power, who seems arrested in the passage from potentiality to actuality—in this case, his potential to speak freely, as an autonomous political subject, as a *parrhesiastes*, or, in keeping with the theme of this book, as a public intellectual.

But this is not the only way to interpret his parting comment. Another comes to us in Giorgio Agamben's treatment of the Greek *adynamia*, meaning "incapacity" or "the potential not to be." Building on Aristotle's account of sensation (*aisthésis*), Agamben insists that every potential to be or do is always also a potential *not* to be or do. If this were not the case—which is to say, if every potentiality (*dynamis*) was not always also an impotentiality (*adynamia*)—"potentiality would always already have passed into act and be indistinguishable from it." It is within this "abyss of potentiality" that freedom takes root. "To be free," Agamben concludes, is *"to be capable of one's own impotentiality."*[63] In this sense, the determining feature of freedom is not our mastery over objective being, as Hegel suggests, but our ability to exist in relation to our own privation, our own incapacity—in short, our own non-Being.

Clearly, Mr. Keuner has the potential to speak out against Power. But it is his ability to remain silent, to *not* actualize this potential, that allows him to escape its grasp and, in so doing, to preserve this ability—along with himself and his livelihood—for future acts of moral menacing. Insofar as Mr. Keuner experiences freedom, then, it is not simply because he retains an ability to speak out against Power. Nor is it simply because he retains an ability to *not* speak out against Power. Rather, his freedom consists in the preservation of his potential to speak out *and* to shut up—to be *and* not to be—depending on the occasion. It is his authority to determine the moment, the means, and the extent of his resistance that allows Mr. Keuner to escape the grasp of Power. And it is his retention of this authority that enables him to outlive it.

When figured in terms of potentiality, Mr. Keuner's conduct appears contingent, not contradictory. It marks an ability to have left undone what he actually did, to have acted in one way or another—or not at all—in the moments before, during, and after his interaction with Power. In retaining this ability, Mr. Keuner preserves not only his potential to speak out and to shut up, depending on the occasion, but also his ability to negate any positive specification of this potential, to override any of its prior actualizations. That he objects to Power in one moment does not preclude his obedience to it in the next—and vice versa. Like Kant before him, Mr. Keuner knows that obedience today can and often does set the stage for opposition tomorrow. It is his authority to conclude without foreclosing either line of conduct that distinguishes Mr. Keuner from the simple servant. And it is his willingness to exercise this authority that distinguishes him from the unwavering dissident.

If he is neither a simple servant nor an unwavering dissident, what, exactly, is Mr. Keuner? All we know for sure is that his identity does not consist in a "single essence." Instead, as Benjamin points out, it involves "a continual readiness to admit a new essence."[64] Like the ēthos of Aristotle's rhetor, the public persona of Mr. Keuner is ever shifting, and always because of his speech, which is itself in constant flux with his rhetorical situation. If his conduct appears "inconsistent," it is because we have pigeonholed him as a "thinking man," allowing our "previous opinion that the speaker is a certain kind of person" to obscure the political identity implicit in his speech.[65] More specifically, it is because we have confined him to the discipline of philosophy, the modality of which is *necessity* and the law of which is *noncontradiction*. To stop here, however, is to miss one of the key features of his interaction with Power. Although it is attributable to a "thinking man," his conduct has little in common with philosophical inquiry. On the contrary, it more closely resembles political engagement, the modality of which is *contingency* and the law of which is *potentiality*. More than violating his identity as a "thinking man," and thus opening himself to the charge of inconsistency, Mr. Keuner leverages the profession of thought for purposes of rhetorical prodding and cunning subterfuge. For why would Power ever doubt a direct public statement—"I was speaking out in favor of Power"—from someone ostensibly bound by the law of noncontradiction?

To be sure, if there is a contradiction to be found in "Measures Against Power," it does not belong to Mr. Keuner's speech and action. Rather, it resides in the disjunction between the conduct we expect from this "thinking man" and the conduct in which he actually engages. Not surprisingly, the roots of this expectation stretch back to antiquity, when the measure of "thinking" men and women was the consistency of their thoughts and discourse. Consistency was also characteristic of their traditional objects of study, the classical canon, which comprised invariable laws, categories, ideas, and the like. Hence the ancient antagonism between the philosopher and the citizen: "To the citizens' ever-changing opinions about human affairs, which themselves were in a state of constant flux, the philosopher opposed the truth about those things which in their very nature were everlasting and from which, therefore, principles could be derived to stabilize human affairs."[66] As a "thinking man" with shifting opinions and a taste for political contention, Mr. Keuner subverts this ancient antagonism. Like the minor political rhetorics discussed in this book, his interaction with Power suggests that the relationship between the philosopher and the citizen—or, more to the point, educated elites and their political cultures—can and should be something other than a "scandalous contradiction between the postulated unity of truth and the factual plurality of opinions."[67]

In this sense, Mr. Keuner is neither a Platonist nor a Cynic, neither a Straussian nor a Marxist, neither a technocrat nor an intellectual. His measures against Power are also measures against our expectation that learned advocates in the academic era will choose between these figures, as though "philosophic politics" and "frank speech" were the only modes of political engagement available to them. Moreover, they are measures against our belief in a radical disjunction between these two practices, the former being presumably "conservative" and the other the latter being presumably "progressive." However precise, this political binary often blinds us to the fact that "philosophic politics" and "frank speech" both thrive on conflicts between the philosopher's commitment to "truth" and the citizen's subservience to "opinion." For if truth seeking were not dangerous to established orders of the political, the philosophic politician would have no excuse to elude the realm of human affairs; and if truth telling were not dangerous to the philosopher, the *parrhesiastes* would derive little moral authority from challenging the opinions of this realm. Like both of these historico-political figures, Mr. Keuner is a "thinking man" engaged in his political culture. And yet he neither seeks the truth nor speaks it to power. It is the threat of political darkness, not the splendor of philosophical truth, that compels him to argue against Power and then, when Power appears, to recant his critique, thereby preserving his ability to resume it at a later date.

So where does this leave us? As we have seen, what qualifies Mr. Keuner's political activity as a mode of dissent is the fact that it comes at the expense of established authority. In speaking out against Power before a mass audience, he deprives Power of its impotentiality, specifically its ability to refrain from action, to *not* reveal itself as a repressive apparatus. And by immediately recanting his critique, just as Power is beginning to assume an executive posture, he deprives it of its potentiality, specifically its ability to actualize its executive potential. In so doing, Mr. Keuner forces Power into the modality of the necessary, leaving it with no choice but to appear and fail to function as a repressive apparatus.

To this extent, it is our "thinking man," not Power, who governs their interaction. And this is precisely what defines his speech and action as "measures against power"—*Maßnahmen gegen die Gewalt*. If *Gewalt* calls our attention to the surplus potential of Power, specifically its ability to control, supervise, prohibit, and constrain Mr. Keuner, Brecht's use of the term *Maßnahmen*, meaning not only "measures" but also "arrangements," "sanctions," and "provisions," allows us to indicate the structural vocation of this thinking man's dissent. In taking measures against Power, Mr. Keuner *authorizes, anticipates,* and *arranges for* the appearance and immediate arrest of its surplus potential—and all before a mass audience of judging spectators intent on critiquing their "so-called leaders," be they "thinkers or politicians."

What we have here is certainly not a politics of emancipation. But neither is it freedom enmeshed in servitude. Rather, it is a form of political contention in which endurance still matters. Like Seneca, Christine, Kant, and Kierkegaard before him, Mr. Keuner refuses to allow self-sacrifice to be the final testament of his convictions. But neither does he allow this refusal to preclude his critique of Power. Against the surplus potential of his adversary, and the control it exerts over his professional life, he posits an incorrigible unwillingness to forfeit his livelihood. For as Mr. Keuner well knows, and as many of today's learned advocates have yet to realize, the profession of thought becomes a resource for political contention when established figures of authority take this profession as their object of scrutiny, prohibition, and constraint. Unlike that of Zola and the Dreyfusards, his opposition does not exceed his livelihood. It is, above all, a *professional opposition*.

Is this a contradiction of terms? Not for academics like Mr. Keuner, whose political and professional identities consist in "multiple and uneven activities, loyalties, obligations, desires, and responsibilities."[68] It is here, in this inconsistent consistency—what Foucault would later champion as "a plentitude of the possible"—that the livelihood of our "thinking man" becomes a vital political force, allowing him to exceed and constrict or, more precisely, *to exceed by constricting* the surplus potential of Power.[69] In this sense, his professional opposition is also a *living opposition*—an opposition that is larger, more extensive, and richer in political potential than his adversary. Cultivating this inordinate political potential is ultimately what it means to outlive Power. And outliving Power, as the figure of "the intellectual" could not, is the foremost challenge of learned advocates in the age of academia.

NOTES

CHAPTER I

1. Russell Jacoby, *The Last Intellectuals: American Culture in the Age of Academe* (New York: Basic Books, 1987); Richard A. Posner, *Public Intellectuals: A Study of Decline* (Cambridge: Harvard University Press, 2001).
2. Ernst H. Kantorowicz, *The King's Two Bodies: A Study in Medieval Political Theology* (Princeton: Princeton University Press, 1957).
3. These characterizations derive from the audience design framework of Allan Bell, "Language Style as Audience Design," *Language and Society* 13, no. 2 (June 1984): 145–204. See also Allan Bell, "Back in Style: Reworking Audience Design," in *Style and Sociolinguistic Variation*, ed. Penelope Eckert and John R. Rickford (Cambridge: Cambridge University Press, 2001), 139–69.
4. Edward W. Said, "The Public Role of Writers and Intellectuals," in *The Public Intellectual*, ed. Helen Small (Oxford: Blackwell, 2002), 28.
5. On the Christian imperative to be in but not of the world, see John 15:19 and 17:11–19; on the Stoic obligation to live as though dead, see Diogenes Laertius, *Lives of Eminent Philosophers*, 7.2.
6. Interestingly, Kierkegaard saw this characteristically Stoic attitude toward death as a feature of radical Christianity: "Believe that you gain everything; you thereby die to the world. And when you are one who is dead, you lose nothing by losing that which in the understanding of the living is everything." Søren Kierkegaard, *Christian Discourses/The Crisis and a Crisis in the Life of an Actress*, ed. and trans. Howard V. Hong and Edna H. Hong (Princeton: Princeton University Press, 1997), 146.
7. Michel Foucault, *The Hermeneutics of the Subject: Lectures at the Collège de France, 1981–1982*, ed. Frédéric Gros, trans. Graham Burchell (New York: Palgrave Macmillan, 2001), 504.
8. Dante, *Inferno*, 4.130–44; Richard Rorty, *Consequences of Pragmatism (Essays: 1972–1980)* (Minneapolis: University of Minnesota Press, 1982), 92.
9. Karl Jaspers, *The Great Philosophers: The Foundations*, ed. Hannah Arendt, trans. Ralph Manheim (New York: Harcourt, Brace & World, 1962), xi.
10. Peter Sloterdijk, *Critique of Cynical Reason*, trans. Michael Eldred (1983; repr., Minneapolis: University of Minnesota Press, 1987), 16.
11. Leo Strauss, *On Tyranny* (1963; repr., New York: Free Press, 1991), 205–6.
12. Leo Strauss, *Persecution and the Art of Writing* (Glencoe: Free Press, 1952), 25. Cf. Leo Strauss, *The City and the Man* (Chicago: Rand McNally, 1964), 54.
13. Strauss was not alone in this argument. On the self-consciously persuasive aspect of philosophical discourse, see also Martin Warner, *Philosophical Finesse: Studies in the Art of Rational Persuasion* (Oxford: Oxford University Press, 1989); John J. Richetti, *Philosophical Writings: Locke, Berkeley, Hume* (Cambridge: Harvard University Press, 1983). A similar faith in the rhetorical agency of thinking men and women may be found in "contextualist" studies such as those contained in James Tully, ed., *Meaning and Context: Quentin Skinner and His*

Critics (Princeton: Princeton University Press, 1988); Anthony Pagden, ed., *The Languages of Political Theory in Early-Modern Europe* (Cambridge: Cambridge University Press, 1987); J. G. A. Pocock, *Virtue, Commerce, and History: Essays on Political Thought and History, Chiefly in the Eighteenth Century* (Cambridge: Cambridge University Press, 1985).

14. Walter Benjamin, "Theses on the Philosophy of History," in *Illuminations*, ed. Hannah Arendt, trans. Harry Zohn (New York: Schocken Books, 1968), 254, 263.

15. See Jacques Derrida, *Who's Afraid of Philosophy? Right to Philosophy I*, trans. Jan Plug (Stanford: Stanford University Press, 2002), 135.

16. On the concept of "minor literature," see Gilles Deleuze and Félix Guattari, *Kafka: Toward a Minor Literature*, trans. Dana Polan (Minneapolis: University of Minnesota Press, 1986). On its revision as "minor rhetoric," see Melissa Deem, "Stranger Sociability, Public Hope, and the Limits of Political Transformation," *Quarterly Journal of Speech* 88 (2002): 444–54.

17. See Gilles Deleuze and Félix Guattari, *A Thousand Plateaus: Capitalism and Schizophrenia*, trans. Brian Massumi (Minneapolis: University of Minnesota Press, 1987), 106.

18. Michel Foucault, "Truth and Power," in *Power*, ed. James D. Faubion (New York: New Press, 2000), 130.

19. Walter Benjamin, *The Arcades Project*, trans. Howard Eiland and Kevin McLaughlin (Cambridge: Harvard University Press, 1999), N9, 4.

20. See Kenneth Burke, *Attitudes Toward History*, 3rd ed. (Berkeley: University of California Press, 1984), 229.

21. Deleuze and Guattari, *A Thousand Plateaus*, 103.

22. Ernest J. Wrage, "Public Address: A Study in Social and Intellectual History," *Quarterly Journal of Speech* 33 (1947): 451–52.

23. Richly annotated discussions of these trends in American higher education may be found in Anthony J. Nocella II, Steven Best, and Peter McLaren, eds., *Academic Repression: Reflections from the Academic-Industrial Complex* (Edinburgh: AK Press, 2010). See also Cary Nelson, *No University Is an Island: Saving Academic Freedom* (New York: New York University Press, 2010).

24. For a pointed account of this recent development in academic culture, see Gaye Tuchman, *Wannabe U: Inside the Corporate University* (Chicago: University of Chicago Press, 2009).

25. On corporate abuses of power in the academy, see Jennifer Washburn, *University, Inc.: The Corporate Corruption of Higher Education* (New York: Basic Books, 2005). Other noteworthy treatments of this topic include Derek Bok, *Universities in the Marketplace: The Commercialization of Higher Education* (Princeton: Princeton University Press, 2003); Geoffrey White, ed., *Campus, Inc.: Corporate Power in the Ivory Tower* (Amherst, Mass.: Prometheus Books, 2000); Lawrence C. Soley, *Leasing the Ivory Tower: The Corporate Takeover of Academia* (Boston: South End Press, 1995).

26. Not surprisingly, these attempts have met with many outcries of "New McCarthyism." See, for instance, Ellen Schrecker, "The New McCarthyism in Academe," *Thought & Action* 21 (Fall 2005): 103–28; Jonathan R. Cole, "The New McCarthyism," *Chronicle of Higher Education*, 9 September 2005, B7–B8; Joel Beinin, "The New American McCarthyism: Policing Thought About the Middle East," *Race & Class* 46, no. 1 (July–September 2004): 101–25; David Cole, "The New McCarthyism: Repeating History in the War on Terrorism," *Harvard Civil Rights–Civil Liberties Law Review* 38, no. 1 (Winter 2003): 1–30.

27. On the activities of these well-funded organizations, see John K. Wilson, *Patriotic Correctness: Academic Freedom and Its Enemies* (Boulder, Colo.: Paradigm, 2008); Bruce L. R. Smith, Jeremy D. Mayer, and A. Lee Fritschler, *Closed Minds? Politics and Ideology in American Universities* (Washington, D.C.: Brookings Institution Press, 2008); John K. Wilson, *The Myth of Political Correctness: The Conservative Attack on Higher Education* (Durham: Duke University Press, 1995).

28. Nelson, *No University Is an Island*, 91.

29. John Dewey, "Academic Freedom," in *John Dewey: The Middle Works, 1899–1924*, ed. Jo Ann Boydston (Carbondale: Southern Illinois University Press, 1976), 59.

30. Randolph Bourne, *The Radical Will: Selected Writings, 1911–1918*, ed. Olaf Hansen (Berkeley: University of California Press, 1992), 331.

31. Michael Bérubé, "Foreword: The Company We Keep," in Nocella, Best, and McLaren, *Academic Repression*, 4. These echoes are especially loud in closed political orders, where higher education systems are often nationally organized, centrally funded, and, not surprisingly, more vulnerable to academic repression. Although it is beyond the scope of this book to address this issue, the need for additional scholarship on the resistant practices of African, Asian, Middle Eastern, Latin American, and even western European academics is worth noting. See, for instance, part 3 of Evan Gerstmann and Matthew J. Streb, eds., *Academic Freedom at the Dawn of a New Century: How Terrorism, Governments, and Culture Wars Impact Free Speech* (Stanford: Stanford University Press, 2006).

32. Andrew Ross, "Defenders of the Faith and the New Class," in *Intellectuals: Aesthetics, Politics, Academics*, ed. Bruce Robbins (Minneapolis: University of Minnesota Press, 1990), 127. See also Bruce Robbins, *Secular Vocations: Intellectuals, Professionalism, Culture* (London: Verso, 1993).

CHAPTER 2

1. Seneca, *Ad Lucilium epistulae morales*, trans. Richard M. Gummere (Cambridge: Harvard University Press, 1917), 75.1 (hereafter cited as *Epistulae morales*).

2. Ibid., 75.1–2. Here, "affectedly" translates the Latin *putide*, from *puditum*—that which, in being overly formal and artificial, offends the taste. On the ancient trope of correspondence as conversation, which persisted well into modernity, see Roger Chartier, Alain Boureau, and Cécile Dauphin, *Correspondence: Models of Letter-Writing from the Middle Ages to the Nineteenth Century*, trans. Christopher Woodall (Princeton: Princeton University Press, 1997), 132–34; David M. Henkin, *The Postal Age: The Emergence of Modern Communications in Nineteenth-Century America* (Chicago: University of Chicago Press, 2006), 109–11.

3. Seneca, *Epistulae morales*, 40.1.

4. See, for instance, ibid., 8.2, 21.5.

5. See Miriam T. Griffin, *Seneca: A Philosopher in Politics* (Oxford: Oxford University Press, 1976), 353.

6. See ibid., 417–18. For an example of the frequency of Lucilius's letters, see Seneca, *Epistulae morales*, 50.1.

7. There was, of course, nothing new in this practice. See Michael Trapp, "Introduction," in *Greek and Latin Letters: An Anthology*, ed. Michael Trapp (Cambridge: Cambridge University Press, 2003), 22: "The use of the letter as a vehicle for what were in effect short treatises offering advice or instruction, addressed to a specified individual but intended from the start for a broader readership too, had been flirted with by Isocrates, and decisively endorsed by Epicurus, already in the fourth century B.C." On Seneca's place in this tradition, see Trapp, "Introduction," 25–26; D. A. Russell, "Letters to Lucilius," in *Seneca*, ed. C. D. N. Costa (London: Routledge and Kegan Paul, 1974), 72–79.

8. M. Luther Stirewalt, *Studies in Ancient Greek Epistolography* (Atlanta: Scholars Press, 1993), 3.

9. Disseminating texts in the first century had little in common with modern publication practices. Copyright laws and other legal safeguards were unheard of in Seneca's day. Although Pliny's letters and Martial's epigrams suggest that a Roman book trade was in place by the end of the century, the circulation of books, letters, poems, speeches, and the like remained a person-to-person enterprise well into the Middle Ages. See E. J. Kenney, "Book Readers in the Roman World," in *The Cambridge History of Classical Literature*, ed. P. E. Easterling and E. J. Kenney (Cambridge: Cambridge University Press, 1982), 3–31.

10. Griffin, *Seneca*, 339.

11. Stirewalt, *Studies in Ancient Greek Epistolography*, 18–19.
12. Seneca, *Epistulae morales*, 38.1.
13. Demetrius, *De elocutione*, in *Ancient Epistolary Theorists*, ed. Abraham J. Malherbe (Atlanta: Scholars Press, 1988), §232.
14. Seneca, *Epistulae morales*, 34.2.
15. Tacitus, *The Annals*, trans. John Jackson (Cambridge: Harvard University Press, 1937), 14.53–56. For a critical inquiry into Tacitus's account of these events, see Theresa K. Roper, "Nero, Seneca and Tigellinus," *Historia: Zeitschrift für Alte Geschichte* 28, no. 3 (1979): 346–57. A summary discussion and literature review is provided in Vasily Rudich, *Political Dissidence Under Nero: The Price of Dissimulation* (London: Routledge, 1993), 268–69.
16. Extensive discussions of face work and politeness theory are provided in Erving Goffman, *Interaction Ritual: Essays on Face-to-Face Behavior* (Garden City, N.Y.: Doubleday, 1967); Penelope Brown and Stephen C. Levinson, *Politeness: Some Universals in Language Usage* (Cambridge: Cambridge University Press, 1987).
17. Tacitus, *Annals*, 14.12.
18. See Jürgen Malitz, *Nero*, trans. Allison Brown (Oxford: Blackwell, 2005), 15–23.
19. Tacitus, *Annals*, 13.4.
20. Andrew Wallace-Hadrill, "*Civilis princeps*: Between Citizen and King," *Journal of Roman Studies* 72 (1982): 43.
21. Cassius Dio, *Roman History*, 57.11.3.
22. See Frank Frost Abbott, *A History and Description of Roman Political Institutions*, 3rd ed. (New York: Biblo and Tannen, 1963), 384.
23. Miriam T. Griffin, *Nero: The End of a Dynasty* (New Haven: Yale University Press, 1984), 90.
24. Léon Homo, *Roman Political Institutions: From City to State* (New York: Barnes & Noble, 1962), 302.
25. Griffin, *Nero*, 60, 89–90.
26. Abbott, *History and Description of Roman Political Institutions*, 383–84.
27. That Nero was concerned about this possibility is well indicated in the speech he later wrote for Thrasea's trial. See Tacitus, *Annals*, 16.27.
28. Ibid., 16.22.
29. See Griffin, *Nero*, 171–77. See also Griffin, *Seneca*, 366.
30. See Ramsay MacMullen, *Enemies of the Roman Order: Treason, Unrest, and Alienation in the Empire* (Cambridge: Harvard University Press, 1966), 46–48.
31. See Griffin, *Seneca*, 102–3, 365–66.
32. Seneca, *De brevitate vitae*, in *Seneca: Moral Essays*, trans. John W. Basore (Cambridge: Harvard University Press, 1932), 18.1. See also Griffin, *Seneca*, 320.
33. Seneca, *De brevitate*, 15.5. Cf. Aristotle's praise of contemplation in *Nicomachean Ethics*, 1177b, and Socrates's statement on exile in the *Republic*, 496d–e. On the subsequent history of this tradition, see Hannah Arendt, *The Human Condition* (Chicago: University of Chicago Press, 1958), 14–15: "To the ancient freedom from the necessities of life and from compulsion by others, the philosophers added freedom and surcease from political activity (*skholē*), so that the later Christian claim to be free from entanglement in worldly affairs, from all the business of this world, was preceded by and originated in the philosophical *apolitia* of late antiquity."
34. Seneca, *De brevitate*, 19.3.
35. Seneca, *De tranquillitate animi*, in Basore, *Seneca*, 5.5.
36. Ibid., 4.1–3.
37. Ibid., 5.4.
38. Ibid., 10.4.
39. Ibid., 14.2–3; see also 15.2–5.
40. Hannah Arendt, *Thinking*, in *The Life of the Mind* (San Diego: Harcourt, 1978), 156. This characterization of Stoicism is the latest in a line of interpretation extending from Hegel's philosophy of history and history of philosophy, to Zeller's articulation of Greek thought, and into the work of T. A. Sinclair and Moses I. Finley. A useful revision of this tradition

may be found in Malcolm Schofield, "Social and Political Thought," in *The Cambridge History of Hellenistic Philosophy*, ed. Keimpe Algra, Jonathan Barnes, Jaap Mansfeld, and Malcolm Schofield (Cambridge: Cambridge University Press, 1999), 739–70.

41. See Michel Foucault, *Fearless Speech*, ed. Joseph Pearson (Los Angeles: Semiotext[e], 2001), 150.

42. Seneca, *De otio*, in Basore, *Seneca*, 3.3–4.

43. Ibid., 4.1.

44. Christopher Gill, "Stoic Writers in the Imperial Era," in *Cambridge History of Greek and Roman Political Thought*, 599.

45. See Malcolm Schofield, *The Stoic Idea of the City* (Cambridge: Cambridge University Press, 1991), chap. 4; Doyne Dawson, *Cities of the Gods: Communist Utopias in Greek Thought* (New York: Oxford University Press, 1992), chap. 5.

46. Seneca, *De otio*, 6.3.

47. See Marcia L. Colish, *The Stoic Tradition from Antiquity to the Early Middle Ages*, vol. 1 (Leiden: Brill, 1990), 1:59. On the communicative ethics and Stoic reverberations of Kantian rhetorical theory, see Samuel McCormick, "The Artistry of Obedience: From Kant to Kingship," *Philosophy and Rhetoric* 38, no. 4 (2005): 302–27.

48. Seneca, *De otio*, 3.5.

49. Ibid., 5.8. This passage is channeling Aristotle's *Politics*, 1325b. On the relationship between the Aristotelian polis and the Stoic cosmopolis, see Martha C. Nussbaum, *The Therapy of Desire: Theory and Practice in Hellenistic Ethics* (Princeton: Princeton University Press, 1996), 343–44. On the moral and political significance of contemplation, see Hannah Arendt, "Thinking and Moral Considerations: A Lecture," *Social Research* 38, no. 3 (Autumn 1971): 417–46; Hannah Arendt, "Truth and Politics," in *Between Past and Future: Eight Exercises in Political Thought* (New York: Penguin, 1980), 227–64.

50. Seneca, *Epistulae morales*, 85.36–38.

51. Seneca, *De otio*, 6.1–3.

52. See Paul Veyne, *Seneca: The Life of a Stoic*, trans. David Sullivan (New York: Routledge, 2003), 26. An extensive discussion of Seneca's career as *amicus principis* is provided in Griffin, *Seneca*, 76–103.

53. Seneca, *Epistulae morales*, 68.2.

54. For a more thorough discussion of this political practice, see Jacques Rancière, *Disagreement: Politics and Philosophy*, trans. Julie Rose (Minneapolis: University of Minnesota Press, 1999).

55. Seneca, *Epistulae morales*, 73.7–8.

56. Ibid., 72.8–9; see also 74.12.

57. Ibid., 73.6, 72.9–10.

58. Ibid., 74.13.

59. See Seneca, *De otio*, 4.2.

60. Seneca, *Epistulae morales*, 73.1–10.

61. Ibid.

62. Ibid.

63. Ibid., 75.1

64. See Griffin, *Seneca*, 337–39.

65. Veyne, *Seneca*, 119.

66. Vasily Rudich, *Dissidence and Literature Under Nero: The Price of Rhetoricization* (London: Routledge, 1997), 100.

67. Griffin, *Seneca*, 338.

68. Seneca, *Epistulae morales*, 43.3–5.

69. Ibid., 94.69–71.

70. Ibid., 19.2–3.

71. Seneca, *De tranquillitate animi*, 5.4.

72. Ibid., 19.3–4.

73. Seneca, *Epistulae morales*, 68.3–5.

74. See Aristotle, *Metaphysics*, 1004a.

75. Interestingly, the story opens with an epigraph ascribed to Seneca: "Nil sapientiae odiosius acumine nimio" (Nothing is more hateful to wisdom than excessive cunning). On the ambiguities of this quotation, not the least of which is its authorship, see Ross Chambers, "Narratorial Authority and 'The Purloined Letter,'" in *The Purloined Poe: Lacan, Derrida, and Psychoanalytic Reading*, ed. John P. Muller and William J. Richardson (Baltimore: Johns Hopkins University Press, 1988), 300–301.

76. Only Alkínoös, the Phaiákian king and host of this sonorous event, notices the sorrow of Odysseus. Because Alkínoös is still unaware of his guest's identity, however, he is unable to discern the connection between Odysseus and the song's content. For more on this event, see Martin Heidegger, *Early Greek Thinking*, trans. David Farrell Krell and Frank A. Capuzzi (New York: Harper & Row, 1975), 106–7.

77. Dennis Spencer to the City Council of Iowa City, Iowa, 18 May 1999, http://www.iowa-city.org/weblink/docview.aspx?id=5489&Page=28.

78. Seneca, *Epistulae morales*, 14.7–8, 103.5.

79. Veyne, *Seneca*, 160, 163.

80. Seneca, *Epistulae morales*, 73.1–2; see also 103.4–5.

81. Griffin, *Seneca*, 362.

82. Rudich, *Dissidence and Literature Under Nero*, 68.

83. Veyne, *Seneca*, 160–61.

84. Tacitus, *Annals*, 14.57. Cf. Griffin, *Nero*, 175, and Griffin, *Seneca*, 363.

85. Veyne, *Seneca*, 161.

86. See *Søren Kierkegaard's Journals and Papers*, vol. 1, ed. and trans. Howard V. Hong and Edna H. Hong (Bloomington: Indiana University Press, 1967), §1030.

87. Seneca, *Epistulae morales*, 22.8–9.

88. Foucault, *The Hermeneutics of the Subject*, 110–11.

89. Seneca, *Epistulae morales*, 26.4–7.

90. See, for instance, ibid., 30.18, 61.3–4, 69.6, 70.17, 101.7–8, 114.26–27.

CHAPTER 3

1. Seneca, *Epistulae morales*, 6.5.

2. Nussbaum, *Therapy of Desire*, 340. See also Stanley K. Stowers, *Letter Writing in Greco-Roman Antiquity* (Philadelphia: Westminster Press, 1986), 38.

3. See, for instance, Gerard A. Hauser, "The Example in Aristotle's Rhetoric: Bifurcation or Contradiction?" *Philosophy and Rhetoric* 1, no. 2 (1968): 78–90; Scott Consigny, "The Rhetorical Example," *Southern Speech Communication Journal* 41 (Winter 1976): 121–34; William Lyon Benoit, "Aristotle's Example: The Rhetorical Induction," *Quarterly Journal of Speech* 66 (1980): 182–92; Michael McGuire, "Some Problems with Rhetorical Example," *Pre/Text* 3 (1982): 121–36; James C. Raymond, "Enthymemes, Examples, and Rhetorical Method," in *Essays on Classical Rhetoric and Modern Discourse*, ed. Robert J. Connors (Carbondale: Southern Illinois University Press, 1984), 140–51; Gerard A. Hauser, "Aristotle's Example Revisited," *Philosophy and Rhetoric* 18, no. 3 (1985): 171–80; William L. Benoit, "On Aristotle's Example," *Philosophy and Rhetoric* 20, no. 4 (1987): 261–67; and Gerard A. Hauser, "Reply to Benoit," *Philosophy and Rhetoric* 20, no. 4 (1987): 268–73. A noteworthy escape from Aristotle's authority is John Arthos, "Where There Are No Rules of Systems to Guide Us: Argument from Example in a Hermeneutic Rhetoric," *Quarterly Journal of Speech* 89 (2003): 320–44.

4. One exception is John D. Lyons, *Exemplum: The Rhetoric of Exemplum in Early Modern France and Italy* (Princeton: Princeton University Press, 1989).

5. See Giorgio Agamben, "What Is a Paradigm?" (lecture, European Graduate School, Saas-Fee, Switzerland, August 2002), http://www.egs.edu/faculty/giorgio-agamben/articles/

what-is-a-paradigm/. See also Giorgio Agamben, *Homo Sacer: Sovereign Power and Bare Life*, trans. Daniel Heller-Roazen (Stanford: Stanford University Press, 1998), 22; Giorgio Agamben, *The Coming Community*, trans. Michael Hardt (Minneapolis: University of Minnesota Press, 1993), 9–10.

6. A more extensive treatment of ambiguity as the basis for transformation may be found in Kenneth Burke, *A Grammar of Motives* (Berkeley: University of California Press, 1945).

7. See Roland Barthes, *The Semiotic Challenge*, trans. Richard Howard (Berkeley: University of California Press, 1988), 56.

8. See Joseph R. Strayer, *On the Medieval Origins of the Modern State* (Princeton: Princeton University Press, 1970), 75.

9. See John Bell Henneman, "Nobility, Privilege, and Fiscal Politics in Late Medieval France," *French Historical Studies* 13, no. 1 (1983): 15.

10. See Richard Vaughan, *Valois Burgundy* (Hamden, Conn.: Archon Books, 1975), 50. Between 1382 and 1403, Philip is estimated to have showered himself with more than 1.3 million livres in royal gifts. Richard Vaughan, *Philip the Bold: The Formation of the Burgundian State* (Cambridge: Harvard University Press, 1962), 57.

11. Joseph R. Strayer, review of *Le domaine du roi et les finances extraordinaires sous Charles VI, 1388–1413*, and *Les finances royales sous Charles VI: Les causes du deficit, 1388–1413*, by Maurice Rey, *American Historical Review* 71 (1966): 935–36.

12. Edmund Fryde, "Royal Fiscal Systems and State Formation in France from the 13th to the 16th Century, with Some English Comparisons," *Journal of Historical Sociology* 4, no. 3 (September 1991): 276.

13. See ibid., 273–74.

14. Strayer, review of *Le domaine du roi et les finances extraordinaires sous Charles VI, 1388–1413*, and *Les finances royales sous Charles VI: Les causes du deficit, 1388–1413*, 935.

15. See Robert J. Knecht, *The Valois: Kings of France, 1328–1589* (London: Hambledon Continuum, 2004), 47.

16. As quoted in R. C. Famiglietti, *Royal Intrigue: Crisis at the Court of Charles VI, 1392–1420* (New York: AMS Press, 1986), 25.

17. It is difficult to understand this perception apart from the gender politics of monarchical France, which did not allow women to succeed to the throne. For a detailed consideration of this issue, and a concise review of the scholarship surrounding it, see Tracy Adams, "Christine de Pizan, Isabeau of Bavaria, and Female Regency," *French Historical Studies* 32, no. 1 (2009): 1–32. See also Katherine Crawford, *Perilous Performances: Gender and Regency in Early Modern France* (Cambridge: Harvard University Press, 2004).

18. As quoted in Famiglietti, *Royal Intrigue*, 28. On the political tradition of election by "maior et sanior pars," see Hilary J. Bernstein, *Between Crown and Community: Politics and Civic Culture in Sixteenth-Century Poitiers* (Ithaca: Cornell University Press, 2004), 101–2; Richard S. Katz, *Democracy and Elections* (Oxford: Oxford University Press, 1997), 20–21.

19. As quoted in Tracy, "Christine de Pizan, Isabeau of Bavaria, and Female Regency," 13.

20. As quoted in Famiglietti, *Royal Intrigue*, 32.

21. As quoted in Tracy, "Christine de Pizan, Isabeau of Bavaria, and Female Regency," 13.

22. Richard Vaughan, *John the Fearless: The Growth of Burgundian Power* (New York: Barnes & Noble, 1966), 41.

23. As quoted in Rachel Gibbons, "Isabeau of Bavaria, Queen of France (1385–1422): The Creation of an Historical Villainess," *Transactions of the Royal Historical Society* 6 (1996): 63.

24. *A Parisian Journal, 1405–1449*, trans. Janet Shirley (London: Oxford University Press, 1968), 48.

25. See George A. Kennedy, *Classical Rhetoric and Its Christian and Secular Tradition from Ancient to Modern Times*, 2nd ed. (Chapel Hill: University of North Carolina Press, 1999), 214. A more thorough explanation of *ars dictaminis* is provided in James J. Murphy, *Rhetoric in the Middle Ages: The History of Rhetorical Theory from Saint Augustine to the Renaissance* (Tempe: Arizona Center for Medieval and Renaissance Studies, 2001), chap. 4. See also

Martin Camargo, "Rhetoric," in *The Seven Liberal Arts in the Middle Ages*, ed. David L. Wagner (Bloomington: Indiana University Press, 1983), 108; Ernst Robert Curtius, *European Literature in the Latin Middle Ages* (Princeton: Princeton University Press, 1990), 75–76.

26. Johan Huizinga, *The Waning of the Middle Ages: A Study of the Forms of Life, Thought, and Art in France and the Netherlands in the XIVth and XVth Centuries* (New York: St. Martin's Press, 1985), 12.

27. Giles Constable, *Letters and Letter-Collections* (Turnhout, Belgium: Brepols, 1976), 11.

28. Martin Camargo, "Medieval Rhetoric: What Was It and Why Should We Care?," unpublished manuscript, 18.

29. As quoted in Donald E. Queller, *The Office of Ambassador in the Middle Ages* (Princeton: Princeton University Press, 1967), 7.

30. See Erin A. Sadlack, "'In Writing It May Be Spoke': The Politics of Women's Letter-Writing, 1377–1603" (Ph.D. diss., University of Maryland, 2005), 51.

31. On the late-medieval tradition of reading aloud in groups, especially among members of the Franco-Burgundian ruling class, see Joyce Coleman, *Public Reading and the Reading Public in Late Medieval England and France* (Cambridge: Cambridge University Press, 1996).

32. An extensive account of the ducal audience of Christine's letter is provided in Sadlack, "In Writing It May Be Spoke," 50–56.

33. Alexander Gelley, "Introduction," in *Unruly Examples: On the Rhetoric of Exemplarity*, ed. Alexander Gelley (Stanford: Stanford University Press, 1995), 5. See also Hegel's discussion of "pragmatical" history in *The Philosophy of History*, trans. John Sibree (New York: Dover, 1956), 6.

34. Earl Jeffrey Richards, "Introduction," in *The Book of the City of Ladies* (1405), by Christine de Pizan, trans. Earl Jeffrey Richards (New York: Persea Books, 1998), xxxiv.

35. Christine de Pizan, "An Epistle to the Queen of France," in *The Epistle of the Prison of Human Life, with an Epistle to the Queen of France and Lament on the Evils of Civil War*, ed. and trans. Josette A. Wisman (New York: Garland, 1984), 71, 73, 75. Throughout this chapter, I work with the French and English texts of Christine's letter based on the 1838 Thomassy edition of B. N. French 580(A): Raymond Thomassy, *Essai sur les écrits politiques de Christine de Pisan, suivi d'une notice littéraire et de pièces inédites* (Paris: Debécourt, 1838). An indispensable resource on MS 580(A) is Charity Cannon Willard, "An Autograph Manuscript of Christine de Pizan?," *Studi Francesi* 27 (1965): 452–57. Other available manuscripts of her epistle to the queen include B. N. French 604(B), 605(C), and Oxford, All Souls MS 182.

36. Pizan, "Epistle to the Queen," 75. See also Pizan, *The Book of the City of Ladies*, 2.34.1.

37. Pizan, "Epistle to the Queen," 77. See also Pizan, *The Book of the City of Ladies*, 2.32.1.

38. Pizan, "Epistle to the Queen," 77.

39. Ibid., 77. See also Pizan, *The Book of the City of Ladies*, 1.13.2.

40. Pizan, "Epistle to the Queen," 77. See also Pizan, *The Book of the City of Ladies*, 2.49.5.

41. Pizan, "Epistle to the Queen," 81.

42. For a more thorough account of intertextuality in Christine's era, see Thomas M. Greene, *The Light in Troy: Imitation and Discovery in Renaissance Poetry* (New Haven: Yale University Press, 1982).

43. See Charity Cannon Willard, *Christine de Pizan: Her Life and Works* (New York: Persea Books, 1984), 135.

44. See Curtius, *European Literature in the Latin Middle Ages*, 59–60.

45. On the iterative function of the example, see Lyons, *Exemplum*, 26–28.

46. See Irene E. Harvey, "Derrida and the Issues of Exemplarity," in *Derrida: A Critical Reader*, ed. David Wood (Oxford: Blackwell, 1992), 193–217.

47. Concise accounts of medieval misogyny may be found in Alcuin Blamires, *The Case for Women in Medieval Culture* (Oxford: Oxford University Press, 1997), 231–44; R. Howard Bloch, "Medieval Misogyny," *Representations* 20 (1987): 1–24; and Eileen Power, "Medieval Ideas About Women," in *Medieval Women* (Cambridge: Cambridge University Press, 1975), 1–26.

48. See Earl Jeffrey Richards, "'*Seulette a part*'—The 'Little Woman on the Sidelines' Takes up Her Pen: The Letters of Christine de Pizan," in *Dear Sister: Medieval Women and the Epistolary Genre*, ed. Karen Cherewatuk and Ulrike Wiethaus (Philadelphia: University of Pennsylvania Press, 1993), 139–70.
49. On the ancestry of this medieval belief—which stretches back to ancient articulations of marriage, the household, and the state, and finds its most explicit pronouncement in the first book of Aristotle's *Politics*—see Elisabeth Schüssler Fiorenza, *In Memory of Her: A Feminist Theological Reconstruction of Christian Origins* (New York: Crossroad, 1983), 254–57.
50. See Lyons, *Exemplum*, xi; and Gelley, "Introduction," 12.
51. See Norbert Elias, *The Court Society*, trans. Edmund Jephcott (Oxford: Blackwell, 1983), 1.
52. See Fredric Jameson, *The Political Unconscious: Narrative as a Socially Symbolic Act* (Ithaca: Cornell University Press, 1989), 29–30.
53. See Lyons, *Exemplum*, 28–31.
54. Ibid., 31.
55. This notion of contamination is developed more fully in Jacques Derrida, "The Law of Genre," *Glyph: Textual Studies* 7 (1980): 202–29.
56. Gelley, "Introduction," 14.
57. On the distinction between determinant and reflective judgments, see Immanuel Kant, *Critique of Judgment*, trans. Werner S. Pluhar (Indianapolis: Hackett, 1987), §4.
58. One notable exception was the ability of elite medieval women to serve as regents and co-regents. But even female regencies were premised on the political entitlement of men. "Regents, royal advisors, opponents, and theorists all assigned incapacities and capacities to each gender," Katherine Crawford explains. "Capacity as a king substituted for incapacity as a woman; capacity as a mother substituted for incapacity as a child" (*Perilous Performances*, 7). Add to this the specific and ongoing competition among rival dukes for official and unofficial regencies during the reign of Charles VI, and the barrier to Isabeau's political leadership becomes even more insurmountable.
59. Pizan, "Epistle to the Queen," 77, 73, 81, 79.
60. See Lauren Berlant, "The Female Complaint," *Social Text* 19/20 (Fall 1988): 237–59; and, more recently, Lauren Berlant, *The Female Complaint: The Unfinished Business of Sentimentality in American Culture* (Durham: Duke University Press, 2008). On the premodern history of the complaint, see Nancy Dean, "Chaucer's Complaint: A Genre Descended from the Heriodes," *Comparative Literature* 19, no. 1 (Winter 1967): 1–27.
61. As translated in Linda Leppig, "The Political Rhetoric of Christine de Pizan," in *Politics, Gender, and Genre: The Political Thought of Christine de Pizan*, ed. Margaret Brabant (Boulder, Colo.: Westview Press, 1992), 143.
62. See Margarete Zimmermann, "Vox Femina, Vox Politica," in Brabant, *Politics, Gender, and Genre*, 113–27.
63. Isa. 25:8; Rev. 7:17, 21:4. On the history of tears, see Tom Lutz, *Crying: The Natural and Cultural History of Tears* (New York: Norton, 1999).
64. Pizan, "Epistle to the Queen," 75.
65. Dante as quoted in John MacQueen, *Allegory* (London: Methuen, 1970), 55.
66. Pizan, "Epistle to the Queen," 75, 83.
67. Arendt, *Human Condition*, 18.
68. Kenneth Burke develops the concept of socioanagogy in *A Rhetoric of Motives* (Berkeley: University of California Press, 1969), 220: "In brief, the socioanagogic sense notes how the things of books and the book of Nature 'signify what relates to worldly glory.'"
69. Pizan, "Epistle to the Queen," 73–75, 77, 79–81.
70. This conception of the future anterior is developed more fully in Bernard Comrie, *Tense* (Cambridge: Cambridge University Press, 1985), 69–75.
71. See Hans-Jost Frey, "On Presentation in Benjamin," in *Walter Benjamin: Theoretical Questions*, ed. David S. Ferris (Stanford: Stanford University Press, 1996), 139–64.
72. Benjamin, *Arcades Project*, Q°, 21.

73. Martin Heidegger, *Being and Time*, trans. John Macquarrie and Edward Robinson (New York: Harper & Row, 1962), 374.

74. Giorgio Agamben, *The Time That Remains: A Commentary on the Letter to the Romans*, trans. Patricia Dailey (Stanford: Stanford University Press, 2005), 74. Paul develops this conception of *typos* in 1 Cor. 10:6 and 10:11.

75. Benjamin, *Arcades Project*, N3,1.

76. See Walter Benjamin, *The Origin of German Tragic Drama*, trans. John Osborne (London: Verso, 1998), 45.

77. Richards, "Introduction," xlix.

78. On the "feminine style," see Karlyn Kohrs Campbell, *Man Cannot Speak for Her* (New York: Greenwood Press, 1989), 52. See also Kathleen Hall Jamieson, *Beyond the Double Bind: Women and Leadership* (New York: Oxford University Press, 1995), 91–98.

79. See Giorgio Agamben, *Potentialities: Collected Essays in Philosophy*, ed. and trans. Daniel Heller-Roazen (Stanford: Stanford University Press, 1999), 184.

CHAPTER 4

1. Peter Gay, *The Enlightenment: An Interpretation* (New York: Norton, 1966), 2:61.

2. See Pamela E. Selwyn, *Everyday Life in the German Book Trade: Friedrich Nicolai as Bookseller and Publisher in the Age of Enlightenment, 1750–1810* (University Park: Pennsylvania State University Press, 2000), 2; James J. Sheehan, *German History, 1770–1886* (Oxford: Clarendon Press, 1989), 175, 203.

3. Gay, *Enlightenment*, 2:79.

4. Jürgen Habermas' treatment of Kant in his *Structural Transformation of the Public Sphere*, trans. Thomas Berger (Cambridge: MIT Press, 1991) is a prime example of this tendency.

5. F. V. L. Plessing to Immanuel Kant, 15 March 1784, in *Kant: Philosophical Correspondence (1759–1799)*, ed. and trans. Arnulf Zweig (Chicago: University of Chicago Press, 1967), 114.

6. See Steven Lestition, "Kant and the End of the Enlightenment in Prussia," *Journal of Modern European History* 65 (March 1993): 64–65.

7. J. G. Kiesewetter to Immanuel Kant, 14 June 1791, *Immanuel Kant: Correspondence*, trans. and ed. Arnulf Zweig (Cambridge: Cambridge University Press, 1999), 378.

8. As quoted in Christopher Clark, *Iron Kingdom: The Rise and Downfall of Prussia, 1600–1947* (Cambridge: Harvard University Press, 2006), 269.

9. As quoted in James Schmidt, "Introduction: What Is Enlightenment?," in *What Is Enlightenment? Eighteenth-Century Answers and Twentieth-Century Questions*, ed. James Schmidt (Berkeley: University of California Press, 1996), 6 and 35n.

10. Michael J. Sauter, "Visions of the Enlightenment: The Edict on Religion of 1788 and Political Reaction in Eighteenth-Century Prussia" (Ph.D. diss., University of California, Los Angeles, 2002), 14–15.

11. Henri Brunschwig, *Enlightenment and Romanticism in Eighteenth-Century Prussia*, trans. Frank Jellinek (Chicago: University of Chicago Press, 1974), 170.

12. Ian Hunter, "Kant's *Religion* and Prussian Religious Policy," *Modern Intellectual History* 2, no. 1 (2005): 12.

13. Clark, *Iron Kingdom*, 270.

14. As quoted in ibid., 271.

15. As quoted in Selwyn, *Everyday Life in the German Book Trade*, 192.

16. George Di Giovanni, translator's introduction to *Religion Within the Boundaries of Mere Reason*, 42, and Allen W. Wood, "General Introduction," xix, both in *Immanuel Kant: Religion and Rational Theology*, ed. and trans. Allen W. Wood and George Di Giovanni (Cambridge: Cambridge University Press, 1996).

17. See Selwyn, *Everyday Life in the German Book Trade*, 194–95.

18. See Lestition, "Kant and the End of the Enlightenment in Prussia," 66.
19. As quoted in Brunschwig, *Enlightenment and Romanticism in Eighteenth-Century Prussia*, 168.
20. See Klaus Epstein, *The Genesis of German Conservatism* (Princeton: Princeton University Press, 1966), 365. On the Ohio requirements, see Robert O'Neil, *Academic Freedom in the Wired World: Political Extremism, Corporate Power, and the University* (Cambridge: Harvard University Press, 2008), 105–7.
21. Immanuel Kant, "On the Miscarriage of All Philosophical Trials in Theodicy," trans. George di Giovanni, in Wood and Di Giovanni *Immanuel Kant*, 37.
22. See Brunschwig, *Enlightenment and Romanticism in Eighteenth-Century Prussia*, 168.
23. Schmidt, "Introduction: What Is Enlightenment?," 13.
24. On the multifarious German response to the French Revolution and its aftermath of Jacobin Terror, see Thomas P. Saine, *Black Bread–White Bread: German Intellectuals and the French Revolution* (Columbia, S.C.: Camden House, 1988).
25. Sheehan, *German History*, 293.
26. J. G. Kiesewetter to Immanuel Kant, 14 June 1791, in Zweig, *Immanuel Kant: Correspondence*, 377.
27. Immanuel Kant to Carl Friedrich Stäudlin, 4 May 1793, in Zweig, *Immanuel Kant: Correspondence*, 458–59.
28. Friedrich Wilhelm II to Immanuel Kant, 1 October 1794, in Zweig, *Immanuel Kant: Correspondence*, 485–86.
29. Immanuel Kant to Friedrich Wilhelm II, 12 October 1794, in Zweig, *Immanuel Kant: Correspondence*, 486–88.
30. Respectively, Manfred Kuehn, *Kant: A Biography* (Cambridge: Cambridge University Press, 2001), 380; Wood, "General Introduction," xx–xxi; Ernst Cassirer, *Kant's Life and Thought*, trans. James Haden (1918; trans., New Haven: Yale University Press, 1981), 395.
31. That Kant indeed saw *The Conflict* as a collection of "minor essays" (*Kleine Schriften*) is indicated in two letters to J. H. Tieftrunk, 13 October 1797 and 5 April 1798, in Zweig *Philosophical Correspondence*, 238–39, 249–50.
32. Immanuel Kant, *The Conflict of the Faculties*, trans. Mary J. Gregor and Robert Anchor, in Wood and Di Giovanni, *Immanuel Kant*, 248, 255.
33. Habermas, *The Structural Transformation of the Public Sphere*, 26. See also John Christian Laursen, "The Subversive Kant: The Vocabulary of 'Public' and 'Publicity,'" *Political Theory* 14, no. 4 (November 1986): 584–603. On the relationship between "publicity" and the public use of reason, see Onora O'Neill, "The Public Use of Reason," *Political Theory* 14, no. 4 (November 1986): 523–51.
34. Immanuel Kant, "An Answer to the Question: 'What Is Enlightenment?'" (1784), in *Kant: Political Writings*, ed. Hans Reiss, trans. H. B. Nisbet (Cambridge: Cambridge University Press, 1991), 55.
35. Kant, *Critique of Judgment*, §40, 161.
36. Kant, "An Answer to the Question: What Is Enlightenment?," 57. See also O'Neill, "Public Use of Reason," 530.
37. Immanuel Kant, *Critique of Pure Reason*, trans. Norman Kemp Smith (New York: St. Martin's Press, 1965), A820/B849, 645.
38. Kant, *Critique of Judgment*, §53, 198n.
39. Ibid., §53, 197; §90, 354–55.
40. Ibid., §53, 197.
41. Ibid., §90, 355.
42. See Karl Jaspers, *Kant* (1957), ed. Hannah Arendt, trans. Ralph Manheim (New York: Harcourt and Brace, 1962), 79. On "pure persuasion," see Burke, *Rhetoric of Motives*, 269–74.
43. J. C. Berens to Immanuel Kant, 5 December 1787, in Zweig, *Philosophical Correspondence*, 126–27.
44. J. E. Biester to Immanuel Kant, 17 December 1794, in Zweig, *Immanuel Kant: Correspondence*, 40–41.

45. Kant, *The Conflict of the Faculties*, 242.

46. Ibid., 242, 255. See also Immanuel Kant, "Perpetual Peace," in Reiss and Nisbet, *Kant: Political Writings*, 115.

47. See Habermas, *The Structural Transformation of the Public Sphere*, 25.

48. As quoted in Sheehan, *German History*, 190.

49. Norbert Elias, *The Civilizing Process: Sociogenetic and Psychogenetic Investigations*, rev. ed., ed. Eric Dunning, Johan Goudsblom, and Stephen Mennell, trans. Edmund Jephcott (Oxford: Blackwell, 2000), 17.

50. Keith Michael Baker, "Politics and Public Opinion Under the Old Regime: Some Reflections," in *Press and Politics in Pre-revolutionary France*, ed. Jack R. Censer and Jeremy D. Popkin (Berkeley: University of California Press, 1987), 213.

51. Benjamin Nathans, "Habermas's 'Public Sphere' in the Era of the French Revolution," *French Historical Studies* 16, no. 3 (1990): 639.

52. Baker, "Politics and Public Opinion," 214.

53. See Habermas, *The Structural Transformation of the Public Sphere*, 48–51. Habermas's identification of the "bourgeois public sphere" as an expansion and completion of the "intimate conjugal family" is hotly disputed among historians of the Enlightenment. Consider, for instance, Margaret C. Jacob, *Living the Enlightenment: Freemasonry and Politics in Eighteenth-Century Europe* (New York: Oxford University Press, 1991), 21: "It may be that rather than the private permitting a new public sphere, however idealized, the reverse is true. We need to consider the possibility that ideologies and behavior intended for the public realm shaped the family, providing it with an egalitarian ethos that never actually redefined the inequality of gender relations."

54. Habermas, *The Structural Transformation of the Public Sphere*, 51.

55. Immanuel Kant, *Gesammelte Schriften* (Berlin: Walter de Gruyter, 1923), 12.406. Cf. Kant, *The Conflict of the Faculties*, 259: "The lower faculty has not only the title but also the duty, if not to state the *whole* truth in public, at least to see to it that *everything* put forward in public as a principle is true."

56. On the "professional oppositionality" of late-modern academics, see Bruce Robbins, "Introduction: The Grounding of Intellectuals," in Robbins, *Intellectuals*, ix–xxvii. A more extensive treatment of this topic is provided in Robbins, *Secular Vocations*.

57. Kant, "An Answer to the Question: 'What Is Enlightenment?,'" 54.

58. Augustine of Hippo, *Confessions*, 2nd ed., ed. Michael P. Foley, trans. F. J. Sheed (Indianapolis: Hackett, 2006), 42.

59. Charles Dickens, *David Copperfield* (1850; repr., London: Penguin, 2004), 581.

60. Immanuel Kant, *Critique of Practical Reason* (1788), trans. Mary Gregor (Cambridge: Cambridge University Press, 1997), 66.

61. Kant, *Critique of Judgment*, §28.

62. Immanuel Kant, *Lectures on Ethics* (1775–80), trans. Louis Infield (Indianapolis: Hackett, 1963), 228.

63. See Robert Hariman, *Political Style: The Artistry of Power* (Chicago: University of Chicago Press, 1995), 172.

64. Gilles Deleuze, *Difference and Repetition* (1968), trans. Paul Patton (New York: Columbia University Press, 1994), 5.

65. Hannah Arendt, *Crises of the Republic* (New York: Harcourt, 1969), 67.

66. Johan Vereycken, Hans Vertommen, and Jozef Corveleyn, "Authority Conflicts and Personality Disorders," *Journal of Personality Disorders* 16, no. 1 (February 2002): 47–48.

67. Theodore Millon and Seth Grossman, *Overcoming Resistant Personality Disorders: A Personalized Psychotherapy Approach* (Hoboken, N.J.: Wiley, 2007), 275.

68. Jared Sandberg, "Passive Aggression May Be the Perfect Office Crime," *The Deseret News* (Salt Lake City, Utah), 27 November 2005.

69. James C. Scott, *Weapons of the Weak: Everyday Forms of Peasant Resistance* (New Haven: Yale University Press, 1985), 273.

70. Ibid., 37.
71. See Onora O'Neill, *Constructions of Reason: Explorations of Kant's Practical Philosophy* (Cambridge: Cambridge University Press, 1989), 37–38.
72. Plato, *Apology*, trans. Hugh Tredennick, in *The Collected Dialogues of Plato*, ed. Edith Hamilton and Huntington Cairns (New York: Pantheon Books, 1961), 38e.
73. Anthony Grafton, *Worlds Made by Words: Scholarship and Community in the Modern West* (Cambridge: Harvard University Press, 2009), 256.
74. See Robbins, "Introduction: The Grounding of Intellectuals," xix; Robbins, *Secular Vocations*, x.
75. Immanuel Kant to J. E. Biester, 18 May 1794, in Zweig, *Immanuel Kant: Correspondence*, 478–79.
76. Kant, *The Conflict of the Faculties*, 313.
77. Plato, *Apology*, 38e–39b.
78. Seneca, *Epistulae morales*, 105.3.
79. Plato, *Apology*, 38c.

CHAPTER 5

1. As quoted in Joakim Garff, *Søren Kierkegaard: A Biography*, trans. Bruce H. Kirmmse (Princeton: Princeton University Press, 2005), 215.
2. As quoted in Ronald M. Green, *Kierkegaard and Kant: The Hidden Debt* (Albany: State University of New York Press, 1992), 218.
3. Kierkegaard, *Christian Discourses/The Crisis*, 420.
4. Stewart Oakley, *A Short History of Denmark* (New York: Praeger, 1972), 170.
5. Frederick VII as quoted in ibid., 176.
6. Heiberg as quoted in Peter Vinten-Johansen, "Johan Ludvig Heiberg and His Audience in Nineteenth-Century Denmark," in *Kierkegaard and His Contemporaries: The Culture of Golden Age Denmark*, ed. Jon Stewart (Berlin: Walter de Gruyter, 2003), 347, 354.
7. Heiberg as quoted in Bruce H. Kirmmse, *Kierkegaard in Golden Age Denmark* (Bloomington: Indiana University Press, 1990), 157.
8. Heiberg as quoted in Alastair Hannay, *Kierkegaard: A Biography* (Cambridge: Cambridge University Press, 2001), 17.
9. Hannay, *Kierkegaard*, 18.
10. Søren Kierkegaard, *Works of Love*, ed. and trans. Howard V. Hong and Edna H. Hong (Princeton: Princeton University Press, 1995), 460.
11. Søren Kierkegaard, *Two Ages: "The Age of Revolution and the Present Age": A Literary Review*, ed. and trans. Howard V. Hong and Edna H. Hong (Princeton: Princeton University Press, 1978), 92, 84, 94, 105, 136.
12. Kirmmse, *Kierkegaard in Golden Age Denmark*, 275.
13. Ibid., 275.
14. Kierkegaard, *Two Ages*, 107, 87, 92, 93, 106, 85, 108; Hannay, *Kierkegaard*, 339.
15. *Søren Kierkegaard's Journals and Papers*, vol. 2, ed. and trans. Howard V. Hong and Edna H. Hong (Bloomington: Indiana University Press, 1978), 636; Kierkegaard, *Two Ages*, 107.
16. Kierkegaard, *Two Ages*, 107–9.
17. See, for instance, Kierkegaard, *Christian Discourses/The Crisis*, 306.
18. *Søren Kierkegaard's Journal and Papers*, vol. 5, ed. and trans. Howard V. Hong and Edna H. Hong (Bloomington: Indiana University Press, 1978), 318; Søren Kierkegaard, *The "Corsair" Affair and Articles Related to the Writings*, ed. and trans. Howard V. Hong and Edna H. Hong (Princeton: Princeton University Press, 1982), 176.
19. As quoted in Howard V. Hong and Edna H. Hong, "Historical Introduction," in Kierkegaard, *The "Corsair" Affair and Articles Related to the Writings*, ix.

20. Kierkegaard, *The "Corsair" Affair*, 176, 224.
21. Paul Rubow as quoted in Hong and Hong, "Historical Introduction," vii.
22. Kierkegaard, *The "Corsair" Affair*, 114, 47.
23. O. P. Sturzen-Becker as quoted in *Encounters with Kierkegaard: A Life as Seen by His Contemporaries*, ed. Bruce H. Kirmmse, trans. Bruce H. Kirmmse and Virginia R. Laursen (Princeton: Princeton University Press, 1998), 94.
24. Nielson as quoted in Kirmmse, *Encounters with Kierkegaard*, 89.
25. Søren Kierkegaard, *The Point of View*, ed. and trans. Howard V. Hong and Edna H. Hong (Princeton: Princeton University Press, 1998), 61.
26. Kierkegaard, *The "Corsair" Affair*, 217, and *The Point of View*, 62.
27. Kierkegaard, *The "Corsair" Affair*, 217.
28. Ibid., 220, 222, 226, 238, 229.
29. Brandes as quoted in Kierkegaard, *The "Corsair" Affair*, 290n107.
30. Kierkegaard, *The "Corsair" Affair*, 238, 223, 209, 239.
31. Kierkegaard, *The Point of View*, 60, and *The "Corsair" Affair*, 222.
32. Kirmmse, *Kierkegaard in Golden Age Denmark*, 357.
33. Kierkegaard, *Christian Discourses/The Crisis*, 402, 418, 359, 415, 419, 416, 425.
34. Jørgen Bukdahl, *Søren Kierkegaard and the Common Man* (1961), trans. Bruce H. Kirmmse (Grand Rapids, Mich.: Eerdmans, 2001), 57.
35. On the role of the Royal Theater in Danish cultural and social life, see W. Glyn Jones, *Denmark* (New York: Praeger, 1970), 64–66.
36. Kierkegaard, *Christian Discourses/The Crisis*, 416.
37. Scholarship on the political function of "The Crisis" is at best glancing. See, for instance, Kirmmse, *Kierkegaard in Golden Age Denmark*, 329–30; Garff, *Søren Kierkegaard*, 548–50; Hannay, *Kierkegaard*, 382. To date, the most rigorous, albeit narrowly aesthetic and authorial, reading of "The Crisis" is Joseph Westfall, *The Kierkegaardian Author: Authorship and Performance in Kierkegaard's Literary and Dramatic Criticism* (Berlin: Walter de Gruyter, 2007), 226–29, 248–70. On the interface between the aesthetic and the religious dimensions of "The Crisis," especially as they relate to other key works in the Kierkegaardian authorship, see Hugh S. Pyper, "The Stage and Stages in a Christian Authorship," in *International Kierkegaard Commentary*, vol. 17, ed. Robert L. Perkins (Macon: Mercer University Press, 2007), 299–319; Joseph Westfall, "The Actress and an Actress in the Life of a Critic: Higher Criticism in 'The Crisis,'" in Perkins, *International Kierkegaard Commentary*, 17:321–43.
38. Kierkegaard, *Christian Discourses/The Crisis*, 179.
39. Klaus-Michael Kodalle, "The Utilitarian Self and the 'Useless' Passion of Faith," in *The Cambridge Companion to Kierkegaard*, ed. Alastair Hannay and Gordon D. Marino (Cambridge: Cambridge University Press, 1998), 410; Søren Kierkegaard, "Of the Difference Between a Genius and an Apostle," in *The Present Age*, trans. Alexander Dru (New York: Harper Torchbooks, 1962), 96.
40. *Søren Kierkegaard's Journals and Papers*, 1:44, 43.
41. Kierkegaard, *Works of Love*, 274, 275, 277.
42. Kierkegaard, *Two Ages*, 109.
43. See Søren Kierkegaard, *Prefaces/Writing Sampler*, ed. and trans. Todd W. Nichol (Princeton: Princeton University Press, 1997), 193n5.
44. *Søren Kierkegaard's Journals and Papers*, 1:280.
45. Kierkegaard, *Works of Love*, 275.
46. *Søren Kierkegaard's Journals and Papers*, 1:280, and *Works of Love*, 258.
47. See Søren Kierkegaard, *Practice in Christianity*, ed. and trans. Howard V. Hong and Edna H. Hong (Princeton: Princeton University Press, 1991), 127–33.
48. *Søren Kierkegaard's Journals and Papers*, 1:281.
49. Plato, *Republic*, trans. Paul Shorey, in Hamilton and Cairns, *Collected Dialogues of Plato*, 361b. That Kierkegaard understands this ancient figure of justice in terms of unrecognizability is indicated in his *Practice in Christianity*, 129.

50. Kierkegaard, *Practice in Christianity*, 128.
51. Kirmmse, *Kierkegaard in Golden Age Denmark*, 318.
52. Kierkegaard, *Practice in Christianity*, 129.
53. Kierkegaard, *The Point of View*, 60, and *Practice in Christianity*, 238.
54. Kierkegaard, *The Point of View*, 60.
55. Kierkegaard, *Practice in Christianity*, 137, 133.
56. Kierkegaard, *Works of Love*, 276.
57. *Søren Kierkegaard's Journals and Papers*, 2:44.
58. Kierkegaard, *Christian Discourses/The Crisis*, 314–15. See also *Works of Love*, 36–37.
59. Kierkegaard, *Christian Discourses/The Crisis*, 315. See also Kierkegaard's discussion of "distinguished corruption" in *Works of Love*, 74–76. Interestingly, in an earlier draft of this discussion, Kierkegaard uses the term "learned" instead of "distinguished," suggesting that the elitism with which he was concerned in the late 1840s was specifically intellectual and perhaps even academic. See *Works of Love*, 432–33.
60. Kierkegaard, *The "Corsair" Affair*, 229.
61. Heiberg as quoted in Vinten-Johansen, "Johan Ludvig Heiberg and His Audience in Nineteenth-Century Denmark," 354.
62. Kirmmse, *Kierkegaard in Golden Age Denmark*, 140.
63. Heiberg as quoted in Vinten-Johansen, "Johan Ludvig Heiberg and His Audience in Nineteenth-Century Denmark," 354.
64. Kierkegaard, *Christian Discourses/The Crisis*, 413, 315–16.
65. William Shakespeare, *1 Henry IV* (1598), in *The Riverside Shakespeare*, ed. G. Blakemore Evans (Boston: Houghton Mifflin, 1974), 3.2.39–59.
66. That the use of seclusion to appear authoritative predates Machiavelli almost goes without saying. Consider, for instance, Plutarch's description of Pericles, who, "to avoid any feeling of commonness, or any satiety on the part of the people, presented himself at intervals only, not speaking to every business, nor at all times coming into the assembly, but, as Critolaus says, reserving himself, like the Salaminian galley, for great occasions." *Plutarch's Lives*, trans. Dryden, ed. Arthur Hugh Clough (Lawrence, Kans.: Digireads.com, 2009), 1:157. Or the pseudo-Aristotelian *Secreta secretorum*: "A kyng owith not to shewe him ouer oftene to his peple, ne ouer oft haunte the company of his sugetis, and specially of chorlis and ruralle folke, for bi ouyr moche homelyness he shalle be the lasse honourid." *Early English Text Society* 74 (1898): 12–13.
67. Hennig Fenger and Frederick J. Marker, *The Heibergs* (New York: Twayne Publishers, 1971), 158. See also Kirmmse, *Kierkegaard in Golden Age Denmark*, 140.
68. Heiberg as quoted in Kirmmse, *Kierkegaard in Golden Age Denmark*, 167–68.
69. Heiberg as quoted in Jon Stewart, *Kierkegaard's Relations to Hegel Reconsidered* (Cambridge: Cambridge University Press, 2003), 428.
70. Kierkegaard, *The Corsair*, 113–14.
71. Signe Læssøe as quoted in Bruce H. Kirmmse, "A Rose with Thorns: Hans Christian Anderson's Relation to Kierkegaard," in *International Kierkegaard Commentary*, vol. 1, ed. Robert L. Perkins (Macon: Mercer University Press, 1999), 76.
72. Eline Haramb Boisen as quoted in Kirmmse, *Encounters with Kierkegaard*, 138.
73. Deleuze, *Difference and Repetition*, 7.
74. Kierkegaard, *Christian Discourses/The Crisis*, 316.
75. Burke, *Rhetoric of Motives*, 39, 167.
76. Kierkegaard, *Works of Love*, 456–57. For a similarly self-referential statement, which takes as its beginning "the secret that *mundus vult decipi*," see Kierkegaard, *The Point of View*, 58–59.
77. Shakespeare, *1 Henry IV*, 3.2.60–78.
78. See Steven Greenblatt, *Renaissance Self-Fashioning: From More to Shakespeare* (Chicago: University of Chicago Press, 1980), 161–63.
79. Shakespeare, *1 Henry IV*, 1.3.202.

80. Kierkegaard, *Christian Discourses/The Crisis*, 316.
81. As quoted in Kierkegaard, *Prefaces/Writing Sampler*, x.
82. Kierkegaard, *The "Corsair" Affair*, 99.
83. Kierkegaard, *Prefaces/Writing Sampler*, 23.
84. Matt. 6:28–29. Cf. 1 Kings 10:4–7 and 2 Chron. 9:4–6, 20–22.
85. Kierkegaard, *Prefaces/Writing Sampler*, 24.
86. Ibid., 6.
87. Kierkegaard, *Works of Love*, 456.
88. Kierkegaard, *Christian Discourses/The Crisis*, 413.
89. Ibid., 318. See Matt. 11:16–17.
90. See, for instance, Hannay, *Kierkegaard*, 483n40.
91. See, for instance, Westfall, *Kierkegaardian Author*, 270; Howard V. Hong and Edna H. Hong, "Historical Introduction," in Kierkegaard, *Christian Discourses/The Crisis*, xvi.
92. On the practice of "congregation by segregation," see Kenneth Burke, "The Rhetorical Situation," in *Communication: Ethical and Moral Issues*, ed. Lee Thayer (New York: Gordon and Breach, 1973), 263–75.
93. On the epistolary origins of the modern newspaper, see David Randall, "Epistolary Rhetoric, the Newspaper, and the Public Sphere," *Past and Present* 198, no. 1 (February 2008): 3–32. See also Gary Schneider, *The Culture of Epistolarity: Vernacular Letters and Letter Writing in Early Modern England, 1500–1700* (Newark: University of Delaware Press, 2005), 143–82, 201–21.
94. On the centrality of reticulate public spheres to ordinary democratic discussion and debate, see Gerard A. Hauser, *Vernacular Voices: The Rhetoric of Publics and Public Spheres* (Columbia: University of South Carolina Press, 1999), 57–81.
95. See, for instance, "The Intellectuals and Power: A Discussion Between Michel Foucault and Gilles Deleuze," trans. Mark Seem, *Telos* 16 (1973): 103–9.
96. Johanne Luise Heiberg as quoted in Hong and Hong, "Historical Introduction," *Christian Discourses/The Crisis*, xvii.
97. Letter of 7 August 1851 to Johanne Luise Heiberg, in Søren Kierkegaard, *Letters and Documents*, trans. Henrik Rosenmeier (Princeton: Princeton University Press, 1978), 389–90.
98. Ibid., 388.
99. Heiberg as quoted in Kierkegaard, *Christian Discourses/The Crisis*, 456.

CHAPTER 6

1. Michael Hardt and Antonio Negri, *Empire* (Cambridge: Harvard University Press, 2000), 212
2. Arendt, *Thinking*, 72.
3. Cicero, *Orator*, trans. H. M. Hubbell (Cambridge: Harvard University Press, 1997), §63–64.
4. Plato, *Philebus*, trans. R. Hackforth, in Hamilton and Cairns, *Collected Dialogues of Plato*, 52b.
5. Dewey, "Academic Freedom," 64.
6. Jacoby, *Last Intellectuals*, 6.
7. Campbell, *Man Cannot Speak for Her*, 52. See also Jamieson, *Beyond the Double Bind*, 91–98.
8. Jacoby, *Last Intellectuals*, 236.
9. Bertolt Brecht, *Stories of Mr. Keuner*, trans. Martin Chalmers (San Francisco: City Lights Books, 2001), 3–4.
10. Seneca, *Epistulae morales*, 73.1–2.
11. Strauss, *On Tyranny*, 205–6.
12. Strauss, *Persecution and the Art of Writing*, 25. See also Strauss, *The City and the Man*, 54.

13. Jeff Goodwin, *No Other Way Out: States and Revolutionary Movements, 1945–1991* (Cambridge: Cambridge University Press, 2001), 9.

14. Exemplary studies of "resistance" include Scott, *Weapons of the Weak*; Robin D. G. Kelley, *Race Rebels: Culture, Politics, and the Black Working Class* (New York: Free Press, 1994); Lisa Wedeen, *Ambiguities of Domination: Politics, Rhetoric, and Symbols in Contemporary Syria* (Chicago: University of Chicago Press, 1999); and Hank Johnston, "Talking the Walk: Speech Acts and Resistance in Authoritarian Regimes," in *Repression and Mobilization*, ed. Christian Davenport, Hank Johnston, and Carol Mueller (Minneapolis: University of Minnesota Press, 2005), 108–37.

15. See Kembrew McLeod, "The Day I Killed Freedom of Expression," *Huffington Post*, 20 July 2010, http://www.huffingtonpost.com/kembrew-mcleod/the-day-i-killed-freedom_b_652094.html.

16. John Durham Peters, *Courting the Abyss: Free Speech and the Liberal Tradition* (Chicago: University of Chicago Press, 2005), 1.

17. See Elizabeth Markovits, *The Politics of Sincerity: Plato, Frank Speech, and Democratic Judgment* (University Park: Pennsylvania State University Press, 2008), 65–68.

18. Burke, *Rhetoric of Motives*, 141. On the incompatibility of persuasion and authority, see Hannah Arendt's "What Is Authority?," in *Between Past and Future*, 92–93, and *Crises of the Republic*, 144.

19. Markovits, *Politics of Sincerity*, 69, 130–31.

20. On the inequities of the bourgeois public sphere and, by extension, those of contemporary democratic political culture, see Nancy Fraser, "Rethinking the Public Sphere: A Contribution to the Critique of Actually Existing Democracy," in *Habermas and the Public Sphere*, ed. Craig Calhoun (Cambridge: MIT Press, 1992), 109–42.

21. Sidney Tarrow, *Power in Movement: Social Movements and Contentious Politics*, 2nd ed. (Cambridge: Cambridge University Press, 1998), 2.

22. Charles Tilly, *Social Movements, 1768–2004* (Boulder, Colo.: Paradigm, 2004), 3.

23. See Scott, *Weapons of the Weak*, xvi.

24. See, respectively, Margaret A. Gibson, *Accommodation Without Assimilation: Sikh Immigrants in an American High School* (Ithaca: Cornell University Press, 1988); Paul E. Willis, *Learning to Labor: How Working Class Kids Get Working Class Jobs* (Westmead, U.K.: Saxon House, 1977), 11–13; Linda Schlossberg, "Rites of Passing," in *Passing: Identity and Interpretation in Sexuality, Race, and Religion*, ed. María Carla Sánchez and Linda Schlossberg (New York: New York University Press, 2001), 1–12, specifically 3; Scott, *Weapons of the Weak*, xv.

25. See, respectively, Erving Goffman, "Felicity's Condition," *American Journal of Sociology* 89, no. 1 (July 1983): 1–53; Brown and Levinson, *Politeness*, 70–71; Robin Lakoff, *Language and Women's Place: Text and Commentaries* (Oxford: Oxford University Press, 2004), 47–51; Kate Burridge and Margaret Florey, "'Yeah-no He's a Good Kid': A Discourse Analysis of Yeah-no in Australian English," *Australian Journal of Linguistics* 22, no. 2 (October 2002): 149–71; Wayne E. Beach and Terri R. Metzger, "Claiming Insufficient Knowledge," *Human Communication Research* 23, no. 4 (1997): 562–88.

26. Jean-François Lyotard, "On the Strength of the Weak," trans. Roger McKeon, *Semiotext* 3, no. 2 (1978): 207.

27. Alain Badiou, *Being and Event*, trans. Oliver Feltham (New York: Continuum, 2005), 110.

28. See, for instance, Kelley, *Race Rebels*, Wedeen, *Ambiguities of Domination*, and Johnston, "Talking the Walk."

29. Pierre Bourdieu, "The Corporatism of the Universal: The Role of Intellectuals in the Modern World," trans. Carolyn Betensky, *Telos* 81 (1989): 109. See also Pierre Bourdieu, *The Field of Cultural Production: Essays on Art and Literature* (New York: Columbia University Press, 1993), 105, 125, 164, 198, 281n11.

30. Plato, *Republic*, 495d–e.

31. Jacques Rancière, "Proletarian Nights," trans. Noel Parker, *Radical Philosophy* 31 (Summer 1982): 12.

32. Ibid., 12.

33. Antonio Gramsci, *Selections from the Prison Notebooks*, ed. and trans. Quintin Hoare and Geoffrey Nowell Smith (New York: International Publishers, 1971), 331–32, 323.
34. Rancière, "Proletarian Nights," 12.
35. Jacques Rancière, *The Philosopher and His Poor*, trans. Andrew Parker (Durham: Duke University Press, 2004), xxvii.
36. Bourdieu, "The Corporatism of the Universal," 109.
37. Plato, *Republic*, 496c.
38. Strauss, *On Tyranny*, 275.
39. Gramsci, *Selections from the Prison Notebooks*, 332. That this tradition of vanguard leadership continues to thrive is well indicated in Henry Giroux, "On Pop Clarity: Public Intellectuals and the Crisis of Language," *Truthout*, 24 March 2010, http://www.truth-out.org/on-pop-clarity-public-intellectuals-and-crisis-language57950.
40. Walter Benjamin, "The Author as Producer," in *Reflections: Essays, Aphorisms, and Autobiographical Writings*, ed. Peter Demetz, trans. Edmund Jephcott (New York: Harcourt Brace Jovanovich, 1978), 237–38.
41. Erik Olin Wright, "Intellectuals and the Class Structure of Capitalist Society," in *Between Labor and Capital*, ed. Pat Walker (Boston: South End Press, 1979), 209.
42. As of 2008, roughly 70 percent of all college instructors were full- or part-time employees off the tenure track, according to JBL Associates, Inc., *Reversing Course: The Troubled State of Academic Staffing and a Path Forward* (Washington, D.C.: American Federation of Teachers, 2008). Add to this the tendency of many administrations to underreport their limited-term employees, and the number may be well over 80 percent. See Marc Bousquet, "Afterword: Management's *Kulturekampf*," in Nocella, Best, and McLaren, *Academic Repression*, 512; Benjamin Johnson, "The Drain-O of Higher Education: Casual Labor and University Teaching," in *Steal This University: The Rise of the Corporate University and the Academic Labor Movement*, Benjamin Johnson, Patrick Kavanagh, and Kevin Mattson (New York: Routledge: 2003), 63. Recent accounts of this development in American higher education may be found in Robin Wilson, "Tenure, RIP: What the Vanishing Status Means for the Future of Education," *Chronicle of Higher Education*, 4 July 2010, http://chronicle.com/article/Tenure-RIP/66114/?sid=wb&utm_source=wb&utm_medium=en; Scott Jaschik, "The Disappearing Tenure-Track Job," *Inside Higher Ed*, 12 May 2009, http://www.insidehighered.com/news/2009/05/12/workforce; "Trends in Faculty Status, 1975–2007," American Association of University Professors, n.d., http://www.aaup.org/NR/rdonlyres/7BAE5D10-3DE3-404D-99A7-23183E9027E4/0/Fig4.pdf.
43. Ellen Schrecker, "Worse Than McCarthy," *Chronicle Review*, 10 February 2006.
44. See O'Neil, *Academic Freedom in the Wired World*, 247.
45. As quoted in Cindy Chang, "Conservative Alumnus Pulls Offer to Buy Lecture Tapes," *New York Times*, 24 January 2006, http://query.nytimes.com/gst/fullpage.html?res=9907E2D6133FF937A15752C0A9609C8B63.
46. O'Neil, *Academic Freedom in the Wired World*, 248.
47. As quoted in Smith, Mayer, and Fritschler, *Closed Minds?*, 17.
48. Rebecca Attwood, "Get It out in the Open," *Times Higher Education*, 24 September 2009, http://www.timeshighereducation.co.uk/story.asp?storycode=408300.
49. Katie Hafner, "An Open Mind," *New York Times*, 8 April 2010, http://www.nytimes.com/2010/04/18/education/edlife/18open-t.html.
50. Ibid.
51. See Arendt, "Truth and Politics," 246.
52. Foucault, "Truth and Power," 127.
53. Giroux, "On Pop Clarity."
54. Walter Benjamin, "Bert Brecht," trans. Rodney Livingstone, in *Walter Benjamin: Selected Writings, Volume 2, Part 1, 1927–1930*, ed. Michael W. Jennings, Howard Eiland, and Gary Smith (Cambridge: Harvard University Press, 2005), 367.
55. Kierkegaard, *Two Ages*, 108.

56. Benjamin as quoted in Martin Chalmers, "Mr. Keuner—and Mr. Brecht; or, Etiquette in Dark Times," in Brecht, *Stories of Mr. Keuner*, 101; Benjamin, "Bert Brecht," 367.
57. Benjamin, "Bert Brecht," 366–67.
58. Ross, "Defenders of the Faith and the New Class," 127.
59. Scott, *Weapons of the Weak*, 285.
60. Peters, *Courting the Abyss*, 249.
61. On the concealment of executive potential, and the mode of domination with which it comes, see Alain Badiou, *Metapolitics*, trans Jason Barker (London: Verso, 2005), 144–50.
62. G. W. F. Hegel, *Phenomenology of Spirit*, trans. A. V. Miller (Oxford: Oxford University Press, 1977), §196.
63. Agamben, *Potentialities*, 215, 183.
64. Walter Benjamin, *Understanding Brecht*, trans. Anna Bostock (London: Verso, 2003), 9.
65. Aristotle, *On Rhetoric: A Theory of Civic Discourse*, trans. George A. Kennedy (New York: Oxford University Press, 1991), 38 (1356a).
66. Arendt, "Truth and Politics," 233.
67. Sloterdijk, *Critique of Cynical Reason*, 18.
68. Ross, "Defenders of the Faith and the New Class," 127.
69. Michel Foucault, *The History of Sexuality, Volume 1: An Introduction*, trans. Robert Hurley (New York: Vintage Books, 1990), 145. See also Gilles Deleuze, *Foucault*, ed. and trans. Seán Hand (Minneapolis: University of Minnesota Press, 1988), 92–93.

INDEX

Abbott, Frank Frost, 27
abscondere (to conceal), 40–43
academic culture. *See also* learned advocates and advocacy
    attacks on autonomy in, 158
    audiences of, 7
    Christine's non-linear style and, 79, 144
    compared to Roman Senate, 26–27
    desertion in, 143–44
    discourse of, 143–44
    dissent in, 17–18, 152–53
    epistolary rhetoric and, 2–3
    future of, 16–18
    German Enlightenment under Friedrich Wilhelm II and, 86–87
    the intellectual and, 2, 153, 155, 163
    oppositional politics within, 107
    rhetoric of exemplarity and, 144
    rhetoric of withdrawal and, 144
    technology and, 158, 160–61
    tenure track and, 188n42
"Academic Freedom" (Dewey), 17
accommodation techniques, 151–52
the "account," 45–46, 49
addressees. *See* audiences
Ad Lucilium epistulae morales (Seneca). *See Letters to Lucilius* (Seneca)
Agamben, Giorgio, 165
ambiguity, 53–54, 69–70
American Council of Trustees and Alumni, 117
"Answer to the Question: 'What Is Enlightenment?'" (Kant), 99
Arendt, Hannah, 30, 73, 143, 174n33
Aristotle, 52–53
astronomy, 128–29, 135–36
audiences
    addressees, 7
    auditors, 7, 63, 157
    for Christine's letter to Isabeau, 5, 62–63
    for *Conflict of the Faculties* (Kant), 5–6
    for "The Crisis and a Crisis in the Life of an Actress" (Kierkegaard), 6, 110, 138–39
    eavesdroppers, 7
    as judges, 70–71
    for *Letters to Lucilius* (Seneca), 4–5
    medieval epistolography and, 69
    required for passive-aggressive resistance, 105–6
    spatial aspects of, 7–8
    temporal aspects of, 8
    witnesses, 7
auditors. *See* audiences
Aufklärer, 82
Augustine, 101
Azo, 62

Badiou, Alain, 152
Baker, Keith Michael, 95
Bathsheba, 64–65, 67
Beck, Andreas Frederik, 109
Benjamin, Walter, 12–14, 76, 78, 161–63, 166
Berens, J. C., 93–94
Berlin Censorship Commission, 86
Biester, Johann Erich, 84, 86–87, 94, 103
Blanche of Castile, 65, 67
Boccaccio, 65–66, 68
The Book of the City of Ladies (Christine de Pizan), 63–66
book trade, 173n9
Bourdieu, Pierre, 153
Brahe, Tycho, 128
Brandes, Georg, 119
Brecht, Bertolt, 18, 146
Bruin Alumni Association, 158–59
Brunschwig, Henri, 85
Burgundy, Duke of. *See* Philip II, Duke of Burgundy
Burke, Kenneth, 139, 150

Cassius Dio, 26
censorship, 86–89
Censorship Edict (1788), 86–87

Charles V, 54
Charles VI, 54–61
"Charlottenlund" (Heiberg), 128
Christian Discourses (Kierkegaard), 119–20
Christianity, 8, 122–23
Christian VIII, 111
Christine de Pizan. *See also* rhetoric of exemplarity
  The Book of the City of Ladies, 63–66
  boundaries between public and private discourse and, 5
  letter to Isabeau: audience for, 5, 62–63; compared to *Letters to Lucilius* (Seneca), 78; as *complainte politique*, 72; *exempla* and *paradeigmata* in, 65–69, 74, 79; exemplary female figures in, 64–69, 73; mediated subjectivity in, 70–71; overview of, 53; potentialities of women in, 78–80; purpose of, 63; temporal aspects of Isabeau's actions, 73–78
  motives for Isabeau's intervention and, 73
  non-linear style of, 79, 144
Chrysippus, 31–32
Churchill, Ward, 159
civil disobedience, 103–4
complainte politique, 72
concealment, 41–44, 46
Conflict of the Faculties (Kant)
  audiences for, 5–6
  on death, 107–8
  "higher" and "lower" university faculties and, 90–91
  preface: as dissent, 93–96, 99–103; illusion of "privacy" in, 97–98; as passive-aggressive resistance, 104–6; as public forum, 5–6, 93–94
The Corsair, 116–19, 128–30
Crawford, Katherine, 179n58
"The Crisis and a Crisis in the Life of an Actress" (Kierkegaard)
  as appeal to public opinion, 6
  audiences for, 6, 110, 138–39
  compared to "Self-Defense," 131–32
  critical elements of, 123
  criticism of Johan Heiberg/elitism in, 110, 116, 125–26, 133–37
  motives for writing, 120–21
  praise of Luise Heiberg in, 124
  and the public, 110, 138–39
  seclusion as deception in, 126–28
  Shakespeare's *I Henry IV* and, 126–28, 130, 132–33

Critique of Judgment (Kant), 92–93
Critique of Practical Reason (Kant), 101
Critique of Pure Reason (Kant), 92
Cynics, 31–32

Dante, 9
death, 8, 50–51, 107–8, 171n6
De brevitate vitae (Seneca). See *On the Shortness of Life* (Seneca)
deconstructionist critiques of philosophy, 10
Deleuze, Gilles, 102, 130
democracy, 110–11, 150–51
Denmark, 110–11
De otio (Seneca). See *On Retirement* (Seneca)
De tranquillitate animi (Seneca). See *On Tranquility of Mind* (Seneca)
Dewey, John, 17, 144
"The Dialectic of Ethical and Ethical-Religious Communication" (Kierkegaard), 122
Dickens, Charles, 101
Difference and Repetition (Deleuze), 102
Di Giovanni, George, 86
dissent
  academic culture and, 17–18, 152–53
  covert acts of, 82, 149–52
  desertion as, 143
  epistolary rhetoric and, 2–3
  in *Letters to Lucilius* (Seneca), 48–49
  letter-writing and, 8–9
  "Measures Against Power" (Brecht) and, 146–48, 151–52, 164
  overt acts of, 148–49
  passive aggression as, 104–6
  resistance, 104–6, 149
  revolt, 148–49
  rhetoric of withdrawal as, 3
  social protest, 148–51
  of Thrasea Paetus, 24–25, 27
Dreyfus Affair, 1

eavesdroppers. See audiences
Elias, Norbert, 95
elites. *See also* the intellectual; the public
  abandonment of Kierkegaard, 119
  in Denmark, 111–12
  Kierkegaard identified as, by *The Corsair*, 118
  Kierkegaard's criticism of, 110, 116, 125–26
  as spokespeople for "the public," 145
Enlightenment, 81–88, 96–97, 99, 182n53
epistolary fiction, 97–98
epistolary rhetoric. *See* rhetoric

epistolography. *See* letter-writing
Esther, Queen, 64, 67
example, use of term, 52–54
exemplary figures. *See* Christine de Pizan; rhetoric of exemplarity
The Fatherland, 109–10, 124, 138

fiction, epistolary, 97–98
Fontenelle, Bernard de, 101
Foucault, Michel, 8, 11, 13, 50, 145, 161, 169
France, corruption of royal fiscal system, 55–56, 59–60
Frederick the Great, 83, 86
Frederick VI, 111
Frederick VII, 111
free speech, 149–51
free will, 121–22
French Revolution, 87–88, 95
Friedrich Wilhelm II
  censorship of Kant, 88–89
  decline of public authority, 95–96
  reign of, 83–88
Fryde, Edmund, 56

Gay, Peter, 82
Gedike, Friedrich, 84
Gelley, Alexander, 70–71
Giroux, Henry A., 161
Grafton, Anthony, 107
Gramsci, Antonio, 154, 156
Griffin, Miriam T., 21, 26–27, 40, 47–48

Habermas, Jürgen, 182n53
habit, 124–25
Hardt, Michael, 143
Hegel, Georg Wilhelm Friedrich, 165
Heiberg, Johan Ludvig. *See also* "The Crisis and a Crisis in the Life of an Actress" (Kierkegaard)
  as addressee of "The Crisis and a Crisis in the Life of an Actress" (Kierkegaard), 6
  "Charlottenlund," 128
  compared to Henry IV, 130
  as critic of Kierkegaard's dissertation, 109
  financial gain and, 134–35
  frustration with "the public," 112–14
  Kierkegaard's critique of, 110, 116, 125–26, 133–37
  response to Kierkegaard's article, 140–41
  "The Starry Heaven," 128
  On the Theater, 112

Urania, 128
vaudeville and, 111–12
Heiberg, Johanne Luise, 6, 110, 139
Heidegger, Martin, 77
I Henry IV (Shakespeare), 126–28, 130, 132–33
historiography, 12
history, Christine's understanding of, 64
Horowitz, David, 117, 159
Hunter, Ian, 85
the intellectual. *See also* academic culture; learned advocates and advocacy
  academic culture and, 2
  law of noncontradiction and, 167
  liminal position of, 153, 155, 163
  origins of term, 1
  the public and, 154–56

International Studies in Higher Education Act (2003), 87
Isabeau of Bavaria, 5, 53, 57–58, 179n58. *See also* Christine de Pizan
iTunes U, 160

Jacoby, Russell, 144
Jaspers, Karl, 9
Jesus, 123, 135
Jezebel, 65, 67
John II, Duke of Burgundy (John the Fearless). *See also* Orléans-Burgundy conflict
  government reform and, 61
  as messenger of Christine's letter, 62–63
  as populist alternative to Louis I, Duke of Orléans, 60
Jones, Andrew, 158–59

Kant, Immanuel. *See also Conflict of the Faculties* (Kant)
  Aufklärer and, 82
  boundaries between public and private discourse and, 5–6
  compared to Socrates, 107–8
  correspondence with Friedrich Wilhelm as public document, 93–94
  "higher" vs. "lower" university faculties, 90–91, 93
  "private" vs. "public" uses of reason, 91–93
  promise of obedience to Friedrich Wilhelm, 90, 94, 96, 98, 99–100
  response to Friedrich Wilhelm's letter of indictment, 89–90
  rhetorical theory and *On Retirement* (Seneca), 32

rhetoric of humility, 100–102
rhetoric of obedience, 3–4, 14, 16, 144–45
rhetoric vs. oratory, 92–93
"subtle deception" as resistance, 90
works: "Answer to the Question: 'What Is Enlightenment?'," 99; *Conflict of the Faculties*, 5–6, 90–91, 93–108; *Critique of Judgment*, 92–93; *Critique of Practical Reason*, 101; *Critique of Pure Reason*, 92; *Lectures on Ethics*, 101; "On the Radical Evil in Human Nature," 88–89; *Religion Within the Limits of Reason Alone*, 89; "Of the Struggle of the Good Principle with the Evil Principle for Sovereignty over Man," 88–89
Kierkegaard, Søren. *See also* "The Crisis and a Crisis in the Life of an Actress" (Kierkegaard)
attitude toward "the public," 113–16
boundaries between public and private discourse and, 6
compared to Richard II, 133
The Corsair's attacks on, 116–19
critique of Danish press, 116
pseudonym of ("Inter et Inter"), 137–38
renunciation of financial gain, 136–37
rhetoric of identification, 3, 14, 16, 131, 139, 145
on Stoicism, 171n6
works: *Christian Discourses*, 119–20; "On the Concept of Irony," 109–10; "The Crisis and a Crisis in the Life of an Actress" (Kierkegaard), 6, 110, 116, 120–21, 123–28, 130–39; "The Dialectic of Ethical and Ethical-Religious Communication," 122; *Either/Or*, 118, 129; *The Point of View*, 118, 123, 140; *Prefaces*, 134–35; "Self-Defense," 131–32
Kiesewetter, J. G., 83
Kirmmse, Bruce H., 114
Kojève, Alexandre, 156

Læssøe, Signe, 129
La Roche, Sophie von, 82
learned advocates and advocacy. *See also* academic culture
contemporary compared to past dilemmas of, 142
dissent and, 147–48, 152–53
obstacles to, 143
online attacks on, 158
self-defense of, 159
as suspicious of online technology, 161
Lectures on Ethics (Kant), 101
Lessing, Gotthold Ephraim, 82
letter-essays, definition of, 21
Letters to Lucilius (Seneca)
as an "account," 45–46, 49
audiences for, 4–5
authenticity of, 20–21
avoiding offense to Nero, 46
compared to Christine's letter to Isabeau, 78
compared to previous writings, 39–40
concealment in, 41–44, 46
on death, 50–51
dissent of, concealed by deference, 48–49
as lesson in advancement, 40
letter 14, 46, 51
letter 19, 42–43, 51
letter 43, 41–42
letter 68, 35–36, 43–44, 51
letter 73, 48–49, 146–47
letter 94, 41–42
as letter-essays, 21
personal agenda of, 39
on philosophical leisure as extension of public life, 35–38
publicity as protection, 44
rhetoric of withdrawal and, 3–5
use of verb *abscondere*, 40–43
letter-writing. *See also* epistolary rhetoric
"audience-oriented subjectivity" of, 97
Enlightenment and, 96–97
medieval, 61–63
as minor political practice, 13–14
spatial/temporal aspects of, 8
as treatises, 173n7
libraries, 86
Louis I, Duke of Anjou, 54–55
Louis I, Duke of Orléans, 5, 55, 57–61. *See also* Orléans-Burgundy conflict
Lyotard, Jean-François, 152

maieutics, 122–23
"Manifesto of the Intellectuals," 1
marginalized groups, 151–52
Markovits, Elizabeth, 150
Marxism, 4, 9–10, 15, 154–57

"Measures Against Power" (Brecht), 146–48
Mr. Keuner: as dominated member of dominating class, 155; final comment of, 165; liminal position of, 151; as political model, 161–62; potentiality and, 166–67; response to power, 157, 162–64, 168
medieval epistolography, 61–63, 69
microhistory, 14
"minor literature," 172n16
misogyny, 66–68, 71
MIT (Massachusetts Institute of Technology), 160
Møller, Peder Ludvig, 116–17, 134–35

Nathans, Benjamin, 95
Negri, Antonio, 143
Nero, 4–5, 22–26
new historicism, 14
"The New Planet," 128–30
New York Times, 160
Nicolai, Friedrich, 86–87
Nielson, Frederik, 117
nobility, 64
NoIndoctrination.org, 159
Nussbaum, Martha C., 52

Odyssey (Homer), 44, 176n76
"Of the Struggle of the Good Principle with the Evil Principle for Sovereignty over Man" (Kant), 88–89
Olufsen, Christian F. R., 128–29
Olympias, 65, 67–68
O'Neil, Robert, 159
On Famous Women (Boccaccio), 65–66, 68
On Retirement (Seneca), 30–33, 35, 40
"On the Concept of Irony" (Kierkegaard), 109–10
"On the Radical Evil in Human Nature" (Kant), 88–89
On the Shortness of Life (Seneca), 28–31, 40
On the Theater (Heiberg), 112
On Tranquility of Mind (Seneca), 29–30, 40, 42
open educational resources movement, 160–61
oratory, 62
Orléans, Duke of. *See* Louis I, Duke of Orléans
Orléans-Burgundy conflict, 57–58, 61

parrhesia. *See* free speech
passive aggression, 104–5
Patriot Act, 86

peace, 37–38
persuasion, 145–46
Peters, John Durham, 149, 163
Philip II, Duke of Burgundy, 5, 55, 57–60
philosophy
deconstructionist critiques of, 10
Marxist critiques of, 9–10
philosophic politics and, 147–48
the public and, 154
revisionist historians and, 11
rhetoric of philosophers and, 11–12
in service of political agendas, 28
Sloterdijk on, 10
Strauss on, 10–11
Plato, 154
Plessing, F. V. L., 83
Poe, Edgar Allan, 44
The Point of View (Kierkegaard), 118, 123
Poirion, Daniel, 72
politeness theory, 23–24
political protest. *See* dissent
potentiality, 165–68
power
abuses of, 160
in "Measures Against Power" (Brecht), 145–48, 162–64
professional oppositionality and, 145, 163, 169
Prefaces (Kierkegaard), 134–35
the press, 138
professional oppositionality, 145, 163, 169
The Professors: The 101 Most Dangerous Academics in America (Horowitz), 117
property, 37
protest. *See* dissent
the public
as addressee of "The Crisis and a Crisis in the Life of an Actress" (Kierkegaard), 138–39
alternate modes of address to, 115–16
emergence of, in Prussia, 95–96
Heiberg's frustration with, 112–13
indirect tutelage of, 115–16, 122
Kierkegaard's attitude toward, 113–16
philosophers and, 154, 157
redemptive potential of, 114–15
rhetoric of identification and, 131, 145
publicity, 44, 145–46
public/private discourse, 4–9. *See also* audiences
"The Purloined Letter" (Poe), 44, 176n75

quinquennium Neronis, 24–27

Rancière, Jacques, 154–55
readers. *See* audiences
reason, "private" vs. "public" uses of, 91–93
Religion Within the Limits of Reason Alone (Kant), 89
Religious Edict (1788), 87
Republic (Plato), 154
resistance. *See also* dissent
    definition of, 149
    passive aggression as, 104–6
retirement. *See also* rhetoric of withdrawal, Nero's denial of Seneca's request for, 23–24
revolt, 148–49
rhetoric
    definition of term, 13
    epistolary, 2–3
    minor, 13
    vs. oratory, 92–93
rhetoric of courtship, 110
rhetoric of exemplarity
    academic culture and, 144
    ambiguity and, 69–70
    Christine's use of, in letter to Isabeau, 3, 14, 64–66
    "otherness" of exemplars and, 70
    persuasion and, 145
    political intervention and, 16
    tying present to future through the past, 54
rhetoric of humility, 100–102
rhetoric of identification
    Kierkegaard's use of, 3–4, 14, 16, 131, 139, 145
    learned advocacy and, 16
    the public and, 145
rhetoric of obedience, 3–4, 14, 16, 144–45
rhetoric of withdrawal
    academic culture and, 144
    concealment and, 48–50
    as dissent, 3–5
    in *Letters to Lucilius* (Seneca), 40–46
    publicity and, 145
    Seneca the Younger and, 28–33
Robbins, Bruce, 107, 145
Roman Senate, 26–27
Rorty, Richard, 9
Rosicrucian Order, 83–84
Rudich, Vasily, 40, 48

Said, Edward, 7
Sauter, Michael J., 85
Schlözer, A. L. von, 82
Schmidt, James, 87
Schrecker, Ellen, 158
Schubart, Christian Friedrich Daniel, 82
Scott, James C., 105, 152
seclusion, 126–28, 185n66
"Self-Defense" (Kierkegaard), 131–32
self-will, 165
Seneca the Younger. *See also Letters to Lucilius* (Seneca); Stoicism
    boundaries between public and private discourse and, 4–5
    defense of Nero's matricide, 24
    on "lesser" and "greater" commonwealths, 30–37
    "Measures Against Power" (Brecht) and, 146
    Nero's denial of retirement and, 23–24, 34
    on peace, 37–38
    on playing dead as mode of resistance, 108
    on political disengagement, 28–33
    rhetoric of withdrawal, 3, 5, 14, 16, 28–33, 40–46, 48–50
    simile of insatiable dog, 37–39
    suicide of, 19
    as teacher and student, 21–22
    use of term *exemplum*, 52–53
    works: *Letters to Lucilius*, 3–5, 20–21, 35–46, 48–51, 78, 146–47; *On Retirement*, 30–33, 35; *On the Shortness of Life*, 28–31; *On Tranquility of Mind*, 29–30
Shakespeare, William, 126–28, 130, 132–33
Sloterdijk, Peter, 10
social protest. *See* dissent
Socrates, 107–8, 123
Solomon, 135
"The Starry Heaven" (Heiberg), 128
Stirewalt, M. Luther, 21
Stoicism
    criminalization of, 27–28, 34
    Kant's obedience to Friedrich Wilhelm and, 108
    Kierkegaard on, 171n6
    "Measures Against Power" (Brecht) and, 146
    use of, to justify resistance, 4–5, 28, 48
    vs. Cynicism, 31–32
Stories of Mr. Keuner (Brecht), 18
Strauss, Leo, 10–11, 147–48, 156
Strayer, Joseph R., 55–56
subjectivity, mediated, 70–71
suicide, 19
Summary Commission of Inquiry (1791), 87

Tacitus, 23–24
technology, 158, 160–61
"temporal differential," 76
tenure track, 188n42
Thrasea Paetus, 4–5, 24–25, 27–28
Tilly, Charles, 151

Urania (Heiberg), 128

vaudeville, 111–12, 135
Vaughan, Richard, 60
Veturia, Princess, 64, 67
Veyne, Paul, 40, 46–49

witnesses, 7
Wöllner, Johann Christoph, 84–87
Wöllner Edict (1788), 84–86

women. *See also* Christine de Pizan; Isabeau of Bavaria
The Book of the City of Ladies (Christine de Pizan) as history of, 63–66
elite medieval, 179n58
political involvement of, 71
potentialities of, in Christine's letter to Isabeau, 78–80
Wrage, Ernest, 15
Wright, Erik Olin, 157

Yale University, 160

Zedlitz, K. A., 84
Zeno, 8, 31–32
Zola, Émile, 1, 144

CPSIA information can be obtained
at www.ICGtesting.com
Printed in the USA
FSOW01n2102091214
3814FS